"*God in the Movies* is an essential text for courageous moviegoers. Paying attention to forty years of cinematic excellence and leading us into the questions raised by art's provocative ambiguities, Barsotti, Johnston, and their community of cinephiles celebrate an incarnational vision. They show us that the Spirit moves in mysterious ways throughout the world of cinema—in movies popular and obscure, commercial and foreign, inspiring and disturbing. With prophetic understanding, they coax us to become wise interpreters of the world's big-screen dreams. They give us 'eyes to see.'"

—**Jeffrey Overstreet**, Seattle Pacific University,
author of *Through a Screen Darkly* and *Auralia's Colors*
and senior film critic at *Christianity Today*
and lookingcloser.org

"Spirituality in movies? You bet! With their book *God in the Movies*, Barsotti and Johnston present a host of insightful essays. Each gives us eyes to see the subtle but powerful nuggets of spiritual wisdom tucked into mainstream Hollywood films. You've seen most of these movies; now take a second look. You'll be amazed at what you'll find!"

—**David C. McFadzean**, writer, producer, partner, Wind Dancer Films
(*Bernie* and TV's *Home Improvement*)

"Catherine Barsotti and Rob Johnston, experts in expressing the profound connections between faith and culture, have opened up the conversation even further in their newest book together, *God in the Movies*. They have drawn together brilliant authors, prophetic films, and fabulous insight into the importance of movies—their messages, their meaning, and their influence on our hearts, minds, and spirits. Christians today must be culturally engaged, and this book challenges us and guides us to connect our appetites for entertainment with our hunger for discussing divine truth."

—**Karen Covell**, film producer and founding director
of the Hollywood Prayer Network

"At their best, films help people engage with the most profound questions of human life. Christianity—and all religion—does this in a much more comprehensive way. In *God in the Movies*, Barsotti and Johnston do a wonderful job of showing how film can stimulate religious discussion and how those discussions can inform our viewing of films."

—**George Nolfi**, screenwriter, producer, and director (*Ocean's Twelve*,
The Bourne Ultimatum, and *The Adjustment Bureau*)

Praise for Barsotti and Johnston's previous book,
Finding God in the Movies

"Robert Johnston and Catherine Barsotti have done a wonderful service in creating a book that teaches believers how to analyze films. They provide excellent examples of thoughtful criticism and great discussion questions to engage our minds. Use it alone, with your family, or, better yet, invite the neighborhood."

—**Charles W. Colson**, founder, Prison Fellowship

"To read God into movies is not difficult. To find God there waiting for us— now, that is something else altogether. *Finding God in the Movies* peels back God's presence in thirty-three compelling films, leading us from superficial analysis and utilitarian agendas to deep, personal engagement. Bravo!"

—**Sally Morgenthaler**, founder, Sacramentis.com and Digital Glass Videos

"Written with humility, grace, and sensitivity, *Finding God in the Movies* will be a tremendous resource for those seeking light inside the cinema. More than just a guide to great films, this book is a window into how to engage with them and find on the other side a deeper understanding of the Lord."

—**Todd Komarnicki**, filmmaker and producer

"An important and insightful book that held me spellbound. Once again, Barsotti and Johnston demonstrate their incredible ability to dialogue with both Hollywood and the community of faith. They offer rich spiritual insights and astute observations on thirty-three films. Unlike other film review books, they appropriate each film's vision of life and invite the reader to interact with it. Here is an invitation to enhance your journey of faith via the silver screen."

—**David Bruce**, host of HollywoodJesus.com

"In every arena of youth ministry today, we are seeing that movies are providing students many of their takes on life. Those of us seeking to minister to youth need effective resources to help them engage in dialogue between faith and film. *Finding God in the Movies* can help you use movies more authentically in your teaching and outreach. I wholeheartedly recommend this book."

—**Cliff Anderson**, vice president of training and strategic resources,
Young Life, Colorado Springs, Colorado

GOD IN THE MOVIES

A Guide for Exploring Four Decades of Film

EDITED BY
CATHERINE M. BARSOTTI
AND **ROBERT K. JOHNSTON**

FOREWORD BY **RALPH WINTER**

Brazos Press

a division of Baker Publishing Group
Grand Rapids, Michigan

Published by Brazos Press
a division of Baker Publishing Group
PO Box 6287, Grand Rapids, MI 49516-6287
www.brazospress.com

Printed in the United States of America

Library of Congress Cataloging-in-Publication Data
Names: Barsotti, Catherine M., 1945– editor. | Johnston, Robert K., 1945– editor.
Title: God in the movies : a guide for exploring four decades of film / edited by Catherine M. Barsotti and Robert K. Johnston.
Description: Grand Rapids, MI : Brazos Press, a division of Baker Publishing Group, [2017] | Includes bibliographical references and index.
Identifiers: LCCN 2017012426 | ISBN 9781587433900 (pbk. : alk. paper)
Subjects: LCSH: Christianity in motion pictures. | Motion pictures—Religious aspects.
Classification: LCC PN1995.9.C49 G63 2017 | DDC 791.43/682—dc23
LC record available at https://lccn.loc.gov/2017012426

Photo captures were made by Steve Vredenburgh.

17 18 19 20 21 22 23   7 6 5 4 3 2 1

For wonderful parents,
Leo and Mary,
who took Cathy to *The Sound of Music*,
her first movie.
And for a great sister, Judith,
whose birthday gift of tickets to *Becket*
changed Rob's life.

The question is not what you look at, but what you see.

Henry David Thoreau, essayist

If without stories we live not, stories live not without us.

Phyllis Trible, Old Testament scholar

The best films are effectively real life wrapped in metaphor.

Travis Knight, director of animated film

If we ask more precisely which moments or events mediate God's Spirit, the answer can only be potentially all experience. The whole world. There is no exclusive zone, no special realm which alone can be called religious.

Elizabeth Johnson, theologian

CONTENTS

The '90s: A Bridge Decade   63
Barry Taylor

FOREWORD

Ralph Winter

Movies are important. Despite the avalanche of new media crashing in around us, movies remain the gold standard of storytelling, taking us on a complete journey in one sitting. Movies affect culture—military pilots cite *Top Gun* as inspiration, and scientists reference *Star Trek*'s seeking of new worlds. Movies also affect individual viewers. Storytelling has had power since the ancients sat around campfires, but the combination of the visual, aural, and narrative in a movie creates a perfect storm that only increases its impact. On Mondays, Christians have trouble recalling the theme of Sunday's word-oriented sermon, but years after a movie comes out, Christians and non-Christians alike can recite lines of dialogue from that film. It is the power of a movie to tell a story that this book engages.

Movies reference deep cultural, human, and spiritual instincts. I can remember working on *Star Trek: The Wrath of Khan* and previewing the movie at the studio. The screening was good, but the ending was a disaster—Spock died and the audience booed. They hated the ending. We gathered as a group in Michael Eisner's office (CEO of Paramount at the time) with all the executives and the filmmakers. I was the lowly junior executive but was invited to tag along. The conversation went late into the night. At the end, the executives articulated the absence of hope and lack of an "Easter morning" moment. Mostly a group of secular Jews, they knew the power of the story of the resurrection and how Good Friday was incomplete without it.

We literally added one shot to the movie, a camera roving through Golden Gate Park as a futuristic garden setting, discovering Spock's casket, and the audience knew exactly what was possible and what was intended. There was hope. A connection was made. And that movie relaunched a troubled franchise that still plays today, tapping into deep narratives where we as Christians see even more significance.

Rob Johnston has been articulating these kinds of observations and driving insights of this sort for years. Rob and his wife, Catherine Barsotti, have provided leadership for both the church and the academy in exploring spirituality in the movies. I know this firsthand, for Rob and I have been talking about film's spiritual possibilities since as far back as the early '90s. Rob's writings (and later Cathy's, along with the writings of Craig Detweiler, Kutter Callaway, and others affiliated with the Reel Spirituality Institute at Fuller Seminary) have filled the gap and started the modern movement to integrate how we engage movies theologically as followers of the Way. Since I began to work in the business, Rob, Cathy, and the Fuller team have helped me think critically about the topics, the approach, and the significance of what I do as a film producer. I am thankful.

Through their writing, teaching, and speaking literally around the world, the Reel Spirituality Institute team has spread the good news of how we can interact with our culture's stories, particularly at the movies. They have helped us grow in our understanding of how engaging popular culture can open us to the deeper things of life. This book will assist you as a reader in doing just that. Enjoy the plunge.

December 2016

CONTRIBUTORS

All of the contributors to *God in the Movies* are part of the creative team of the Reel Spirituality Institute of the Brehm Center for Worship, Theology, and the Arts at Fuller Theological Seminary, Pasadena, California. For a sample of their reviews and articles, see ReelSpirituality.com.

Kutter Callaway

Kutter is assistant professor of theology and culture at Fuller Theological Seminary and codirector of its Reel Spirituality Institute. His musings are typically focused on film, music, television, and contemporary culture. His book *Scoring Transcendence: Contemporary Film Music as Religious Experience* was published by Baylor University Press in January 2013. More recently, he published *Watching TV Religiously: Television and Theology in Dialogue* (Baker Academic, 2016). His next project, *Sex, Spouses, and Singleness*, is scheduled for release in 2017 (InterVarsity). He also serves on the editorial board for the *Journal of Religion and Film* and on the steering committee for the Religion, Film, and Visual Culture group at the American Academy of Religion.

Elijah Davidson

Elijah Davidson is codirector of the Reel Spirituality Institute, a Brehm Center initiative of faith and film at Fuller Theological Seminary, and Brehm Center web manager. He is the author of *How to Talk to a Movie: Movie-Watching as a Spiritual Exercise* (Cascade Books, 2017). He has also written over four

hundred film and television articles, reviews, and discussion guides for the
Reel Spirituality website, as well as for other outlets including *Christianity
Today*, *Think Christian*, *Patheos*, *Motive Entertainment*, and *Imaginatio et
Ratio*. He holds a master's degree in intercultural studies from Fuller Theo-
logical Seminary and lives with his wife, Krista, an elementary teacher, in
Pasadena.

Craig Detweiler

Craig is professor of communication and creative director of the Institute for
Entertainment, Media, and Culture at Pepperdine University. He's written
comedies for the Disney Channel and directed documentaries featured on
ABC. *Foreword* honored *iGods: How Technology Shapes Our Spiritual and
Social Lives* (Brazos, 2014) as the 2013 silver winner for best books about
popular culture. His additional books include *Into the Dark* (Baker Academic,
2008), a study of the top-ranked films on the Internet Movie Database, and
Halos and Avatars (Westminster John Knox, 2010), about the connection
between video games and faith. *Variety* named Craig their 2016 Mentor of
the Year. A former director of the Reel Spirituality Institute at Fuller Theological Seminary, he also received a master of divinity and a PhD in theology
and culture from that institution.

Lauralee Farrer

Lauralee is president of Burning Heart Productions and the writer/director
of award-winning documentary and narrative films including *The Fair Trade*,
Laundry and Tosca, and *Not That Funny*. She recently finished production
on the *Praying the Hours* film series, which has been in development for
over a decade. An author, speaker, and film festival juror, Farrer is in senior
management at Fuller Theological Seminary as storyteller and chief creative,
responsible for its award-winning magazine and innovative *FULLER* Studio
content platform.

Joseph C. Gallagher

Joe, a graduate of Harvard Law School, served as a senior executive with
Universal Studios, as senior vice president of production and administration
at Twentieth Century Fox, and as the founding president of Industrial Light

& Magic (ILM). Joe currently is the operations director of the Brehm Center at Fuller Theological Seminary. He and his wife, Joanne, an actress, live in Los Angeles and are active in the Presbyterian church.

Mathew P. John

Originally an electrical engineer from India, Mathew received his PhD from Fuller Theological Seminary. His book *Film as Cultural Artifact: Religious Criticism of World Cinema* (Fortress, 2017) focuses on developing a methodology for the cultural exegesis of film. He is an avid film enthusiast and a graduate of the Professional Program in Producing at the UCLA School of Theater, Film and Television. He is also the founding director of Focus Infinity, an independent film and television production house engaged in development projects in the United States and in Canada.

Avril Z. Speaks

Avril is a producer and director of award-winning film and new media projects including *Sophisticated Romance, Defining Moments*, and *Sisters—The Web Series*. She earned her MFA in film directing from Columbia University and a second master's degree in theology and the arts from Fuller Theological Seminary, where she focused on the intersections of race, film, and theology. As an advocate for film education, Avril has been a professor at schools such as Howard University and Azusa Pacific University. Currently she is working as an associate producer for the television series *The Race Card* (TNT) while also producing the upcoming feature film *Jinn*.

Eugene Suen

Eugene is codirector of Reel Spirituality at Fuller Theological Seminary and a filmmaker. Originally from Taiwan, Eugene has codirected the City of Angels Film Festival and worked as a development executive for an Asian entertainment company. As a writer, he has contributed to *FilmCraft: Editing* (2011), a volume on leading film editors published by Focal Press; and *Don't Stop Believin'* (Westminster John Knox, 2012), a dictionary of religion and popular culture. His filmmaking credits as a producer include *Abigail Harm*, starring Amanda Plummer and Will Patton; *This Is Comedy*, a French documentary about modern American comedies; and an upcoming documentary set in

Rwanda. His films have been official selections at such international film festivals as Busan, Torino, and Tribeca.

Barry Taylor

Barry is an artist-in-residence at Fuller Theological Seminary's Brehm Center, where he also teaches courses on the intersections of theology, faith, and culture. He also regularly teaches classes on creativity and concepting at Art Center College of Design in Pasadena, California, in the School of Advertising. Barry's books include *A Matrix of Meanings: Finding God in Pop Culture* (with Craig Detweiler, Baker Academic, 2003); *Entertainment Theology* (Baker Academic, 2008); and *Don't Stop Believin'* (coedited with Craig Detweiler and Rob Johnston, Westminster John Knox, 2012). He speaks at conferences, seminars, and events around the world; he also writes songs, composes theme music, and acts as a music supervisor for a number of independent movies (*The Third Miracle*, *Method*, *Ballistic*).

Ralph Winter

Ralph produced *Star Trek III* through *VI*, with the original cast, and the first four *X-Men* movies, among many others. Recently he executive-produced *The Giver*, starring Jeff Bridges and Meryl Streep, and *Crouching Tiger, Hidden Dragon: Sword of Destiny*, for Netflix. Awaiting release in 2017 is *The Promise*, with Christian Bale and Oscar Isaac, directed by Terry George (*Hotel Rwanda*), about the Armenian genocide in 1915. Ralph has cotaught theology and film classes at Fuller Seminary with Rob Johnston. Each year, Ralph also teaches a six-week Sunday-school class at his local church on the theological importance of each of the Oscar nominees for Best Picture. He is an active member of the Academy of Motion Picture Arts and Sciences, the Directors Guild of America, and the Producers Guild of America.

Catherine M. Barsotti (Coeditor)

Cathy has taught in both Spanish and English in the areas of theology, ethics, spirituality, and theology and film in various settings: since 1993 at Centro Hispano de Estudios Teológicos (CHET), a Latino ministry training center in Compton, California; from 2000 to 2015 for Young Life International; and since 2005 as an affiliate professor at Fuller Theological Seminary. The coauthor of *Finding God in the Movies: 33 Films of Reel Faith* (Baker Books, 2004), she wrote movie reviews for the *Covenant Companion* and *Faith@ Work* for eighteen years. She was a contributor to *Reframing Theology and Film* (Baker Academic, 2007) and *Vivir y servir en el exilio* (Ediciones Kairos, 2008). Baptized, confirmed, and married in the Roman Catholic Church, she is also a licensed minister in the Evangelical Covenant Church.

Robert K. Johnston (Coeditor)

Rob is professor of theology and culture at Fuller Theological Seminary and the founder and codirector of Fuller's Reel Spirituality Institute. His book *Reel Spirituality: Theology and Film in Dialogue* (Baker Academic, 2000, 2006) is the standard textbook in the field. Recent books include *God's Wider Presence* (Baker Academic, 2014), a constructive theology of revelation in and through creation, conscience, and culture; *Don't Stop Believin'* (coeditor, Westminster John Knox, 2012), a reflection on the religious significance of one hundred cultural icons over the last fifty years; *Reframing Theology and Film* (editor, Baker Academic, 2008), an evaluation of the current scholarship and future directions of theology and film scholarship; and *Useless Beauty* (Baker Academic, 2004), a conversation between film and the book of Ecclesiastes. In 2017 he was a member of the ecumenical jury at the Locarno Film Festival.

INTRODUCTION

Faith and Film

Welcome to a Maturing Conversation

We have been teaching in the area of theology and film for twenty-five years—propelled by separate experiences that we both had in which God spoke to us through a movie story. For Rob, it was an experience he had as a freshman in college when he heard God's call into the ministry while at a movie theater watching *Becket*. He had been struggling with whether he was "holy" enough—like his high school youth leaders—to consider ministry as a calling. But as he watched Thomas à Becket respond to God's call to be archbishop, he heard God say to him, "You don't need to be holy. Thomas wasn't. You only need to be obedient, and I will help you become holy." The next day, Rob switched his major from engineering to history (so he could learn how better to read and write!) and began preparation for seminary and a career as an ordained minister and professor of theology.

For Cathy, it was while watching Peter Weir's *The Year of Living Dangerously*, in which the biblical question from Luke 3 (by way of Tolstoy) "What then must we do?" is voiced by Billy Kwan three times. Kwan is trying to help a young boy and mother who are living in abject poverty, only to watch the boy die from drinking polluted water. People, events in her life, and the Holy Spirit had prepared her to watch the film, she says. The result was that she immediately began to see the world through Billy's eyes and his question, so much so that she resigned from her full-time position with a large bank and started her own independent appraisal firm so she would have time to work with immigrant women and children, something she has now done for over thirty years. Here was "what then must she do."

Given these encounters with God in the movies, we both have continued to explore how such cultural stories, whether seen on the giant screen or on one's computer, might interact both with God's story and with your and our own personal stories. It is a similar exploration to the one C. S. Lewis describes in his autobiography, *Surprised by Joy*. In that book, Lewis explores how one might understand those spiritual experiences he had, not in the church, but in the course of his everyday life—when smelling a currant bush as a boy, or listening to Wagner, or reading the Greek play *Hippolytus*. How was he to understand what happened to him when he read George MacDonald's *Phantastes*? How did his own life story and God's story interlace with Mac-Donald's story? It is this three-way conversation that *God in the Movies* also seeks to facilitate for its readers.

When we started teaching theology and film in a seminary context in the nineties, after Rob had taught for some time the stories found in American literature—particularly the American novel—there was still some suspicion in the church about the enterprise. Wasn't Hollywood anti-Christian in the main and often immoral? Wasn't reason to be preferred over the imagination, truth more primary than beauty? Many Christians believed that propositional texts in the Bible should be given priority over narrative. They also thought the arts to be ornamental—only incidental to life. The ordering of the transcendentals clearly reflected their perceived importance: truth, goodness—and then beauty. But things have changed, haven't they? The importance of putting our faith stories into conversation not only with Scripture and church doctrine but also with the wider culture, particularly with the arts, is being recognized by an increasing number of Christians. Most Christians recognize the importance of narrative both in Scripture and in sermons, and spirituality is a culturally important topic that movies regularly explore.

To give two examples: at Fuller Seminary, where we both teach, over 20 percent of the student body currently report that they came to Fuller because of our coursework and degree programs in worship, theology, and the arts. It is Fuller's commitment to the aesthetic, not just the rational or ethical, that is appealing to many Christians today. Or again, George Barna in his book *Revolution* (2000), reported that over 20 percent of all American adults found in media, culture, and the arts their primary means of spiritual expression and growth, with that percentage on the upswing such that by 2025 over one-third of all adults in the United States are projected to turn to media, culture, and the arts for their primary spiritual experiences. But we don't need Barna to tell us this; we encounter this turn to the aesthetic daily in our own lives.

The discussion between film and faith is no longer "should we engage" in the dialogue but "how should we best engage" in the dialogue. Thus the focus of *God in the Movies* is not on the validity of such conversation—that is taken for granted—but on assisting those wanting dialogue with theologically significant movies either personally or professionally, whether in individual or group settings.

The conversation between theology and film has been going on for over one hundred years, ever since the Congregational minister Herbert Jump wrote a pamphlet titled "The Religious Possibilities of the Motion Picture" in 1911. But the dialogue took on new possibilities with the advent of film rentals that were affordable for most in the late seventies. Thus we are going on forty years in which films have been available on demand for re-viewing and subsequent analysis and theological dialogue. Since those early days, movies have been understood religiously, whether as parable or as icon. But regardless of the debate as to how movies function in the viewer's life, there is wide agreement as to their unique power to fully engage their audience.

The Centrality of Movies in World Culture

When we ask students in our classes or audiences at our speaking engagements, "How many movies did you see last month?" the typical answer is five to ten, with responses ranging to a high of fifty-five! The average number of movies watched nationally is between forty-five and fifty a year. Most of these are seen not in the theater but on TV or on one of a number of our ubiquitous personal devices. But even theater attendance remains strong, not only in the United States but increasingly around the world. Globally, box-office receipts for films released around the world reached $38.3 billion in 2015, up 5 percent from 2014. China's box-office increases were particularly startling, rising 49 percent. Admissions to movie theaters in the United States totaled 1.32 billion tickets, and on average, every American over the age of two saw 3.8 movies in a theater in 2015.

Just as interesting as these numbers relating to movie audiences are those focusing on the number of films produced. The total number of films released commercially rose to 708 in 2015, up from 462 in 2001. And as we know, movies are seen not just in Cineplexes. Films totaling billions of dollars are shot yearly but never released commercially. And countless others are made on a credit card budget. (The democratization of film means that anyone today—even the teen in your church—can make a movie.) Amazon and Netflix, streaming and DVDs, iPads and iPhones, have all become part of the film industry, revolutionizing film viewing from that of a previous generation. Not only have digital devices made a wider selection of movies, past and present, available to almost everyone, they have changed the typical cinema experience. Rather than experience laughter, tears, surprise, and anger together with an audience, today's movie viewer watches many movies alone. Rather than movie watching being a communal activity, it is for many a solitary pursuit.

While most of us still go to movie theaters to see some movies, the twenty-four-hour movie has also come to us. Digital technologies have transformed not only how movies are shot and edited, distributed and exhibited; they have also changed how movies are watched. Though we still might commune with others about the movies we see—whether later in a conversation with friends or online—this isn't the same as being with an audience while watching a film together. Moreover, rather than the local theater choosing what we watch, today the individual is sovereign—we choose. But though choices are legion, as with much else in the information age, there also is the need for help in what is best to watch. *God in the Movies* is, thus, a small protest against what has been lost, even while recognizing the amazing gains that digital access allows. *God in the Movies* invites you to benefit both from the wisdom of those connected with the Reel Spirituality Institute in choosing what movies to watch and from the material in each chapter that provides a dialogue partner for you as you watch the movie yourself. We also encourage you to join with others in a communal experience of film viewing and dialogue. Movies are not meant to be seen alone.

The Power of Story

In 2013, *Blackfish* was released, documenting how orcas are treated in captivity at SeaWorld. Three years later, the film had grossed $2.1 million and had been shown thirty times on CNN to nearly thirty million viewers. But more significant than the success in screening this documentary was the backlash it created against this theme park—a backlash sufficient to reduce attendance at the company's eleven parks by 4.2 percent the next year and ultimately to cause SeaWorld to halt the breeding of their twenty-nine orcas. Eventually, these magnificent, intelligent, complex animals will no longer be part of the theme park's shows.

Other examples are easily recalled. The prominence of Pinot Noir wine in *Sideways*, as both a plot device and a major metaphor, ushered in a permanent increase in sales of this wine since the movie's release. Similarly, in *About Schmidt*, Warren Schmidt's sponsoring of an African child through Childreach caused a spike in child sponsorships through that organization. One of our favorite examples has to do with the Sundance Audience Award winner in 2014, *Alive Inside*, which inspired many across the country, including our friend Terri Bullock, to raise funds for the use of iPods in institutions caring for persons suffering from memory loss.

The power of film resides in its storytelling. Few debate the power of the stories we see on film and television to shape our beliefs and actions. For movies image life. Through words, sound, and image, through screenplay and editing, framing and music, they give expression to memorable stories. As a central art form in our culture, we might even say that movies tell our collective stories. C. S. Lewis (in "On Stories") recognized that "the story does what no theorem can quite do. It may not be 'like real life' in the superficial sense, but it sets before us an image of what reality may well be like at some more central region." In their particularity, movies have the capacity to portray something universal about life and to convey it convincingly.

A good movie helps us make sense of our world, even as it provides a temporary respite from it. As we watch a movie, we are invited to look closely at life in ways we otherwise might miss. Even the simplest of stories present viewers options concerning life (the lives seen on the screen and by extension the viewers' own lives). As we wrote in a previous movie study guide, *Finding God in the Movies*, "By focusing reality for the viewer, a movie provides us metaphors for understanding life."

Mark Burrows has pointed out that in modern Greek cities, the word for mass transportation vehicles—whether buses, trams, or trains—is *metaphoria*. That is to say, one takes a "metaphor" if one wants to go from one place to another. By telling our stories, by providing our culture its metaphors, movies give us a "ride." They fill us with the dreams, hopes, and fears of others, enabling us to move from here to there. The movies we highlight in this book all provide viewers such a ride—they are *metaphoria*, metaphors of life.

There is a second sense in which movie stories are also *metaphoria*—transportation vehicles. Not only do they transport viewers into the lives of others and in the process help us move forward in our own lives, but their stories, which are rooted in the ordinary experiences of living (even if imaginatively expressed through science fiction or animation), also have the potential to usher us into the realm of the Spirit. It is not just biblically based stories (in fact, it is rarely biblically based movies) that prove spiritual to the viewer. Rather, God is more typically encountered at the Cineplex amidst the everyday stuff of life. When we are led from one place to another with the result being forgiveness, reconciliation, or true friendship, this can prove to be a spiritual experience for the viewer. The movies we highlight in this book have primarily been chosen because they invite us as viewers to take such a ride. All are *metaphoria* in this second sense as well.

The Spiritual Possibilities of Movies

Those writing about the spiritual possibilities of movies have used a variety of descriptors to explain what takes place. Some have spoken of cinema as a medium of *contemplation*, even the occasion of prayer. Others have viewed movies not as our opening ourselves outward to God in prayer but as a *means of grace* whereby God speaks to us. Protestants have most typically understood movies to be the occasion for *common grace*; Catholics have more often spoken of movies' *sacramental* possibilities. Some have viewed movies in *analogical* terms, exploring the *dialogical* possibilities between a movie and the theological themes it raises. Others have understood the divine possibilities of movies to reside in an *incarnational* model of everyday life, whether that grace is received through the film narrative and its theme or through the experience of movie viewing. All of these descriptors help us understand film's spiritual possibilities.

The approach contributors to this volume have taken might be labeled *interactional*. Movies, as a major source of cultural insight, when combined with the personal experiences a viewer brings to the screening, invite a theological exchange with Scripture, the insights of the Christian community, and ultimately with the Spirit of God. This interaction, or conversation, between our culture and our faith will at times take the form of a *dialogue*; at other times, moviegoers will be drawn to *appropriate* certain aspects of the movie's portrayal of life; and at still other times, the movie might trigger a *divine encounter* for the moviegoer as the Spirit graciously and freely chooses to speak to us through the movie event. As contributors to this volume, we also recognize that not all movies might be suitable for all people. Thus, for example, we have suggested that *caution* might need to be exercised as to whether one chooses to view a movie like *Breaking the Waves*. In this way, "God in the movies" will mean different things to different readers. Let us explain.

Rather than come to a movie with a skeptical eye, seeking protection from its cultural and personal impact, the interactional model we have adopted opts to instead receive a movie's story on its own terms before engaging the movie theologically. It recognizes that we must first listen and look before we speak, if our response to a movie is to have integrity. C. S. Lewis was right when in his

An Experiment in Criticism he warned, "We are so busy doing things with the work [the movie] that we give it too little chance to work on us. Thus increasingly we meet only ourselves." Says Lewis, as with any dialogue, one must be willing to "Look. Listen. Receive. Get yourself out of the way. (There is no good asking first whether the work before you deserves such a surrender, for until you have surrendered you cannot possibly find out.)" Having engaged the movie on its own terms (much like someone listening attentively to a friend before they seek to respond), the theological critic will then put what she has seen and experienced into dialogue with her own understanding, with Scripture, and with the insights of the Christian community. This might include critique as well as affirmation. Thus, in each of the chapters, we have provided not only a brief synopsis of the movie but also a reflection on its theological significance, together with suggested biblical texts that might become dialogue partners with it as one reflects theologically on the movie viewed. We have also provided questions that encourage viewers to respond personally.

An intellectual *dialogue* does not end the possibility for theological interaction with a movie. Viewers also *experience* a film's vision of life and are invited to share that vision. That is, film does not simply provide alternate perspectives that invite disinterested dialogue from a faith perspective. Rather, movies also expand one's vision, providing new vistas by which to appropriate the truth, beauty, and goodness found in life. Through movies Christians sometimes find their human spirits enlarged, their orientation toward life challenged, their attitudes and beliefs deepened. One's interaction with movies need not just invite dialogue; it can also lead to the *appropriation* of perspectives experienced while movie watching (or the active rejection of perspectives found wanting).

And again, the spiritual possibilities of a movie need not end with a viewer's spirit being renewed, challenged, or enlarged. A movie can also provide the occasion for the Spirit to be present, for an *encounter* with the Spirit of God to take place. Movie watching can be the occasion for God's wider presence to be disclosed, as God chooses to speak through and within our human creations. When this takes place, theology moves from a second-order experience to that of a primary experience, from "knowing about God" to "knowing God" more fully.

In these three ways, movie watching can participate in the spirituality (and sometimes Spirituality) of everyday life, where our encounters provide occasions for new reflection, for spiritual growth, and for encounter with the Spirit of God. It is our prayer that *God in the Movies* will provide you with many such occasions. The films selected in the book have been chosen because of their potential for just such experiences.

God in the Movies

As the millennium turned, the first edition of Rob's book *Reel Spirituality* was published. The book's title was also incorporated into our film and theology institute at Fuller Seminary, suggesting that there was an important connection between faith and film, between movies and spirituality, between Hollywood and the church, between theology and art. And though this book was one of the first to explore such interaction in a comprehensive way, it has hardly been alone in making such a claim. Andrew Greeley cowrote *God in the Movies*, also in 2000, the same year that Ken Gire published his *Reflections on the Movies: Hearing God in the Unlikeliest Places*. Later Gareth Higgins published *How Movies Saved My Soul* (2003); Cathy and Rob cowrote *Finding God in the Movies* (2004); Craig Detweiler wrote *Into the Dark: Seeing the Sacred in the Top Films of the 21st Century* (2007); and Roy Anker wrote *Of Pilgrims and Fire: When God Shows Up at the Movies* (2010). And more books have followed.

But as these claims have been made, we have also felt the need to deal with the ambiguity of what exactly we mean by "God in the movies." How is a movie's spirituality to be described? How is it that God is present? In what way does God show up at the movies? As a theme? As an encounter? Surely not just as an idea. But is God's presence perhaps only a "trace" or an "echo"—that is, a reverberation of some past action by God? If it is an encounter, can such a numinous event be important, even foundational, to faith? Or, given humankind's sin, does such spirituality remain simply confused and confusing?

In responding to such questions about a movie's spirituality, we understand that three distinct answers are possible: (1) a movie deepens our theological understanding, (2) it transforms our spirit, and (3) it is the occasion for our encountering God. All three of these responses inform *God in the Movies*. This multiplicity of perspective is present in how contributors understood the movies they wrote about and how they framed the clip conversations and discussion questions. In most of the chapters, the movie functions for the writers first as a theological parable, giving support for, or perhaps inviting the maturing of our understanding of an aspect of, the Christian faith. The movie is a visual reenactment of Christian truth, a metaphor of Christian theology that can deepen one's knowledge, making one's understanding more holistic. Here, for example, is how the Rwandan film *Munyurangabo* is seen in this book to function, showing the power, possibility, and problematic of reconciliation (see chap. 23). Here also is the discussion of vocation in *Amadeus* (see chap. 1) or in *Chariots of Fire* (see chap. 3).

In many of the theological reflections as well as in the questions and clip conversations that each chapter presents, a given movie is also seen as an occasion for the viewer's spirit to be challenged, even transformed. Through the moviegoing experience, something greater, or other, or whole, might be experienced. Spiritual insight can be gained, which can be life-changing. When we showed *Lars and the Real Girl*, for example, in one of our theology and film classes, a woman wrote that after "meeting" Lars, a broken and awkward young adult who is nurtured back toward wholeness by his church community (see chap. 22), she went online the very next day to find a PhD program in psychology so she could help people like Lars and her brother. The film stories in the forty chapters to follow have become for many the occasion for the re-centering and grounding of their spirits, for personal transformation. Here is the testimony of Elijah Davidson in his chapter on *12 Years a Slave* (see chap. 39) or of hundreds of viewers of *Field of Dreams* (see chap. 7).

But again for others, the viewing of one of the forty movies highlighted in this book has become the occasion for an encounter with the Spirit of God, which proved transformative in the viewer's life. Through the movie's expression of human creativity, viewers discovered themselves to be in the presence of the Creator. The movie, that is, proved revelatory, the movie's story merging with their own stories, resulting in a divine encounter that changed lives. When lecturing in China, for example, we met a political science student who told of her experience upon seeing *Life of Pi* (see chap. 34). As she found herself with Pi on the raft looking up at the heavens, she said she knew that her Marxist, materialistic understanding of life up to that moment was bankrupt. Having encountered the Spirit as Creator, she entered upon a pilgrimage that led to her Christian faith. Again, when we showed *Magnolia* (see chap. 16) one year in class, a male student wrote about seeing the movie when it first came out. He had had an active Christian faith as a teenager but had turned away from this when in college. In fact, it had been almost a decade when he heard the characters in *Magnolia* sing along with the radio in serial fashion the song "Wise Up," recognizing the song as "their" song (and his). At the end of the movie, as Jim's love and acceptance for Claudia in her brokenness is shown on the screen and the Aimee Mann song "Save Me" is foregrounded, the student said God became present to him. He wrote,

> I see a lot of myself in Claudia's character and a lot of Jesus in Jim. The fact that Anderson kept Jim out of the frame for much of the scene while his voice bestowed grace from off camera was simply brilliant. This enabled the scene to transcend the film and become a conversation between me and Jesus. This film served as a catalyst for my return to faith after a decade of apostasy.

The movies in this book have been chosen because they invite theological interpretation and reflection. As such they have both pedagogical and missional potential. They even can be revelatory as the Spirit of God chooses to be present in and through them. For this to take place, however, movies must be "interpreted" rather than "used." An interpretation is already potentially present in the movie viewed; it only is awaiting discovery. While we know there is more than one possible interpretation of a movie we have seen (just ask your friend or spouse who accompanies you to a movie and goes to Starbucks with you afterward to discuss it), there also are a limited number of ways of seeing a film, if we are to be true to its story.

An *interpretation* is always legitimated by the audiovisual text. Not so when *using* a movie story. Here, the viewer deals loosely with the movie text, making choices motivated chiefly by her or his own interests. The result is like looking into a mirror and not through a window. Rather than being allowed to look freshly at human life, the user only sees what he or she already knows. *God in the Movies* seeks to interpret, not use, forty of the most spiritually compelling movies from the last four decades. It offers its readers interpretations so that they can look closer at the life that God has given us. That is to say, movies offer their viewers human expressions about life—about human needs and relationships and possibilities—and invite our responses.

Of course, there is no such thing as a strictly objective interpretation of a movie, nor would we want there to be. Movies are dependent for their meaning not only on their makers but also on their viewers. And both are embedded in a particular culture that is both influenced by popular culture and itself influences popular culture. But while movie watching is an "imprecise science," we also have the ability as viewers of suspending judgment while looking closely and listening carefully to a movie. *God in the Movies* seeks to help its readers avoid the theological mistake of using a film for one's own ends and purposes. Its goal instead is to help readers break open the theological significance of forty superb movies that on their own terms invite such engagement.

How to Make Use of This Book

We intend *God in the Movies* to serve as a resource. The goal of our Reel Spirituality team in choosing the movies and then writing this book is to assist Christians in bringing their faith and life together, to link their experiences of a story on the screen with their experience of the Triune God.

A diversity of movies. Over several months, those of us connected with the Reel Spirituality Institute proposed movies that had been significant

theologically for us. Our end goal was to choose ten movies from each of
the last four decades that invited theological dialogue, spiritual appropriation, and even divine encounter. Of course the final list we voted on is not
exhaustive. (So many films to see, so little time and space!) It is certainly true
that all of us saw one of our favorites removed from the final listing. One of
us (Cathy!) is extremely disappointed that none of the films of her favorite
Mexican and Italian filmmakers—*Babel* (d. Iñárritu, 2006), *Pan's Labyrinth*
(d. del Toro, 2006), *Cinema Paradiso* (d. Tornatore, 1988), *La Gran Belleza*
(*The Great Beauty*, d. Sorrentino, 2013)—made it into the book. Without a
doubt, all of us on the writing team have our own lists of favorites that were
not included—and we suspect you do as well. It is also the case that since
forming the list in early to mid-2015, new options from the current decade
have been released.[1] Nevertheless, the book offers readers forty outstanding
visual parables of our age that invite our best theological engagement.

Some of the chosen films open viewers to life's wonder amidst its pain and
chaos; others are rooted in a spirituality of everyday life. Some are honest about
faith's quandaries; others show what it is to truly be human. The redemptive
possibilities of art and play are displayed. Some discover love beneath the ruins;
others show the power of forgiveness or make the meaning of reconciliation
live. Many reveal a fragile spirituality that opens one to the possibility of the
transcendent. This theological dialogue is rooted in the life stories portrayed
on the screen, and as such, it is rich, varied, and multifaceted.

Some of the movies you no doubt have seen. They probably are even some
of your favorites. Movies that are judged excellent by the culture (and some
that aren't!) are seen by millions of viewers, whether in the Cineplex or in
their homes. Others of these visual stories will be new to you. Perhaps you do
not live in a major media center and some of the smaller yet superb movies
highlighted in the book did not receive any press in your town. Regardless,
these movies have been chosen because their stories engage our lives of faith
in significant ways, and we write with the expectation that they will engage
yours as well.

A diversity of contributors. The authors of this book are all part of the
theology and film community of the Reel Spirituality Institute of the Brehm
Center at Fuller Seminary. As such, we share our own individual perspectives
but also a collective approach to the discipline. While it can be described in

---

1. If we had continued our discussion and selection process, we no doubt would have considered these 2015 films: *Inside Out* (d. Docter, Del Carmen), *Ex Machina* (d. Garland), *Rams*
(d. Hákonarson), and *Room* (d. Abrahamson). Films we might have considered in 2016 include
Silence (d. Scorsese), *Hacksaw Ridge* (d. Gibson), *The Birth of a Nation* (d. Parker), and *Dr.
Strange* (d. Derrickson). Happy viewing!

many ways, perhaps chief is our love for both movies and God. We are unapologetic in our enthusiasm for both. Rather than pit one against the other as some in our culture are prone to do, we seek to embrace both, learning from each and allowing a fruitful conversation between the two. Thus, this book does not take up the important question of how movies might also be harmful—or for that matter, how the misuse of faith can also be harmful. Instead, we have provided readers a guide for reflection and use in group settings of forty movies that invite (perhaps even demand) a theological engagement. We are sure you will enjoy this invitation to hours of delightful viewing and reviewing.

We believe that you will find a strength of the book to be the diversity of contributors, each writing from their own vantage points. Though moviemaking and movie criticism have been disproportionally done by white male Americans, the eleven contributors to this volume include three women, an Indo-Canadian, a Taiwanese American, an African American, and a chap from England(!). The book's contributors include those who are filmmakers, those who are film bloggers, and those who teach in the area of theology and film (a few are all three). This diversity provides a richness of perspectives. To have Asians writing on Asian film, or women writing on movies by women directors, or filmmakers writing on movies they were connected with, provides a sensitivity and viewpoint that proves illumining. But equally illumining is to have a Southern white male write on *12 Years a Slave* (chap. 39), an African American woman write on the male perspective of *American Beauty* (chap. 11), or a Taiwanese American write on a Woody Allen movie (chap. 4).

A similar format. But though the contributors write from their diverse backgrounds and life experiences, each of the chapters also has a similar format. We trust this will help make the book more easily accessible to you. On the first page of each chapter, you will notice a list of theological themes and subthemes that seem pertinent to the power and meaning of the movie story. The boldface theme is the one we consider most central; the regular type indicates other important themes in the movie. Appendix 2 lists the movies by topic and will assist you in searching for a given theme.

Also at the beginning of each chapter are the basic production notes of a given movie, including date, length, actors, director, screenwriter, and rating. The ratings of the Motion Picture Association of America (G, PG, PG-13, and R) are notoriously subjective and inconsistent. So, in addition to these ratings, we have given brief descriptions of what might prove unsuitable for certain age groups. When an R-rated movie is included, its thematic and visual material is adult in nature and needs to be noted accordingly.

The production notes are followed by a synopsis of and theological reflection on the film. Here our authors guide readers into the heart of each movie, looking for what we might learn from the movie that will deepen and extend our faith. Why is it that a Christian should want to engage this particular movie's story? We are convinced that God is present in and through all of life. Where a story helps viewers experience authentically some aspect of beauty, goodness, or truth (or the lack of it), there is the energizing presence of God's Spirit. As these visual stories connect us with the human story at its bedrock, they thus become the occasion for us to find God. (Leaders, you might find this section helpful as you preview and select movies for study and discussion.)

Next we have listed a group of biblical texts that raise themes similar to those in a given movie. These texts are not meant to be exhaustive, and we hope we have not made them susceptible to misuse ("proof texting") by listing one verse after another. But when used appropriately given their biblical contexts, these verses can be suggestive of themes similar to or complementing those found in the movie. In some cases a text reflects a scene in the movie quite directly; other times, the texts reflect a theme that is present in the movie; occasionally they present a biblical alternative. In several chapters the verses come directly from the movie, for if a filmmaker thought a biblical citation relevant, we did too.

If there is a discernible pattern to the biblical texts chosen for dialogue (you will note that several texts are used by multiple authors; see appendix 1), perhaps it is that they center on those parts of Scripture that help us better understand our God-given humanity (e.g., Genesis, the Wisdom literature—Job, Proverbs, Ecclesiastes—Psalms, Jesus's parables and wisdom). For here is where the movies chosen from the last forty years also focus.

Following the biblical texts are the discussion questions and clip conversations. These include questions of a more general nature, flowing from the whole movie, its major themes, and the filmmaker's intentions. This section also includes questions arising from particular moments in the movie's storytelling. For your convenience as you make use of the movies in your teaching, small groups, and personal reflection, we have made all of the clips available on our Reel Spirituality Institute website (ReelSpirituality.com/Books/God-In-The-Movies). You can go online to see and use these clips. The timestamp range for the clips (assuming you set your counter at 00:00 when the studio logo appears on the screen) has also been listed, if you care to use your own DVDs. Together these questions and conversations are meant to take you into the heart of the visual stories and suggest fruitful areas for theological discussion and personal engagement.

In most chapters, we have also included "Bonus Material." This section is intended to help readers understand something of the making and the reception of the movie. Awards that have been given to the movie are often listed, as is personal information about cast or crew members. Sometimes an aspect of a movie that is important but was not otherwise covered is mentioned. What all the comments have in common is that they provide additional, interesting background for understanding the movie being considered. Finally, some chapters provide "Selected Additional Resources" that the interested reader can turn to for more conversation about the movie and/or its theological importance. Many of these are easily found online with the links provided.

It is important to remember in reading the movie discussions that they are meant only as a guide. Some of our questions will not connect with you. Movies strike different viewers in different ways. A clip might not work for you. Use what is useful, and feel free to contextualize the questions in ways that will be helpful in your setting. There is more than enough material to lead a vibrant discussion, to use a particular movie to embody a point, or to meditate on movies and Scripture as they are allowed to be heard in conversation with each other. Each chapter is intended to give the interested movie viewer a sufficient body of material to enter into a robust dialogue between faith and film.

A Resource and Guide

God in the Movies can be used as a personal resource for your own movie watching. Here are forty movies that we have found both entertaining and spiritually provocative. They have challenged and informed us, inviting us into the lives of others who share God's image. We believe they will provide you a similar experience. We suggest that you invite a friend or neighbor to watch these movies with you. (Use us as your excuse, if you like. You can say the movie was recommended as being worth viewing.) Movie watching invites conversation and response. To hear a story and have no means of responding to it is to risk aborting its power and significance in your life.

Though individual viewers can benefit from the conversation generated within the pages of this book, the volume is intended primarily as a resource for use by those in group or public settings, particularly those speaking to or leading groups in the church or community. The book is intended mainly as a guide for those teaching an adult study group, for youth workers leading discussions after viewing movies with students, for those wanting to begin a neighborhood discussion group for Christians and non-Christians alike, or for those wanting help in how to use film clips and Scripture to focus a group's meditation and prayer.

The book is also meant as a resource for church leaders and pastors who would like to use film clips and stories in their speaking, teaching, and preaching. Just as many sermons unfortunately misinterpret a biblical text, using it for unintended purposes, so many in the church who want to connect the Christian faith with wider popular culture often misinterpret film clips and stories and use them to illustrate something other than what a movie is portraying. Thus we have tried to engage each movie at the center of the story's power and meaning and to suggest how it might prove useful for those charged with the teaching and preaching ministries of the church.

Leading a Discussion Group

Leading a movie group discussion is a subject worthy of a much longer treatment than we can give here, but the following are insights (à la David Letterman) we have found useful in groups we have led:

10. As the leader, you are not the "expert" but the guide for the discussion.

9. See the movie yourself before the event so you can prepare adequately to be the discussion guide.

8. If you are going to see the film together as a group (something we strongly recommend), keep your initial comments very brief. Let the movie introduce itself. Those bonus materials we have provided or other tidbits you uncover might best be used as part of the discussion following the movie.

7. After seeing the movie, begin with a question that helps participants express their experience with the film. Ask them to share their response to a scene that was particularly moving to them, or even ask why they liked or didn't like the movie. There are no right or wrong answers here. If participants start to analyze the movie in an abstract way, politely ask them to respond to their own experience with the movie.

6. Remember, *God in the Movies* is a resource for you and your community. Don't feel the need to use everything provided. And feel free to adapt/contextualize the questions for your group.

5. Groups can create their own momentum and process. Don't sweat it if questions arise from the group, as long as faith and film are put in conversation.

4. Always be respectful. Because movies are viewer oriented, what moves one person will leave another cold. We all know this. If someone says something that seems not in keeping with the movie, ask the group if they agree. Let the wisdom of the group carry you forward.

3. Don't be the "answer man or woman." Your background reading, viewing, and preparation should be directed toward helping the group break open the movie's story and begin a theological dialogue with it. There is no need for closure. Remember that Jesus usually left his parables open-ended. The power of story is in its ability to invite ongoing reflection and engagement.

2. Create a space where everyone can participate, which is especially impor tant in intergenerational groups. If needed, respectfully ask the "talkers" to allow the quieter folks to share their ideas.

1. In the pursuit of beauty, goodness, and truth, have fun!

Robert K. Johnston
Catherine M. Barsotti

A **DECADE**
OF **CHANGES**

Like most decades, the 1980s were a mixture of often-contradictory ideas. The turmoil of the previous decades—the countercultural movements of the sixties, the Vietnam War, Watergate, Middle East unrest, and oil embargoes—had damaged American self-confidence, grinding people down in a spiral of economic inflation and social unrest. No wonder, then, that in the 1980s attitudes seemed to swing in the opposite direction, with the embrace of a new conservatism in most areas of life, including religion. The eighties were marked by the rise of the Moral Majority, which fought with renewed vigor for religion's voice in society and politics.

Many have tended to characterize the eighties as the "decade of greed," citing its rampant materialism (Gordon Gekko's "greed is good" war cry from Oliver Stone's *Wall Street*) and consumerism. But it might be better to use that descriptor of the next decade, because the 1990s saw an economy fueled by tech innovations go bust and witnessed an explosion of corporate greed and corruption. Instead, the eighties was a decade of change—the Iranian hostage crisis, the collapse of the Soviet empire, Chernobyl, AIDS. It was

1

also the decade in which computers became a household item and moved us all toward the digital age.

The eighties also witnessed the emergence of the yuppie (young urban professional). Often derided as self-centered and materialistic, these college-educated baby boomers with money and a hankering for the good things in life were also riddled with self-doubt and anxiety about the state of things (consider movies made about them, such as *The Big Chill* and *Bright Lights, Big City*). These yuppies may have been more consumerist than their fore-bears, but they certainly didn't seem to be happier for it. Their rise to cultural prominence was aided by the ongoing emergence of popular culture as a shaping force. With the emergence of MTV in 1981, which gave us the music video and launched the careers of many iconic pop artists, such as Michael Jackson and Madonna, popular culture continued its two-decade shift from being a marginal effect of youth culture to being a defining aspect of late twentieth-century cultural life in the West, if not globally.

In the movies it was arguably the decade of both the blockbuster (films like *E.T.* and *Raiders of the Lost Ark*) and the teen movie (films like *Pretty in Pink* and *The Breakfast Club*). But perhaps most surprisingly, the 1980s also saw a number of films with religious themes—*The Elephant Man, Chariots of Fire, Places in the Heart, Tender Mercies, The Mission, Witness, Babette's Feast*. In spite of the claim by some critics that Hollywood was "anti-church," religious-themed films abounded. It may be true that suspicion of organized Christianity was a focus in popular culture in general (a theme that has only gained currency as the decades have passed), but it was by no means that simple. Not all of the films that focused on religious themes could be characterized as "religious films"; rather, religious ideas even permeated many of the massive blockbusters of the period (perhaps evidence of the power of telling old stories in new ways). The end of the decade also saw the release of two controversial religious films that garnered much public attention, if not major audiences—*Jesus of Montreal* and *The Last Temptation of Christ*. Religion was making its surprising journey back into the center of public and social life, and cinema was both mirroring and contributing to this trend.

Barry Taylor

1

Amadeus

US, 1984
160 Minutes (Extended Cut), Feature, Color
Actors: F. Murray Abraham, Tom Hulce,
  Elizabeth Berridge
Director: Miloš Forman
Screenwriter: Peter Shaffer
Rated: R (brief nudity)

Vocation
Art/Play Mediating
God's Presence,
Beauty, Idolatry, Jealousy

Synopsis and Theological Reflection

In more ways than one, the Oscar-winning film *Amadeus* asks a number of profoundly theological questions. What exactly is it about Mozart's music that, even centuries after its creation, prompts not just appreciation among those who hear it but actual devotion? Was Mozart somehow mediating the music of the heavens? And if so, how on earth could *this* man of all people be the vessel through whom God voices creation's praise?

Amadeus doesn't attempt to answer these questions in the abstract. Rather, it dramatizes the (transcendent?) power of his music by locating it within an all-too-human story about ambition, jealousy, murder, love/lust, and the desire for our creative work to somehow matter.

Set in eighteenth-century Vienna, *Amadeus* tells Mozart's story from the perspective of an aging Antonio Salieri, Mozart's slightly less talented contemporary. Initially, Salieri is convinced that Mozart's success as a respected and financially well-off court composer in Austria is due to his pious devotion. But upon meeting Mozart, Salieri begins to question why God would favor such a creature, especially one so wantonly vulgar and immoral. By the film's conclusion, Salieri's envy of Mozart has driven him to seek the death of God's chosen instrument and, in doing so, to enact a kind of vengeance against God for Salieri's musical mediocrity.

Amadeus was originally released in theaters in 1984, which makes it a thirty-year-old movie telling a three-hundred-year-old story. But like so many classics, *Amadeus* is far from dated. In fact, many of its core themes directly address our contemporary situation.

For instance, a 2007 Pew Research Center poll suggested that the number one life goal for 51 percent of eighteen- to twenty-five-year olds in the United States is to be famous. A similar survey in the United Kingdom noted that, when asked to name their vocational aspirations, the most common response among middle-school-aged students was that they wanted nothing more than to be a celebrity—a notable change from thirty years prior when the leading responses were doctor, lawyer, and teacher.

But what is it that inspires this kind of ambition? Is there something unique about modern culture that allows fame and celebrity to be held out as viable options for living a full and flourishing life? Or could it be that our desire for public recognition and all the trappings that go with it is a core human impulse? Interestingly, echoes of this same sensibility can be heard in the prayer of the young Salieri early on in the film: "Make me famous through the world. Make me immortal. Let people speak my name forever with love. In return I will give you my chastity."

In Salieri's mind, his is an earnest prayer for God to use him as an instrument for proclaiming God's glory to the entire world. But as Salieri recounts these formative moments of his life, we realize that the true motivation for his prayer is not about his calling or a genuine aspiration to serve God with his gifts and talents. It's about his desire for fame—his yearning both to create something and become someone whom others would recognize, love, and perhaps even worship.

Next to the story of creation, this is the oldest story in the book. Like countless other tales that have come before and after, *Amadeus* is a movie about one of God's creatures—ephemeral, limited, contingent, and finite— seeking permanence. Much like Salieri, regardless of the mental gymnastics we perform in order to justify (or disguise) our true aims, it seems that human beings cannot help but overreach. We continually attempt to place ourselves in a position reserved only for God. So whether it's an eighteenth-century court composer or a twenty-first-century YouTube star, fame and celebrity reveal themselves to be expressions of a core human dilemma: idolatry.

The tragedy of course is that, as a contemporary of Mozart, Salieri never really had a chance. Although it is quasi-apocryphal and reflects a nineteenth-century romanticized understanding of musical production, part of Mozart's notoriety had to do not simply with the breathtaking music he created but with the process by which he created it. Mozart had an exceptional musical memory and keen improvisational skills. The by-product was his ability to create music on the spot, as if music lived ready-made in his head and all he had to do was perform it or write it down to make it a reality.

Regardless of the exact historical details, though, the end result of Mozart's creative process was and continues to be some of the most enduring music in the Western world. So it's not surprising that a man like Salieri would both adore this music and hate the one who made it. Indeed, it is this hatred of Mozart and his music—this jealousy rooted in a blind ambition for unending fame—that eventually undoes an otherwise talented musician in his own right.

In the end, much like Mozart's final requiem mass, Salieri's own life never arrives at a proper end. Given his unquenchable ambition and the jealousy it inspired, his life remained unfinished and incomplete. It simply faded into nonexistence, which, if the biblical testimony is right, is exactly where our selfish ambitions will eventually lead us all. If followed long enough, our individual quests for celebrity will have us uttering something strikingly similar to Salieri as he sums up his life's work: "[God] killed Mozart and kept me alive to torture. Thirty-two years of torture, thirty-two years of slowly watching myself become extinct. My music becoming fainter, all the time, becoming fainter, till no one plays it at all. While his . . ."

Dialogue Texts

If then there is any encouragement in Christ, any consolation from love, any sharing in the Spirit, any compassion and sympathy, make my joy complete: be of the same mind, having the same love, being in full accord and of one mind. Do nothing from selfish ambition or conceit, but in humility regard others as better than yourselves. Let each of you look not to your own interests, but to the interests of others. Let the same mind be in you that was in Christ Jesus,

> who, though he was in the form of God,
>   did not regard equality with God
>   as something to be exploited,

but emptied himself,
     taking the form of a slave,
     being born in human likeness.
And being found in human form,
     he humbled himself
     and became obedient to the point of death—
     even death on a cross.

Philippians 2:1–8

Then I saw that all toil and all skill in work come from one person's envy of another. This also is vanity and a chasing after wind.

Fools fold their hands
     and consume their own flesh.
Better is a handful with quiet
     than two handfuls with toil,
     and a chasing after wind.

Ecclesiastes 4:4–6

Who is wise and understanding among you? Show by your good life that your works are done with gentleness born of wisdom. But if you have bitter envy and selfish ambition in your hearts, do not be boastful and false to the truth. Such wisdom does not come down from above, but is earthly, unspiritual, devilish. For where there is envy and selfish ambition, there will also be disorder and wickedness of every kind. But the wisdom from above is first pure, then peaceable, gentle, willing to yield, full of mercy and good fruits, without a trace of partiality or hypocrisy. And a harvest of righteousness is sown in peace for those who make peace.

Those conflicts and disputes among you, where do they come from? Do they not come from your cravings that are at war within you? You want something and do not have it; so you commit murder. And you covet something and cannot obtain it; so you engage in disputes and conflicts. You do not have, because you do not ask. You ask and do not receive, because you ask wrongly, in order to spend what you get on your pleasures.

James 3:13–4:3

Then he said to them all, "If any want to become my followers, let them deny themselves and take up their cross daily and follow me. For those who want to save their life will lose it, and those who lose their life for my sake will save it. What does it profit them if they gain the whole world, but lose or forfeit themselves? Those who are ashamed of me and of my words, of them the Son of Man will be ashamed when he comes in his glory and the glory of the Father and of the holy angels. But truly I tell you, there are some standing here who will not taste death before they see the kingdom of God."

Luke 9:23–27

Discussion Questions and Clip Conversations

All clips are available for viewing at ReelSpirituality.com/Books/God-In-The-Movies. We have also listed the timestamp range of the scenes for your reference.

1. "Everyone Liked Me . . . until He Came" [05:00–14:04]. In his opening monologue, Salieri demonstrates that he has confused his God-given vocation with his desire for fame and notoriety. Consider the words of his prayer as a young boy: "Make me famous through the world. Make me immortal. Let people speak my name forever with love. In return I will give you my chastity." Have you ever confused your own ambitions with God's calling? What happened as a result? What motivates contemporary persons' desire for fame and celebrity? What core human longing does this desire reflect? Is there any kind of recognition or accolade that is not "motivated by selfish ambition or vanity" (Phil. 2:3 NET)? If so, what would that look like? How does the model Christ provides us in Philippians 2:5–8 shape the way we understand our desire for fame—both as individuals and as a community?

2. "Here Again Was the Voice of God . . . in a Boastful, Lustful, Infantile Boy" [51:28–58:38]. Who is qualified to serve as God's instrument? What are the criteria that we use to make this judgment? Are they the same criteria that God uses? In your own life, how do the words of Ecclesiastes 4:4–6 ring true? That is, how much of your own work is motivated by competition with someone else—someone you might think has been unfairly "gifted" by God? In what ways does this quest put you at odds with God's work in the world? Are there good or helpful kinds of competition? At what point does our dedication to "skillfulness" or "excellence" get in the way of our ability to enjoy our work and what we make?

3. "I Thought You Did Not Care for My Work or Me" [2:23:31–2:24:51]. Do you ever feel as Mozart did—that no one around you likes what you do, much less likes you? Could it be that our jealousy of others is connected somehow to a more basic insecurity with who we are and whether we are likable? If so, how does James address this source of

conflict among the Christian community? Mozart asks Salieri for forgiveness. James 4:1–3 says that we do not have because we do not ask. What hinders you from asking others to forgive you, especially those whom you envy?

4. "I Speak for All the Mediocrities in the World. I Am Their Patron Saint" [2:32:39–2:34:43]. Does our "mediocre" work still matter when placed next to the brilliance of others? How can we rightly appreciate inspiration without diminishing our own work? How do we find joy regardless of fame? Did Salieri "gain the whole world but lose himself"? If so, how? How might *Amadeus* shed new light on our reading of Luke 9:23–27 about losing our life in order to save it rather than gaining the world but losing our soul (or in Salieri's words, "my music")?

Selected Additional Resources

Brown, Peter. "*Amadeus* and Mozart: Setting the Record Straight." *American Scholar* 61, no. 1 (Winter 1992): 49–66.

Ebert, Roger. Review of *Amadeus*. September 19, 1984. http://www.roger ebert.com/reviews/amadeus-1984.

Myers, Cathleen. "Amadeus." http://www.peersdance.org/revamade.html.

"Synopsis of *Don Giovanni*: An Opera by W A Mozart." http://www.music withease.com/don-giovanni-synopsis.html.

Kutter Callaway

2

Babette's Feast

Original title: *Babettes gæstebud*
Denmark, 1987
102 Minutes, Feature, Color
Actors: Stéphane Audran, Bodil Kjer, Birgitte
    Federspiel
Director: Gabriel Axel
Screenwriter: Gabriel Axel (based on the
    novel of the same name by Karen Blixen)
Rated: G

*Art/Play Mediating
God's Mercy*
*Beauty, Community,
Forgiveness,
God's Mercy vs.
Human Judgment,
Gratitude, Vocation*

Synopsis and Theological Reflection

Babette's Feast opens on a gray ocean, widening to reveal a dozen buildings huddled against the bleak northernmost seaside of Denmark. Gutted cod, mouths agape, hang to dry in the sun—framing the entrance of the film's gentle protagonists, Filippa and Martine. Elderly, they are the daughters of the tiny enclave's long-dead minister, whose spirit of austerity hovers over their implacable community. With two simple shots, aided by spare notes from composer Per Nørgård, Danish film director Gabriel Axel reveals a spirituality dedicated to a "higher and purer life" that is also willfully ignorant of abundance and bliss. The narrator's first words hint at the results of such

Babettes gaestebud (Babette's Feast) © 1987 A-S Panorama Film International

The community gathers at Babette's feast

lopsided devotion: "In this remote spot, there once lived two sisters." *There once lived*: it is easy to imagine that the two aging virgins were once alive in a way that they are no longer when we meet them.

It is quite some time before we meet the titular French refugee Babette Hersant, who arrives in dire need, hoping to gain shelter with the sisters. First, the storyteller takes pains to flash back on the once-alive life of the daughters when they were young and beautiful women. Their father ruled them and his congregation with an ice-covered righteousness matching the countryside in which they worshiped their harsh Savior. The young beauties are offered many opportunities for love and life beyond the Jutland coast, but paralyzed by doubt and afraid of their feelings, they sublimate desire and choose to devote their lives in service to their father and his church. Two particular suitors are most painfully rejected, leaving a mark on each sister's soul that no amount of community service can hope to erase. As one rejected suitor puts it, he has been "defeated by some pious melancholics who can't afford salt for their soup."

Decades after their father's death—as they struggle to keep a shrunken congregation from bitter infighting with little more than endless meals of saltless ale-bread soup—they are given another miraculous chance at life. On a dark and stormy night, a hooded French woman appears at their door with a missive from Filippa's long-ago rejected admirer who begs the sisters to shelter the bedraggled refugee. It will be some years before they discover that the risk they take to receive Babette, fueled by their Christlike kindness, is also an answer to their prayers. On that rainy night they welcomed the finest culinary artist from the most extravagant, pleasure-seeking capital of the world: Paris. But the letter she carries simply says, "Babette knows how to cook."

The sisters teach Babette to make soup from pieces of stale rye bread and rehydrated cod, boiled into the consistency of a bricklayer's mortar. Over the years, she transforms it with herbs growing wild on the rocky shore, and with loving care. Her longing, as she gathers her seasonings in the sinking sun, is palpable. For fourteen years she keeps her yearning tucked in the "hidden regions of the heart."

"God's paths run by the sea and the snowy mountain peaks where the human eye sees no tracks," the minister teaches his congregation early in the film, reminding them of the unpredictability of the Spirit. And so, many years later, an old Paris lottery ticket pays Babette a small fortune, destined to change their little village. A celebration of the one-hundredth anniversary of the Lutheran prophet's birth becomes a transformational event for the sisters, the congregation, and Babette as she receives permission to make the celebratory meal. The handful of remaining church members are the fearful beneficiaries of her largesse, as Babette purchases, prepares, and serves the gastronomic delight of a lifetime. They bring to her table many lifetimes of bitter regret and shriveled hopes—fueled by a misbegotten collusion to deny the pleasures of the meal, as if by silence and denial their pleasure will not exist. Yet Babette's feast works its wonders on them all—including the servants who wait in the kitchen—and all leave transformed.

Dialogue Texts

All this I laid to heart, examining it all, how the righteous and the wise and their deeds are in the hand of God; whether it is love or hate one does not know. Everything that confronts them is vanity, since the same fate comes to all, to the righteous and the wicked, to the good and the evil, to the clean and the unclean, to those who sacrifice and those who do not sacrifice. As are the good, so are the sinners; those who swear are like those who shun an oath. . . . But whoever is joined with all the living has hope, for a living dog is better than a dead lion. The living know that they will die, but the dead know nothing; they have no more reward, and even the memory of them is lost. Their love and their hate and their envy have already perished; never again will they have any share in all that happens under the sun.

Go, eat your bread with enjoyment, and drink your wine with a merry heart; for God has long ago approved what you do.

Ecclesiastes 9:1–7

Welcome those who are weak in faith, but not for the purpose of quarreling over opinions. Some believe in eating anything, while the weak eat only vegetables. Those who eat must not despise those who abstain, and those who abstain must not pass judgment on those who eat; for God has welcomed them.

Romans 14:1–3

Listen! I am standing at the door, knocking; if you hear my voice and open the door, I will come in to you and eat with you, and you with me.

Revelation 3:20

Set apart a tithe of all the yield of your seed that is brought in yearly from the field. In the presence of the LORD your God, in the place that he will choose as a dwelling for his name, you shall eat the tithe of your grain, your wine, and your oil, as well as the firstlings of your herd and flock, so that you may learn to fear the LORD your God always. But if, when the LORD your God has blessed you, the distance is so great that you are unable to transport it, because the place where the LORD your God will choose to set his name is too far away from you, then you may turn it into money. With the money secure in hand, go to the place that the LORD your God will choose; spend the money for whatever you wish—oxen, sheep, wine, strong drink, or whatever you desire. And you shall eat there in the presence of the LORD your God, you and your household rejoicing together.

Deuteronomy 14:22–26

Discussion Questions and Clip Conversations

All clips are available for viewing at ReelSpirituality.com/Books/God-In-The-Movies. We have also listed the timestamp range of the scenes for your reference.

1. In the Old Testament, God's people are urged to spend their tithes on what they desire and to rejoice in the meal they are to share together. In the New Testament, Jesus says that if the door is opened to him, his promise is to enter and share a meal. How (and why) is eating together of central importance in the Christian faith? How do the Scriptures above inform us about the sacred act of the shared meal? What role does food play in bringing the film's congregants to gratitude, forgiveness, and renewed love? What role does food play in your life?

2. "Achille Tempts Filippa and She Reluctantly Withdraws" [22:18–29:16]. Achille Papin rehearses the famous duet from Mozart's *Don Giovanni*

with Filippa, telling her, "You will be the only star in the heavens!" She sings, "I tremble but I listen, I'm fearful of my joy! Desire, love, and doubting are battling in my head!" He assures her that he will make her a great lady. She keeps singing, "My soul weakens already." He sings his reply, "Love will unite us!" Why does Filippa say, after this passionate lesson, that she wishes to quit studying with Papin? What is it about Papin's sorrow that amuses their father? How does Filippa feel about her decision and what does she do with those feelings? How do you feel about her decision? Why?

3. "Babette Arrives with a Letter on a Stormy Night" [29:25–36:05]. In an impossible storm, Babette arrives, bedraggled and weary, with one last hope left to her for salvation. In a letter of recommendation and remembrance to the pious sisters, Achille Papin speaks glowingly of Filippa, saying that after the bloody uprisings in Paris, he can think of no place where Babette might find charity other than from the generous women devoted to God. He imagines their lives are filled with family while he, with his career over and his name forgotten, bemoans his choices. It seems that everyone in the film has similar regrets. What is the importance of illuminating these forlorn choices?

4. "The General Realizes Who Babette Is" [1:18:00–1:21:53]. During the meal, one of the congregants reminisces about a miraculous event in the life of the prophet that they are honoring, when the fjord froze over so that the minister could "walk across the waves" to serve distant villagers who had all but given up hope of his arrival. Immediately after this story, Babette removes from the oven the signature dish that will convince the general beyond doubt whose food he is eating—another holiday miracle. He describes Babette in her heyday as someone who could "transform a dinner into a love affair between bodily appetites and spiritual appetites." How does this observation reflect on the film's theme? How does it inform your answers to question 1? Has eating a meal ever been a spiritual experience for you? When?

5. "The General Reflects on the Meal's Transcendent Power" [1:26:43–1:28:46]. General Löwenhielm reflects on the transformation of the evening in a toast that reads like a homily:

> Mercy and truth have met together. Righteousness and bliss shall kiss one another. Man, in his weakness and shortsightedness, believes he must make choices in this life. He trembles at the risks he takes. We do know fear. But no, our choice is of no importance. There comes a time when your eyes are opened and we come to realize that mercy is infinite. We

need only await it with confidence and receive it with gratitude. Mercy imposes no conditions. And lo! Everything we have chosen has been granted to us—and everything we rejected has also been granted. Yes, we even get back what we rejected. For mercy and truth are met together and righteousness and bliss shall kiss one another.

How does the author of Ecclesiastes (see above) mirror General Löwen-hielm's sentiments? What do you think of his conclusions?

6. "Babette Explains Her Gift" [1:38:00–1:41:01]. When Babette explains to the sisters that the lottery money was her chance to do her very best as an artist, what did she mean? She had created that meal many times before under easier circumstances—what was it that made this experience something she waited her whole life for? In what ways does the artist bring something unique to the life of faith that none other can bring?

Selected Additional Resources

Fuller Theological Seminary's Brehm Center director Makoto Fujimura puts *Babette's Feast* in dialogue with T. S. Eliot's *Four Quartets* and Olivier Messiaen's composition "Quartet for the End of Time" in his 2013 address for the IAM (International Arts Movement) Inhabit conference in New York City. http://fujimurainstitute.org/wp-content/uploads/2014/03/MF-Inhabit -Keynote-Notes.pdf.

One of the contributors to this book, Elijah Davidson, writes about *Babette's Feast* in a series on Advent, noting, "*Babette's Feast* reminds us that devotion to truth and righteousness must be tempered by mercy and bliss. A little gruel is good, but so is a lavish feast." Find his devotional at http:// www.brehmcenter.com/initiatives/reelspirituality/film/study-guides/coming -attractions-week-4-filled-with-good-things.

Lauralee Farrer

3

Chariots of Fire

US/UK, 1981
124 Minutes, Feature, Color
Actors: Ian Charleson, Ben Cross, Ian Holm,
    John Gielgud, Alice Krige
Director: Hugh Hudson
Screenwriter: Colin Welland
Rated: PG

Vocation
Art/Play Mediating
God's Presence,
Faith/Belief, Play, Sabbath

Synopsis and Theological Reflection

I was vice president of production at Twentieth Century Fox when we produced *Chariots of Fire*. We knew the screenplay by Colin Welland was exceptional, and we were thrilled by the high quality of the performances and by the visual elegance of director Hugh Hudson's film. But none of us expected the acclaim, or the enduring legacy, that resulted for the film. The year 1981 produced some great movies—Stephen Spielberg's *Raiders of the Lost Ark*, Warren Beatty's *Reds*, Louis Malle's *Atlantic City*, and Mark Rydell's *On Golden Pond*. Those four were also nominated for the Academy Award for Best Picture, but to the surprise of almost everyone in the movie business, the fifth nominee, *Chariots of Fire*, won.

Chariots of Fire is based on a true story, set against the background of the 1924 Olympics. The movie depicts the stories of two outstanding runners with strikingly different motivations. Eric Liddell (Ian Charleson) is a Scottish Presbyterian university student (later to become a missionary in China) who runs to honor the gift of athletic skill that God has given him. Harold Abrahams (Ben Cross) is a secular Jewish student at Cambridge University who runs for himself in order to prove to his prejudiced upper-class schoolmates that a Jew can compete and excel at sports (and, metaphorically, at all levels of enterprise and society). While superficially that sounds as if Liddell is the hero and Abrahams is his foil, nothing could be less true. The movie is a story of two courageous men of integrity, each running for a worthy purpose.

As the story unfolds, Liddell and Abrahams meet in an important race leading up to the Olympics. When Liddell wins, Abrahams hires a professional trainer (Ian Holm, who received an Academy Award nomination as Best Supporting Actor) to help him prepare. Abrahams is unfairly criticized by anti-Semitic aristocrats for seeking this assistance, which they claim is unsportsmanlike. Meanwhile, Liddell trains on his own, running through the Scottish countryside and along the sandy beach.

Liddell's and Abrahams's Olympic preparations are challenged by personal dramas involving women who love them. Abrahams's girlfriend is troubled by his obsessive focus on training, and Liddell's sister warns Eric that his running is interfering with his missionary call to bring the gospel

The race of Abrahams's life—100-meter Olympic final

to China. Yet both men are selected for the English Olympic team that will compete in Paris. The film has led us to cheer for both, arguably with equal fervor.

Liddell, the gold-medal favorite, is informed that his best event is scheduled to be run on a Sunday. Because of his Christian conviction, he announces that he will not compete since it will be the Sabbath. The British Olympic Committee, and even the Prince of Wales (later King Edward VIII), attempt to persuade Liddell to run, the prince saying he should do so "for the good of the country." But in one of the movie's most powerful moments, Liddell replies, "God made countries, God makes kings, and the rules by which they govern. And the rules say that the Sabbath is his. And I for one intend to keep it that way."

History—some would say destiny—favored both runners. Abrahams won a gold medal in his event. Liddell, holding firmly to his Christian conviction not to compete on Sunday, is given the opportunity by another member of his team—in one of the film's many poignant scenes of selfless brotherhood and nobility of spirit—to run in his teammate's place in an event two days later. Liddell accepts and wins his gold medal.

Chariots of Fire raised the bar for major studio movies about people of faith. Many of the movies in this book have built on its foundation. Liddell's character—defined by integrity formed by unshakable Christian beliefs—is portrayed as dignified, humble, and heroic. His depiction centers on character and values, not ideology. For this reason, the film has received wide praise, even among secular audiences. Although it is rooted in (at times quite severe) Christian conviction, the movie's humanity and deep spirituality have a universal appeal. Here is a portrayal of Christian conviction appropriate for the public arena. As *New York Times* critic Vincent Canby wrote, "'Chariots of Fire' is simultaneously romantic and commonsensical, lyrical and comic. . . . It is an exceptional film, about some exceptional people."

Dialogue Texts

So let us not grow weary in doing what is right, for we will reap at harvest time, if we do not give up.

Galatians 6:9

I press on toward the goal for the prize of the heavenly call of God in Christ Jesus.

Philippians 3:14

Remember the sabbath day, and keep it holy. Six days you shall labor and do all your work. But the seventh day is a sabbath to the LORD your God; you shall not do any work.

Exodus 20:8–10; cf. Deuteronomy 5:12–15

Jesus said to them, "Give to the emperor the things that are the emperor's, and to God the things that are God's."

Mark 12:17

Discussion Questions and Clip Conversations

All clips are available for viewing at ReelSpirituality.com/Books/God-In -The-Movies. We have also listed the timestamp range of the scenes for your reference.

1. Why do you think the running scenes are in slow motion? What scriptural message does running alongside the water suggest? What is your theology of sport/play?

2. "Muscular Christianity" [25:54–27:44]. Early in the film, after Eric Liddell wins a race, he speaks to an admiring crowd of fans and says, "I have no formula for winning the race. Everyone runs in her own way, or his own way. And where does the power come from, to see the race to its end? From within. Jesus said, 'Behold, the Kingdom of God is within you. If with all your hearts you truly seek me, you shall surely find me.' If you commit yourself to the love of Christ, then that is how you run a straight race." Does the movie portray Liddell as a great preacher? How does the crowd respond? Would he still be a hero even if he were not a champion athlete? What is your opinion about such "muscular Christianity"?

3. "Another Two Yards" [48:20–51:57]. After Harold Abrahams loses a race to Eric Liddell, his coach/trainer, Sam Mussabini, tells him, "I can find you another two yards." Are we always seeking "another two yards" in the struggles we face? Can that be the difference between success and failure? How can prayer and faith enable us to find the "something extra" in our lives?

4. "When I Run I Feel His Pleasure" [56:07–1:00:21]. When Eric Liddell's sister Jenny warns him that he is losing track of his primary call to return to China as a missionary, that "your mind is not with us anymore, it is full of running and starting and medals and pace," he responds gently,

saying, "I believe God made me for a purpose, but he also made me fast. And when I run I feel his pleasure." In what pursuits do you feel God's pleasure? Is it difficult to balance developing your individual talents and self-confidence with surrendering your life to God's will? How do you balance your play and your work—both God-given?

5. How does Liddell honor God by running? Does his faith give him a competitive edge? Why? Are Abrahams's motives any less honorable than Liddell's? Why? Was it wrong for Abrahams to use a professional trainer? If Abrahams's race had been scheduled on Saturday, the Jewish Sabbath, do you think he would have run? Is this a relevant question?

6. It is easy to see who wins a race. But how can we tell if we are winning the race that God has called us to run? How do we know if we have even entered the right event? Is there a finish line? Besides gold medals, what else did Eric Liddell and Harold Abrahams win? Are the values that Liddell and Abrahams represent still present in competitive sports today? Was 1924 a time of higher moral standards than 2016? As a movie set almost one hundred years ago, is *Chariots of Fire* still an example of how Christians should live their lives and use their gifts?

Bonus Material

In September 2015, I met Mark Joseph, a respected film producer who is now developing a "sequel" to *Chariots of Fire*. Mark's movie will focus on Eric Liddell's heroic missionary service and death as a prisoner during World War II. Ironically, another unofficial sequel to *Chariots of Fire* is also in development, one that is not explicitly Christian and that focuses far less on Liddell's faith. I find this continuing interest in Liddell's story to be a fascinating example of the lasting impact of, and broad admiration for, the movie. Christians celebrate *Chariots of Fire* as a breakthrough major studio movie that honors Christian conviction. Others see it simply as a wonderful movie that employs eloquent language, beautiful imagery, and memorable music to tell a story of character and perseverance. It is, of course, both.

If, over the past four decades, mainstream Hollywood has become increasingly receptive to redemptive stories with explicitly Christian protagonists, then *Chariots of Fire* is the front page. It never occurred to any of us involved with the film that this was a Christian movie. It was simply a values-affirming story, beautifully executed, and we were all proud to be part of it.

Chariots of Fire, while a coproduction of Twentieth Century Fox and Warner Bros., was a lower budgeted movie. It featured no box-office stars (the great John Gielgud notwithstanding) and a relatively unknown director in Hugh Hudson. But somehow the mystical alchemy of collaborative filmmaking produced a remarkable movie.

If I may add a personal note, the success of *Chariots of Fire* also produced a healing between two people I deeply care about. Alan Ladd Jr. ("Laddie") was my first boss at Fox, and he, as president, promoted me to vice president of production and administration. Laddie had championed the development of *Chariots of Fire* at Fox, but he resigned as president and left to become a producer (Ladd Company) at Warner Bros. Laddie's departure was triggered by a bitter falling out with Dennis Stanfill, Fox's chairman and CEO, who subsequently promoted me to senior vice president. Given that *Chariots of Fire* was perceived by all of us as an art film, not a blockbuster, financing the movie was not easy. Laddie facilitated Warner's joining Fox in putting up part of the production budget. The balance of the budget was provided by Dodi Fayed, who later died with Princess Diana in their tragic car crash in Paris. The complicated coproduction deal gave Warner Bros. US distribution rights and Fox international rights. The movie's extraordinary critical reception resulted in commercial success. That, in turn, helped to heal the harsh feelings between my friends and mentors, Dennis and Laddie.

In addition to winning the Academy Award for Best Picture, *Chariots of Fire* also won the Oscars for Best Original Screenplay (Colin Welland), Best Costume Design (Milena Canonero), and Best Original Score (Vangelis). Vangelis's electronic score accompanying the running scenes together with Eric Liddell's noble character and inspirational speech remain the most remembered and cherished elements of the movie.

Joseph C. Gallagher

4

Crimes and Misdemeanors

US, 1989

104 Minutes, Feature, Color

Actors: Martin Landau, Woody Allen, Alan
Alda, Mia Farrow, Anjelica Huston, Sam
Waterston, Joanna Gleason, Jerry Orbach

Director: Woody Allen

Screenwriter: Woody Allen

Rated: PG-13 (sex, violence, language)

The Meaning of Life
Justice, Life's Mystery,
Life's Vanity,
Morality/Amorality,
Sin and Its Consequences

Synopsis and Theological Reflection

Throughout his prolific, five-decade-long career, Woody Allen has written
and directed some of the most acclaimed and theologically interesting films in
American cinema. Some of these films, such as *Banana* (1971), *Sleeper* (1973),
and *Love and Death* (1975), are high-concept slapstick comedies designed
to amuse and entertain, while others, such as *Interiors* (1978), *September*
(1987), and *Another Woman* (1988), are serious spiritual dramas with strong
resemblance to the works of his filmmaking hero Ingmar Bergman. Allen's
best-known films, though, are those that seamlessly combine the tragic and the
comedic. Works like the Oscar-winning *Annie Hall* (1976), *Manhattan* (1979),
and *Hannah and Her Sisters* (1986) all feature complex characters wrestling

with various forms of existential and romantic crises, and they expertly balance comedy with pointed philosophical inquiries about the meaning of life and the existence of God.

Allen's 1989 film *Crimes and Misdemeanors* is perhaps the purest example of this unique brand of philosophical tragicomedy. Loosely inspired by Dostoyevsky's novel *Crime and Punishment*, the film contains two distinct but parallel stories—one a drama, the other a comedy—that together offer a thought-provoking examination of the nature of morality and the justice of God.

In the movie's dramatic first story, an Oscar-nominated Martin Landau plays Judah, a distinguished ophthalmologist with a loving family and a community of admiring friends and colleagues. Beneath that veneer of respectability, however, Judah has been involved in an extramarital affair with Dolores (Anjelica Huston), a former flight attendant who has become increasingly unstable due to Judah's reluctance to leave his wife. When she threatens to expose their affair along with knowledge she has of his financial misconduct, Judah solicits his estranged mobster brother's help to have the woman killed. When this is accomplished, he becomes stricken with guilt and haunted by the religious beliefs from his Jewish upbringing, which teach him that "the eyes of God are on us always." Judah fears that he will face divine punishment, and he wonders if he can ever live a normal life again.

In the movie's comedic second story, Woody Allen himself plays Cliff, an unsuccessful documentary filmmaker with a wife who regards him with disdain. Cliff's efforts to produce meaningful, socially conscious films have been met with little attention. His crass and pompous brother-in-law Lester (Alan Alda) is a highly successful television producer. Out of pity and as a favor to his sister, Lester hires Cliff to produce a vanity documentary about his life and career. Cliff reluctantly agrees. During the production, Cliff falls in love with the film's producer, Halley (Mia Farrow), who is also being casually pursued by Lester. Cliff attempts to win her affection and begins showing her footage from a documentary he has been working on about a philosopher who speaks with eloquence and insights about the human condition. Cliff wonders if things will finally come together for him.

Connecting these two stories is the character of Ben (Sam Waterston), a rabbi who happens to be Judah's patient and Cliff's brother-in-law. Ben is a genuinely good man, and he offers sincere counsel to Judah during his moral crisis, but he is also rapidly losing his eyesight and inching closer toward total blindness.

Crimes and Misdemeanors is a multilayered film with intricate ideas and rich metaphors. Take the character of Ben: Is the rabbi's loss of eyesight

Crimes and Misdemeanors © 1989 Orion Pictures Corporation

Judah recalling a family Seder: Does the universe have a moral order?

a reflection of the universe's injustice and indifference? Or is this a sign of his spiritual blindness with respect to the struggles and suffering of others? The answer could well be both. This is a highly philosophical movie that asks ultimate questions about human existence without offering easy answers. The viewers are invited to consider the following: Is morality a matter of choice, or is there a higher law that governs our conscience and actions? Does the universe have a moral order, or is it indifferent and devoid of meaning? How do our choices affect the way we live? Why do bad people triumph and good people suffer? Indeed, what makes someone "good" or "bad"?

In the film, Allen makes a strong distinction between the "idealized" world of religious faith and the "real," complicated world of everyday moral decisions. On the one hand, we have Rabbi Ben and Judah's father—sincere believers who lead rich and peaceful lives because of their faith; they believe in God's justice, and they unfailingly urge Judah to be righteous. On the other hand, Allen shows us characters who have difficulty subscribing to religious thinking, who either have to struggle with tough moral decisions or contend with the seeming injustice of the universe: Judah can confess to his affair and risk losing everything, or he can get rid of his problem by committing an immoral act and face the consequence. Judah ultimately gets away with the crime, and in the film's central irony, not only is he untroubled by his conscience, but he also ends up prospering. Cliff tries to make a difference in the world by making meaningful documentaries, but the person who has all the success (and gets the girl in the end) is Lester, the arrogant and vulgar television producer. What we are presented with is a world where unjust deeds go unpunished, where a thoughtful philosopher is doomed to commit suicide while a blind rabbi is able to enjoy life and happily see his daughter being married off.

Allen's film is, however, more than just a didactic treatise on the injustice of the universe. What makes it compelling is the way it depicts each major character and their predicament with nuance and insight. Some may find Rabbi Ben and Judah's father naive, but they are also clearly decent and upright, their lives filled with the sort of peace and gladness that Cliff and others strive for but are unable to attain. Cliff may be less pompous and obnoxious than Lester, but he can also be sanctimonious and self-pitying. Dolores is hysterical and menacing, but she is also shown to be full of feelings and longings. This is a world in which everyone has a reason for doing what they do, and they are confronted with the consequence of their choices. "God is a luxury I can't afford," says Judah at one point, and when explaining his decision to ignore his conscience, he tells Cliff that in life "we rationalize, we deny, or we couldn't go on living." Allen's film laments his characters' inability to believe, just as it laments the terrible implication of their beliefs about the world.

Crimes and Misdemeanors invites viewers to soberly examine the state of the world. It is a brilliant tragicomedy and an essential movie for Christians who wish to think seriously about faith, about morality, and about life itself.

Dialogue Texts

The reader is encouraged to read the whole book of Ecclesiastes to explore another reflection on the apparent amorality of life. Yet unlike *Crimes and Misdemeanors*, the narrator, an ancient student of life's vagaries and injustices, never loses sight of the Creator and the Creator's gift of life. Here are two sample texts from Ecclesiastes and two from the New Testament.

> In my vain life I have seen everything; there are righteous people who perish in their righteousness, and there are wicked people who prolong their life in their evildoing.
>
> Ecclesiastes 7:15

> There is something else meaningless that occurs on earth: the righteous who get what the wicked deserve, and the wicked who get what the righteous deserve. This too, I say, is meaningless. So I commend the enjoyment of life, because there is nothing better for a person under the sun than to eat and drink and be

glad. Then joy will accompany them in their toil all the days of the life God has given them under the sun.

Ecclesiastes 8:14–15 (NIV)

Anyone, then, who knows the right thing to do and fails to do it, commits sin.

James 4:17

What good is it for someone to gain the whole world, yet forfeit their soul?

Mark 8:36 (NIV)

Discussion Questions and Clip Conversations

All clips are available for viewing at ReelSpirituality.com/Books/God-In -The-Movies. We have also listed the timestamp range of the scenes for your reference.

1. "Dark Night of the Soul: Judah Decides to Go Through with the Murder" [40:03–43:35]. What does Judah mean when he says that God is "a luxury [he] can't afford"? What do you think about Rabbi Ben's response to Judah's struggle? Is he naive, or does he have a point? How would you compare Judah's and Ben's views on God and morality?

2. "The Heretical Aunt: Judah Remembers His Childhood Seder" [1:09:55–1:13:22]. This childhood Seder scene encapsulates the film's central philosophical debate. Judah's aunt challenges the religious worldview of his father. She believes morality is a matter of choice— for those who want to abide by it, they will have it, and for those who choose to ignore it (and can get away with their misdeeds), they can live carefree. In contrast, Judah's father believes the wicked will always be punished, that the justice of God will eventually be carried out. When pressed on the reasonableness of his religious beliefs, Judah's father says that even if he is wrong, he would still live a better (and presumably happier) life than those who doubt. He concludes, "If necessary, I will always choose God over truth." Who do you agree with here? Is the cynical aunt right when she says that "might makes right"? Do you think the world is as unjust as she thinks it is? Is Judah's father's unwavering faith a sign of strength, or is he foolish in ways that he is unaware of? Or has Allen failed to explore a third way that combines the two positions, something that his Jewish tradition finds in Ecclesiastes?

3. "Climax: Judah and Cliff's Conversation about Morality" [1:34:45–
   1:39:24]. In this final meeting between Judah and Cliff, Judah describes
   hypothetically, but personally, a murder and how the perpetrator became
   free from the guilt that initially plagued him. The man finds that his
   life has prospered and that his awful deed has gone unpunished. He's
   learned to live happily despite his sins. Cliff tells him that this would
   mean that his worst beliefs about the injustice and meaninglessness of
   the universe have been realized. Judah admits that this is chilling, but
   argues that in the real world, this is how people have to live. How do
   your own beliefs compare to what Judah and Cliff are expressing here?
   How does this conversation shed light on the rest of the story?
4. The distinction between the "real" world and the "idealized" world is
   a running theme in this film (think of Cliff discussing movies with his
   niece, or Cliff's movie about Lester, or Professor Levy saying platitudes
   but committing suicide). How else is this dichotomy represented in the
   story? What does it say about human existence? How do you handle
   this disparity in your own life?
5. The motif of sight and blindness is also prominent in the film. Where
   do you see this motif? In your opinion, who in the film is blind? Who
   can actually see? Reflect on this with particular attention to the authority figures in the story (Rabbi Ben, Professor Levy, Aunt May, Judah's
   father, Judah, Lester, etc.).

Bonus Material

Fifteen years after this film, Woody Allen revisited many of the same themes
and plot points in his acclaimed 2004 drama *Match Point*. Set in the world of
upper-class London, the film similarly focuses on an unfaithful protagonist
who contemplates murdering his mistress. Like Judah, the character here
is forced to come to grips with the existential significance of his action.
Or is he?

The role of Professor Louis Levy, the subject of Cliff's documentary in
the film, is played by Martin Bergmann (1913–2014). Before he passed away,
Bergmann was a world-renowned psychotherapist and professor of clinical
psychology at New York University.

Allen's plan was always to create two parallel story lines, with one being
a drama and the other a comedy. However, he allegedly rewrote and reshot
a significant portion of the comedic story line because of his dissatisfaction
with the initial result.

The film was nominated for three key Academy Awards: Best Director (Allen), Best Original Screenplay (Allen), and Best Supporting Actor (Martin Landau).

Selected Additional Resources

Barnett, Christopher B. "Crimes and Misdemeanors." *Theology + Movies* (blog). October 19, 2014. https://theologyandmovies.wordpress.com/2014 /10/19/crimes-and-misdemeanors-dir-woody-allen-1989/.

Ebert, Roger. Review of *Crimes and Misdemeanors*. September 11, 2005. http:// www.rogerebert.com/reviews/great-movie-crimes-and-misdemeanors -1989.

Fisch, Sarah Lucille. "The Eyes of God: Guilt, Belief and Existentialism in Fyodor Dostoevsky's *Crime and Punishment* and Woody Allen's *Crimes and Misdemeanors*." *Sarah Lucille Fisch's Blog*. August 22, 2010. https:// sarahlucillefisch.wordpress.com/tag/crimes-and-misdemeanors/.

Eugene Suen

5

Do the Right Thing

US, 1989
120 Minutes, Feature, Color
Actors: Danny Aiello, Ossie Davis, Ruby Dee,
    Richard Edson, Giancarlo Esposito, Spike
    Lee, Bill Nunn, John Turturro, Rosie Perez,
    Joie Lee
Director: Spike Lee
Screenwriter: Spike Lee
Rated: R (brief nudity, strong profanity, violence)

Who Is My Neighbor?
Justice, Otherness,
Prejudice/Oppression,
Reconciliation

Synopsis and Theological Reflection

I was a fourteen-year-old African American woman when I first saw Spike Lee's film *Do the Right Thing*. It was one of those formative films that not only influenced my desire to become a filmmaker but also changed how I saw and thought about race from that point forward. Growing up in a New Jersey town outside Manhattan, I remember watching the news in 1985 when six New York transit officers were acquitted in the murder of Michael Stewart, a young black man who died while in police custody. That same year another young black man, Edmund Perry, was killed at the hands of a white, off-duty cop. And how could I forget 1986, when two black men walked out of a pizzeria in Howard Beach, New York, and were brutally beaten and killed by a mob of white youths wielding baseball bats and yelling racial epithets. If any of these headlines sound remotely similar to today's headlines, it should bear witness to why this film is included in this book as a cinematic work that warrants theological reflection.

Scripture gives us constant reminders that we must love our neighbors; this film challenges viewers to examine who our neighbors are and how we should interact with them. A slice-of-life drama situated on the hottest day of the year in the Bedford-Stuyvesant neighborhood of Brooklyn, *Do the Right Thing* centers on Sal (played by Danny Aiello), an Italian American man who owns a pizzeria in the neighborhood, and his two sons, Pino and Vito. Mookie (played by Spike Lee) is his delivery guy who sometimes feels like an adopted son, but who also serves as the link to the primarily African American community surrounding the restaurant. The neighborhood is filled with other colorful characters such as Buggin' Out, the rabble-rouser who tries to stand up for his community, no matter how big or small the issue, and Radio Raheem, the quiet storm whose presence alone speaks volumes. Radio Raheem carries a giant boom box with him wherever he goes, blasting the movie's theme, "Fight the Power."

In fact, Public Enemy's song "Fight the Power" is played twenty-seven times throughout the film. Lee said he used it to demonstrate the rage of African American males. But before the opening credits even roll, while the Universal logo globe still spins, there is also heard the soft tinge of James Weldon Johnson's "Lift Every Voice and Sing," an African American hymn originally written as a poem in 1899. And just as the film begins with this juxtaposition of hope and anger, it ends with conflicting quotes from Martin Luther King Jr. and Malcolm X on the benefits and the danger of nonviolent tactics. The film begins and ends, that is, with the same contradictions that exist in a nation that, 150 years after the abolition of slavery, remains crippled by the blows from its own corporate sin.

Throughout the film, there are glimpses of the deeply embedded prejudices that everyone has against one another, often bringing inner monologues about race to the surface and onto the street. As the temperature gets warmer throughout the day, so do tempers on the street. After discovering that there are no African Americans on Sal's Wall of Fame despite the fact that he does business in a black neighborhood, Buggin' Out rounds up Radio Raheem and they decide to boycott Sal's pizzeria. What follows is a series of events that lead to a showdown in the pizzeria between Sal and the community that he thought he was once part of, ultimately snowballing into a destructive street riot.

Radio Raheem's options

The film is bold and unapologetic in depicting racial biases that boil beneath the surface among the various neighborhood racial groups. Although the title of the film might seem to suggest the filmmaker is giving a command that seems definitive, the movie never gives any prescription or remedy to prejudice and hatred. As Roger Ebert stated in his review of the film, "'Do the Right Thing' doesn't ask its audiences to choose sides; it is scrupulously fair to both sides, in a story where it is our society itself that is not fair."

Some may find this film offensive because of its profanity and violence. But it is honest. If we as a church are serious about reconciliation, we need to have honest conversations about how to move forward in a culture that is so divided over race. *Do the Right Thing* can help us deal with our injustices by facing them head-on.

In portraying our ongoing prejudices, *Do the Right Thing* is told from an African American perspective. It thus reflects internal arguments within the black community—issues of gentrification, police brutality, self-determination, generational differences, and indifference. While the language may be harsh, I have heard family and friends within our community make the same arguments as the people in the film. As urban ministries continue to situate themselves in the middle of gentrified communities, this film challenges us to think about difference and how the church positions itself in the midst of it.

It has been said that white viewers and black viewers see the film and its characters very differently. During the riot, white people tend to side with Sal, while black people usually side with Mookie and Radio Raheem. This reveals how different communities view events. Any modern-day viewing of this film should ask the question, "How much has changed?" For we see these differences continue to play out each time there is a new police brutality case in the news. What is the church's response to our different perceptions? Such vast differences in opinion are what keep our neighborhoods and our churches divided. Surely a deeper examination is in order. Are we able to dive into such difficult conversations in order to hear someone else's pain?

Dialogue Texts

Do not judge by appearances, but judge with right judgment.

John 7:24

Whoever says, "I am in the light," while hating a brother or sister, is still in the darkness.

1 John 2:9

But wanting to justify himself, he asked Jesus, "And who is my neighbor?" Jesus replied, "A man was going down from Jerusalem to Jericho, and fell into the hands of robbers, who stripped him, beat him, and went away, leaving him half dead. Now by chance a priest was going down that road, and when he saw him, he passed by on the other side. So likewise a Levite, when he came to the place and saw him, passed by on the other side. But a Samaritan while traveling came near him; and when he saw him, he was moved with pity."

Luke 10:29–33

"You shall love your neighbor as yourself." There is no other commandment greater than these.

Mark 12:31

Discussion Questions and Clip Conversations

All clips are available for viewing at ReelSpirituality.com/Books/God-In -The-Movies. We have also listed the timestamp range of the scenes for your reference.

1. "Why No Black People on the Wall?" [18:40–22:52]. Buggin' Out challenges Sal about having black people on the Wall of Fame. Discuss Sal and Buggin' Out's treatment of one another. Do they have any level of

respect for one another as neighbors? Does Sal have a point about the pictures on the wall? What about Buggin' Out?

2. "Not in OUR Neighborhood" [35:00–36:46; 38:20–41:50]. Buggin' Out confronts a white man in his neighborhood, and the three old men on the corner discuss their lack of power within their own community. What do you make of Buggin' Out's statement to the biker that he doesn't belong in "his" neighborhood? What is Willie's point about the Korean grocery store owners, and how does it tie in with the previous scene with Buggin' Out? What do these two brief scenes suggest in terms of disenfranchisement and self-determination of minorities? Also, discuss how the depiction of the cops in the latter scene reflects the relationship of the police to the community. Is it positive or negative and why? Do these scenes still reflect life in the United States today?

3. "Getting Out of Bed-Stuy" [57:55–1:02:16]. Sal has a heart-to-heart with Pino about his decision to keep the pizzeria open in Bed-Stuy. Why does Sal stay in this community? Based on this scene, what does Sal value?

4. "Pain Breeds Violence" [1:28:20–1:40:20]. Biblical theologian Walter Brueggemann has said, "Pain brought to speech turns to energy, and pain not brought to speech turns to violence." Try to trace the progression of the fight in Sal's pizzeria. How and why did things start peacefully and end in death? What do Sal and Radio Raheem value as important in this scene? How might those values affect the way different groups see the events? Consider the riot as well. Is Mookie's throwing the garbage can through the window a form of justice? Who is the voice of reason in this scenario? If you were a minister in this community, how might you go about bringing reconciliation in the days to follow?

5. Years after the film's release, Spike Lee says that the one question people still ask is why Mookie threw the trash can through Sal's pizzeria window, causing the riot. But Lee says that question typically only comes from white viewers. According to Lee, there is more concern for loss of property than there is for loss of Radio Raheem's life. Why do you think Mookie threw the garbage can through the window? Did he think he was doing the right thing? Does understanding Mookie's actions necessarily equate to condoning his actions? How is our response to these events related to our response to social justice issues happening today?

6. Do you sympathize with Sal or Radio Raheem? Why? Was anyone in this film justified in their behavior toward their neighbor?

Bonus Material

Spike Lee once read a statistic that said when the heat rises, the murder rate goes up—he wanted to make a movie showing that kind of anger coming to a boil. Racial tensions in New York City were high in the 1980s. In addition to the incidents already noted, around the time that Lee wrote his film, there were headlines about a fight between black and white students at Brooklyn College over what music would be played on the jukebox, and five black teenagers were wrongfully accused of attacking a white female jogging in Central Park.

When *Do the Right Thing* premiered, many critics believed that it would cause more race riots. One reviewer in *New York* magazine predicted that the film would negatively influence the upcoming mayoral election and specifically that it would hurt David Dinkins's chances at winning. However, no riots occurred and David Dinkins went on to become New York City's first African American mayor. Instead of the negativity that was predicted, the film fared very well among viewers.

The film was a crowd favorite at Cannes Film Festival and was nominated for the Palme d'Or (it lost to Steven Soderbergh's *Sex, Lies, and Videotape*). It won Best Picture at the Los Angeles Film Critics Association Awards. The film was not nominated at the Oscars, which caused an uproar among some viewers, but twenty-six years after releasing *Do the Right Thing*, Spike Lee received an honorary Oscar for his overall work as a filmmaker, and this movie is considered a classic.

Much detail went into the style of the film. Since the film takes place on the hottest day of the year, Lee had to figure out how to express heat visually. He decided to interpret the block as an urban desert, and as a result, production designer Wynn Thomas says they carefully chose a street with few trees. They tried to have the trees that were present cut down because they didn't want any place where people could escape the heat or the tension.

Selected Additional Resources

Ebert, Roger. Review of *Do the Right Thing*. May 27, 2001. http://www.roger ebert.com/reviews/great-movie-do-the-right-thing-1989.

Klein, Joe. "Spiked? Dinkins and Do the Right Thing." *New York*, June 26, 1989, 14–15.

Wall, James M. "Do the Right Thing." *Christian Century* 106, no. 24 (1989): 739–40.

Avril Z. Speaks

6

The Elephant Man

US/UK, 1980
123 Minutes, Feature, Black and White
Actors: Anthony Hopkins, John Hurt, Anne
   Bancroft, John Gielgud
Director: David Lynch
Screenwriters: Christopher DeVore, Eric
   Bergren, David Lynch
Rated: PG

The Nature of the Human
God's Mercy vs. Human
Judgment, Human Dignity,
Human Suffering,
Prejudice/Oppression,
Who Is My Neighbor?

Synopsis and Theological Reflection

The Elephant Man, set in Victorian London in the 1880s, is based on the true story of a grotesquely deformed man, Joseph Merrick (John Merrick in the film), known as the Elephant Man. It is the story of his brave dignity despite his afflictions, and of those who abused him and those who befriended him.

Merrick (John Hurt) is kept in a freak show—masked most of the time to hide his deformity—by the show's cruel owner, Mr. Bytes. In the life-changing event that initiates the movie's story, Merrick is beaten by Bytes and must be taken to a hospital. There he is treated and protected by a kind surgeon, Dr. Treves (Anthony Hopkins). The hospital's governor (John Gielgud) is about

The Elephant Man © 1980 Brooksfilms Limited

John at afternoon tea

to release Merrick as incurable, but Merrick recites the Twenty-Third Psalm, proving that he can read and that he is, therefore, capable of treatment and potential improvement. Merrick is, truly, delivered from the valley of the shadow of death, demonstrating a soulful, courageous humanity that is both heartbreaking and universally affirming.

Merrick is allowed to remain at the hospital under Dr. Treves's care. As a friendship develops between Merrick and Treves, Merrick builds a small model of a church that he watches from his hospital room. Merrick meets regularly in his hospital room with Dr. Treves and other visitors, demonstrating surprising intelligence and social grace. He becomes well known in London and is befriended by a distinguished actress, Mrs. Kendal (Anne Bancroft). In one of the film's most touching scenes, Merrick and Mrs. Kendal read a scene from *Romeo and Juliet* together, which ends with Mrs. Kendal saying, "You are not an Elephant Man. You are Romeo." As more members of London high society come to visit Merrick, Dr. Treves becomes increasingly concerned that he has not done well by Merrick, fearing that he has turned him from a sideshow freak into a more genteel object of curiosity.

The villainous Mr. Bytes kidnaps Merrick and takes him on the road again as part of the hideous show, but Merrick escapes back to London. In London, Merrick is attacked and unmasked in a train station, crying out, in perhaps the movie's best-known scene, "I am not an elephant! I am not an animal! I am a human being!" Merrick is returned to Treves's care at the hospital, but he is dying because of his degenerative genetic disease.

Dr. Treves brings Merrick to a performance by Mrs. Kendal at a famous London theater. She dedicates the performance to him, and he is filled with pride and gratitude. Shortly thereafter, after finishing his project of constructing the church model, Merrick dies, seemingly at peace.

Dialogue Texts

Blessed are the merciful, for they will receive mercy.

Matthew 5:7

Jesus replied, "A man was going down from Jerusalem to Jericho and fell into the hands of robbers, who stripped him, beat him, and went away, leaving him half dead. Now by chance a priest was going down that road; and when he saw him, he passed by on the other side. So likewise a Levite. . . . But a Samaritan while traveling came near to him; and when he saw him, he was moved with pity. He went to him and bandaged his wounds, having poured oil and wine on them. Then he put him on his own animal, brought him to an inn, and took care of him. . . . Which of these three, do you think, was a neighbor to the man who fell into the hands of robbers?" He said, "The one who showed him mercy." Jesus said to him, "Go and do likewise."

Luke 10:30–37

So God created humankind in his image,
   in the image of God he created them;
  male and female he created them.

Genesis 1:27

The Lord is my shepherd, I shall not want.
   He makes me to lie down in green pastures;
he leads me beside still waters;
   he restores my soul.
He leads me in right paths
   for his name's sake.

Even though I walk through the darkest valley,
   I fear no evil;
for you are with me;
   your rod and your staff—
   they comfort me.

You prepare a table before me
   in the presence of my enemies;
you anoint my head with oil;
   my cup overflows.
Surely goodness and mercy shall follow me
  all the days of my life,
and I shall dwell in the house of the Lord
   my whole life long.

Psalm 23

Discussion Questions and Clip Conversations

All clips are available for viewing at ReelSpirituality.com/Books/God-In-The -Movies. We have also listed the timestamp range of the scenes for your reference.

1. "The Twenty-Third Psalm" [46:02–51:47]. Why did Merrick recite the Twenty-Third Psalm? How do Treves and the governor respond when they hear Merrick reciting the psalm? Were they impressed by the content or simply by the fact that he could read? Is this text especially appropriate for his situation? How does Merrick respond when the governor tries to shake his hand? Why? What does this scene tell us about his faith? What other scenes seem relevant to portraying his faith?

2. "Afternoon Tea" [57:00–58:54]. How does Mrs. Treves treat Merrick? How does he respond when she takes his hand? Can we see a parallel to Jesus and the lepers? Others? Why were the photographs so important to Merrick? Would Treves and his wife have been as kind to Merrick if he were less polite, less charming, and less intelligent? What preconditions are there for Christian kindness and generosity?

3. "I Am a Human Being!" [1:44:34–1:46:42]. When Merrick is being chased through the train station, do we see any parallels to biblical mobs? When Merrick cries out, "I am a human being," how does the crowd react? How should they have reacted? How would we react today? Who are today's objects of ridicule? Do we treat people who are "different" better now than was the case in Victorian England?

4. Was Merrick ever treated as an equal—as normal? If so, by whom? How did Merrick maintain his dignity? From where did he draw his courage? Did Dr. Treves make a mistake by allowing Merrick to become so visible? What should he have done? Was it his choice or Merrick's? Did Merrick have any character flaws?

5. Why do you think the film was shot in black and white? Were you shocked by the appearance of the Elephant Man? Would you invite him to your church? Your home?

6. "You Are Romeo" [1:07:21–1:10:08]. Why did Mrs. Kendal choose to have them read *Romeo and Juliet*? Was this a sensitive choice? What does she mean in telling Merrick, "You are Romeo"?

Bonus Material

The Elephant Man was nominated for eight Academy Awards but did not win in any category. Competition that year was very strong: *Ordinary People* won

Best Picture. John Hurt's excellent performance "lost" to Robert De Niro for *Raging Bull*. David Lynch and Martin Scorsese (*Raging Bull*) saw the Best Director award go to Robert Redford for *Ordinary People*. *The Elephant Man* did win the BAFTA (British Academy of Film and Television Arts) Award for Best Film, and John Hurt received the BAFTA Award for Best Actor.

Mel Brooks personally cofinanced *The Elephant Man* and arranged for its distribution. He was originally credited as executive producer but asked for his credit to be removed because he believed his comedic reputation might confuse audiences and compromise the marketing of the movie.

My colleague Rob Johnston has written a small book, *Psalms for God's People*, that includes a chapter on Psalm 23 and references this movie. I quote from the chapter:

> *The Elephant Man* . . . is an eloquent witness to the original intention and meaning of Psalm 23, for the psalm is a cry to God in a time of great need. The simplicity of its imagery and the peacefulness of its message have made the psalm a favorite of believers. It is often repeated in a variety of circumstances. But what needs to be understood is that Psalm 23 is not a general affirmation of faith by someone reflecting on his life. It is not a psalm written when all is well and God seems near at hand. Rather, it is the poetic cry of one shaken, one in the midst of danger, one in need of help. It is a psalm for us to sing when crisis threatens. . . . In his crisis, David [the probable author] turns to his God who reveals His nature to be like that of a good shepherd. . . .
>
> In the image of the shepherd we have one of the most meaningful and comprehensive word pictures of God in the Psalms. In other psalms God is portrayed as a rock or shield or king; that is, God's glory and strength are graphically represented. But in the metaphor of the shepherd, it is not only God's strong protection that is highlighted, but also His continuing care. Not only His majesty represented, but also His grace. . . . God, the great God of the universe, is "my shepherd." The contrast is simple and yet profound. God is presented as *my* God, one who cares for me.
>
> David [Merrick], in his crisis [with the hospital administrator], dwells upon God's character as provider. Having experienced God's fullness in days past [with his mother], he can assert—despite the seeming evidence to the contrary—that God, his shepherd, will certainly provide for all his needs.
>
> Joseph C. Gallagher

7

Field of Dreams

US, 1989
106 Minutes, Feature, Color
Actors: Kevin Costner, Ray Liotta, James Earl
    Jones, Burt Lancaster
Screenwriter: Phil Alden Robinson
Director: Phil Alden Robinson
Rated: PG

Reconciliation
Art/Play Mediating
God's Presence,
Father/Son Relationships,
Loss, Play, Vocation,
Wonder

Synopsis and Theological Reflection

Occasionally a line from a movie will enter the lexicon of American culture. "I'm going to make him an offer he can't refuse" (*The Godfather*, 1972). "May the Force be with you" (*Star Wars*, 1977). "Houston, we have a problem" (*Apollo 13*, 1995). So it is with "If you build it, he will come" (*Field of Dreams*, 1989).

   Field of Dreams tells the story of a novice Iowa corn farmer, Ray Kinsella (Kevin Costner), who hears a voice in his cornfields saying those iconic words. Interpreting them as meaning he is to plow up part of his farm in order to build a baseball field, Ray risks both his brother-in-law's scorn and his very livelihood to do just that. And after a painful wait of almost a year, the "he" does in fact come to his field to play—Shoeless Joe Jackson (Ray Liotta) and the other seven players of the 1919 Chicago White Sox who were banned from major league baseball for allegedly throwing a game in the World Series.

Later the voice speaks to Ray again, leading him to go to Boston in search of a famous civil rights writer, Terence Mann (James Earl Jones), a recluse who has stopped writing because he couldn't be the "answerer" for his generation's problems. But Mann too turns out to have unreconciled memories attached to baseball, the American pastime. As a child he had dreamed of one day playing at Ebbets Field for the Dodgers.

And as they travel together back to the ball field in Iowa, Ray and Terence stop in a small town in Minnesota to look for Archie "Moonlight" Graham (Burt Lancaster in his last role), a former major league player (in)famous for having only played half an inning in one game back in 1922. When things didn't work out, Graham retired from baseball to become a dearly loved small-town doctor. Although the men discover that Graham died in 1972, Ray is undeterred. Magically transported back to 1972, he meets the elderly Graham. Graham tells Ray that it was OK that he never fulfilled his dream, because he had saved lives and helped others as the town doctor. Nevertheless, he has unfulfilled dreams. He wishes he could have gotten to bat once in the big leagues.

Ray and Terence leave Minnesota to complete their trip back to Iowa. Along the way, they pick up a hitchhiker who turns out to be the young Moonlight Graham. This unlikely trio—all connected by their love of baseball and Ray's faithfulness in following the voice's commands—eventually shows up in Iowa on Kinsella's cornfield baseball diamond.

But the "he" that Ray hears in that initial call turns out ultimately to be neither Shoeless Joe nor Moonlight Graham, nor even Terence Mann. The "he" is much closer to home. John Kinsella, Ray's dad, appears on the cornfield diamond near home plate in his catcher's equipment. As a rebellious teenager, Ray had rejected his dad's offer to continue to play catch with him. His dad, a lifelong White Sox fan and minor league baseball player, had always told him stories about his hero, Shoeless Joe. However, Ray chose to reject all things having to do with his dad, and the rupture continued until John's death. Now, however, John is the "rookie" playing with Shoeless Joe.

As Ray's wife encourages Ray to introduce their daughter to her grandfather, Ray can at first only do so in formal terms. But on this field of dreams, Ray too finds the courage to be healed and forgiven. As his father turns to leave the field, Ray asks him, "Hey, dad . . . do you want to have a catch?" It is the first time in years that he has been able to say "dad," and the movie ends with something that, to this day, bonds countless fathers and sons (and sometimes daughters): a game of catch.

What all four characters in *Field of Dreams* have in common is their need for a healing of memories and a rekindling of their hopes and dreams. In this sense, the movie is ultimately not a "baseball" movie at all. Baseball, the great American pastime, becomes simply the crucible in which hopes can be gathered and reconciliation achieved. As Ray and his dad play catch, John asks his son, "Is this heaven?" To which Ray responds, "It's Iowa." When his dad responds that he could have sworn this was heaven, Ray says, "Is there a heaven?" And his dad answers, "Oh yeah. It's the place where dreams come true." As Ray stands next to his father, looking at his wife and daughter, he senses he has had a glimpse of heaven. He responds, "Maybe this is heaven."

Each character in the movie needs to suspend his or her skepticism and enter fully into the wonder of the story's magical realism before reconciliation can take place. And so do we as viewers. What makes *Field of Dreams* a classic is that an overwhelming number of its viewers do just that, often through tears. The movie is about the universal experiences of loss, disappointment, reconciliation, redemption, and hope. It is a story that invites viewers to reconsider their own losses and to reach out in courage to seek redemption.

Phil Alden Robinson, the writer and director, spoke at the City of Angels Film Festival, an event cosponsored by Fuller Seminary's Reel Spirituality Institute. When asked if he had any spiritual intention for his movie, he answered, "No." The audience was shocked, for many who had seen the movie reported just such an experience. Robinson then went on to chronicle how he had received hundreds of letters from viewers whose lives had been transformed by his film. He even received letters thanking him for giving viewers a picture of God the Father. Having entered the theater expecting to be entertained by another baseball movie (*Bull Durham* had been a rousing success the year before Robinson's movie came out), they departed feeling compelled to reach out to a father or child and seek a fresh start—a new relationship. There was no way to describe their experience other than to say their spirits had been touched and their lives transformed.

Evidence of the film's power to affect viewers spiritually goes beyond the letters Robinson has received. The baseball diamond in the cornfield outside Dubuque, Iowa, that was used in the filming of the movie has become something of a shrine, a destination site attracting thousands of moviegoers each year from across the country. It is, in fact, the major tourist attraction in Dubuque! Perhaps Terence Mann was more prescient than he knew when he opined:

> Ray, people will come, Ray. They'll come to Iowa for reasons they can't even fathom. . . . They'll arrive at your door as innocent as children, longing for the past. . . . You'll say, "It's only $20 per person." They'll pass over the money

without even thinking about it: for it's money they have and peace they lack. . . . It'll be as if they dipped themselves in magic waters. . . . People will most definitely come.

Dialogue Texts

Hope deferred makes the heart sick,
    but a desire fulfilled is a tree of life.

                              Proverbs 13:12

A wise child makes a glad father,
    but a foolish child is a mother's grief.

                              Proverbs 10:1

The wicked are overthrown by their evildoing,
    but the righteous find a refuge in their integrity.

                              Proverbs 14:32

Honor your father and your mother, so that your days may be long in the land that the LORD your God is giving you.

                              Exodus 20:12

All this is from God, who reconciled us to himself through Christ, and has given us the ministry of reconciliation.

                              2 Corinthians 5:18

Discussion Questions and Clip Conversations

All clips are available for viewing at ReelSpirituality.com/Books/God-In -The-Movies. We have also listed the timestamp range of the scenes for your reference.

1. A few critics and viewers have found the movie far-fetched, even corny (pun intended!). But the overwhelming majority of viewers have been willing to suspend their judgment and enter into the film's magical story. What is there about the film that conveys its sense of wonder? Is it James Horner's music? Or John Lindley's ethereal photography? Or the superb acting by Costner, Liotta, Jones, and Lancaster? Or is it also the fact that the story resonates deeply with most of us, for most of us

have unfulfilled dreams as well? Despite its fantasy-based plotline, is the movie nonetheless true to life? To your life?

2. "If You Build It, He Will Come" [09:00–10:25]. How does this prophecy expand as the movie unfolds? Who becomes the "he"? Does this prophecy extend outward beyond the film itself to take in the viewer as well? Is there a larger Christian principle or value that is embodied by this aspect of the story? Servanthood? Courage? Faith? Tenacity? As the movie's story nears its end, we hear Ray asking Shoeless Joe Jackson what is in it for Ray. Is this his motivation? Can there be mixed motives?

3. "People Will Come" [1:22:35–1:26:07]. Terence Mann's soliloquy about the place of baseball in the American experience serves as a major plot device. But it also provides direction as to how we are to interpret the whole movie. In what way does baseball provide spiritual possibility in the movie? In what way is baseball simply the particular referent for something more transcendent, even sacramental? Does the fact that each year thousands of viewers still come to Dubuque, Iowa, on a pilgrimage to see the ball field where *Field of Dreams* was shot add further veracity to Mann's soliloquy? Or is it simply a fun coincidence?

4. "Is This Heaven?" [1:36:30–1:40:45]. The voice also told Ray to "ease his pain" and to "go the distance." How do these requests/commands relate to the final scene of the movie, if at all? Can you relate the film's ending to the biblical texts quoted above?

5. There are a number of sports-themed movies that seek to portray something other than simply the thrill of the game. *Field of Dreams* is certainly one, but so too Norman Jewison's *The Hurricane* (1999) and Robert Redford's *The Legend of Bagger Vance* (2000), not to mention Barry Levinson's *The Natural* (1984), which also starred Redford. All of these seek some sense of transcendence, perhaps what T. S. Eliot wrote of as "the still point of the turning world" ("Burnt Norton" in *Four Quartets*). All invite wonder. What, if any, connection might there be between our play and our spirituality?

Bonus Material

1. There really was a baseball player by the name of "Moonlight" Graham who played only half an inning in major league baseball. See http://wikipedia.org/wiki/Moonlight_Graham and http://www.baseball-reference.com/g/grahamo01.shtml. In the scene in which Terence Mann

is interviewing the men at the bar, the people interviewed were actually old-timers who had known Graham.

2. Terence Mann is fictitious. In W. P. Kinsella's novel *Shoeless Joe*, on which the movie is based, the writer that Ray goes to see is J. D. Salinger, who is a recluse. Salinger was offended by his portrayal in Kinsella's story and let it be known through his lawyer that he would be "unhappy" if the story appeared in other media with this portrayal still in it. So the studio had the character of Terence Mann created.

3. When the movie was given a test screening, audiences complained that the title *Shoeless Joe* made them think the movie was about someone who was homeless. So the studio changed the title to *Field of Dreams*. When Phil Alden Robinson, the director, called W. P. Kinsella to relay the news, Kinsella informed him that the title *Shoeless Joe* was not his original choice but the publisher's. His original title was *Dream Field*.

Robert K. Johnston

8

The Mission

UK/France, 1986
125 Minutes, Feature, Color
Actors: Robert De Niro, Jeremy Irons, Ray
   McAnally
Director: Roland Joffé
Screenwriter: Robert Bolt
Rated: PG

Who Is My Neighbor?
The Church, Peaceful/
Violent Resistance,
Repentance, Sin and
Its Consequences,
Theology of Religions

Synopsis and Theological Reflection

The Mission is a haunting film. Long after the credits roll, it stays with you. Part of the reason is the music. In one of Ennio Morricone's more memorable scores, we hear hints of the primary musical theme from the opening frames. But it isn't until Father Gabriel (Jeremy Irons) reaches beyond the top of the waterfall for the first time and plays the corresponding melody on his oboe that the music becomes truly otherworldly. In this incredibly tender moment, we not only come to understand who Father Gabriel is as a human being and a priest, but we also bear witness to the power of music in its ability to transcend the many barriers that divide us—language, culture, customs, and ethnicity.

The music in the film thus comes to represent that which it also makes possible: communion. Father Gabriel's entire approach to his missionary work could be cast in these terms. That is, he offers up his music to the Guarani, not with the goal of persuading or proselytizing them, but as an invitation for them to join his music-making. All of his efforts with the indigenous people are rooted in the kind of mutual give-and-take that is required for anyone to truly play in harmony with someone else. It involves a willingness not just to know but also to be known—a willingness not just to transform the other but also to be transformed by the other.

So it is no small matter that, as the film progresses and Father Gabriel's life becomes "inextricably linked" with the Guarani, a jaunty, syncopated beat punctuated by vocal chanting joins Father Gabriel's oboe melody. In certain respects, these two musical pieces don't fit. They refuse to meld into an indistinct synthesis. Rather, the music signals the ways in which both Father Gabriel and the Guarani people bring their unique voices into a shared space. Neither one overwhelms the other, but both live in mutual interdependence. And as Cardinal Altamirano reminds us, this kind of (musical-missional) collaboration is the primary means by which "the Indians of the Guarani were brought finally to account of the everlasting mercies of God."

More so than any other character, it is Rodrigo Mendoza (Robert De Niro) who experiences the transformative effects of Father Gabriel's and the Guarani's collaborative communion. Mendoza begins the film as a ruthless slave trader, known by the Guarani as the quintessential Spaniard whose only concern is the violent conquest of the land and its inhabitants. But it isn't until he murders his brother in a fit of revenge that Mendoza recognizes his desperate need for (and the seeming impossibility of) redemption.

Mendoza's redemption is realized (at least symbolically) when he ascends the waterfall with his past life of violence quite literally dragging behind him. One of the Guarani cuts this burden from his back, thereby forgiving him and embracing him as a member of their community. In this way, Mendoza's journey reflects that of the apostle Paul, a man who was also called to love and serve the very community he once persecuted. And just as it is in Paul's story, God's amazing grace is captured most fully, not by Mendoza's transformation, but in the fact that this community could bring themselves to love and accept a man who once sought to murder and enslave them.

Yet underlying the stories of Father Gabriel's missionary work among the Guarani and Captain Mendoza's restoration is another, perhaps more insidious, reality that makes this film truly haunting. That is, *The Mission* offers us a visceral depiction of the many ways in which the spread of Christianity was bound up with European colonialism. Historically speaking, the church and the state have sometimes made too easy bedfellows, and as theologian Willie Jennings reminds us in *The Christian Imagination* (2010), the Christian church

Mendoza paying his self-imposed penance

continues to suffer from the wounds inflicted by its complicity with colonial efforts. Indeed, it may be that our very imaginations have been fundamentally shaped by this fractured history.

In light of this convoluted and violent past, it may be tempting to echo Mendoza's sentiment—that "there is no redemption" for us. But as the story of the slave trader who became a Jesuit priest reminds us, even the Western church is not beyond the scope of God's redemptive love. Of course, the kind of penance we need to pay is something that we will have to discern together, and this is perhaps the question that Cardinal Altamirano is posing to the audience as he breaks the fourth wall and stares into the camera after the credits roll. Given this history—our violent past—what does it look like to make music with those we have wounded? How are we to be light in a context where darkness is the product of our own doing? Beyond the story of the Jesuits and the Guarani who are caught between the competing commitments of two European states, these are the enduring questions that *The Mission* presents. May they continue to haunt us.

Dialogue Texts

> Blessed are the poor in spirit, for theirs is the kingdom of heaven.
> Blessed are those who mourn, for they will be comforted.
> Blessed are the meek, for they will inherit the earth.
> Blessed are those who hunger and thirst for righteousness, for they will
> be filled.
> Blessed are the merciful, for they will receive mercy.
> Blessed are the pure in heart, for they will see God.
> Blessed are the peacemakers, for they will be called children of God.

> Blessed are those who are persecuted for righteousness' sake, for theirs
> is the kingdom of heaven.
> Blessed are you when people revile you and persecute you and utter
> all kinds of evil against you falsely on my account. Rejoice and be
> glad, for your reward is great in heaven, for in the same way they
> persecuted the prophets who were before you.
>
> Matthew 5:3–12

I am grateful to Christ Jesus our Lord, who has strengthened me, because he judged me faithful and appointed me to his service, even though I was formerly a blasphemer, a persecutor, and a man of violence. But I received mercy because I had acted ignorantly in unbelief, and the grace of our Lord overflowed to me with the faith and love that are in Christ Jesus. The saying is sure and worthy of full acceptance, that Christ Jesus came into the world to save sinners—of whom I am the foremost. But for that very reason I received mercy, so that in me, as the foremost, Jesus Christ might display the utmost patience, making me an example to those who would come to believe in him for eternal life. To the King of the ages, immortal, invisible, the only God, be honor and glory forever and ever. Amen.

1 Timothy 1:12–17

While he was still speaking, Judas, one of the twelve, arrived; with him was a large crowd with swords and clubs, from the chief priests and the elders of the people. Now the betrayer had given them a sign, saying, "The one I will kiss is the man; arrest him." At once he came up to Jesus and said, "Greetings, Rabbi!" and kissed him. Jesus said to him, "Friend, do what you are here to do." Then they came and laid hands on Jesus and arrested him. Suddenly, one of those with Jesus put his hand on his sword, drew it, and struck the slave of the high priest, cutting off his ear. Then Jesus said to him, "Put your sword back into its place; for all who take the sword will perish by the sword."

Matthew 26:47–52

Do not think that I have come to bring peace to the earth; I have not come to bring peace, but a sword.

> For I have come to set a man against his father,
> and a daughter against her mother,
> and a daughter-in-law against her mother-in-law;
> and one's foes will be members of one's own household.

Whoever loves father or mother more than me is not worthy of me; and whoever loves son or daughter more than me is not worthy of me; and whoever does not take up the cross and follow me is not worthy of me. Those who find their life will lose it, and those who lose their life for my sake will find it.

Matthew 10:34–39

In the beginning was the Word, and the Word was with God, and the Word was God. He was in the beginning with God. All things came into being through him, and without him not one thing came into being. What has come into being in him was life, and the life was the light of all people. The light shines in the darkness, and the darkness did not overcome it.

John 1:1–5

Discussion Questions and Clip Conversations

All clips are available for viewing at ReelSpirituality.com/Books/God-In-The -Movies. We have also listed the timestamp range of the scenes for your reference.

1. "A Man Whose Life Was to Become Inextricably Intertwined with Their Own" [00:45–06:23]. As he enters a context in which he is knowingly facing potential violence, what strategies does Father Gabriel use in approaching the Guarani? What does it mean that his life became "inextricably bound up with their own"? How is his posture like or unlike the way other Europeans (Christians or not) entered these environments? In what ways does Father Gabriel embody Jesus's words in the Beatitudes? How does this approach put him at risk? Are you willing to risk being treated violently for the sake of others? Put differently, are the Beatitudes a life rule, or are there exceptions to the rule? When and where are you willing to live according to Jesus's words in Matthew 5, and how do you decide when it is appropriate to act differently? In the modern world, is it realistic to expect people to be merciful and peaceful? What "good" does it do for Christians to live this way?

2. "For Me There Is No Redemption" [28:30–31:46]. In what ways is Mendoza's story similar to the apostle Paul's? What would it require from the communities they served to receive teaching and wisdom from "the worst sinners"—the very men who once persecuted them violently? Have you ever been in a similar place to that of Mendoza, feeling as if "there is no redemption for me"? How is your current life shaped by that moment? Think of the image of Mendoza carrying his armor up the waterfall to pay his penance. What does "penance" look like for you? How does one move from a life of sin to a life of freedom in Christ? What role does the

community play in this process (think of the Guarani cutting the burden from his back)? What do you make of Paul's point that the mercy of Christ was demonstrated in even greater measure because of how terrible a sinner he was? How does it help you to make sense of your own story when you hear stories about others whom Christ has redeemed?

3. "Subdued by the Sword . . . and the Whip" [54:35–59:35]. Father Gabriel and Mendoza offer us two ways of responding to oppression, injustice, and violence: the way of peaceful nonresistance and the way of violent resistance. From a Christian perspective, which way is right? Jesus clearly demonstrated nonviolent resistance, going so far as to say that if we respond with the sword, it will end in our own death. Does this teaching apply to the Jesuit order and the Guarani people? Does it apply to us today? Mendoza chooses to take up the sword against violent injustice. Is there a sense in which he is simply following faithfully the teachings of Jesus in Matthew 10? Could we say that Mendoza is siding with the oppressed and experiencing the very violence and rejection from his brothers that Jesus describes? Is he not just losing his life in order to save it? How does our involvement with the state and with politics complicate our ability to answer these questions?

4. "Thus Have We Made the World. Thus Have I Made It" [1:55:00–2:04:55]. The film ends with a direct quotation on the screen from John 1:5 ("The light shines in the darkness, and the darkness has not overcome it," NIV). Given the overarching narrative of *The Mission*, how does this passage shape our understanding of the film as a whole? And how does the film help us read this passage in a new light? Why is it important for Christians to acknowledge that "we have made the world thus"? Or is it? The post-credits sequence features Cardinal Altamirano signing his letter to the papacy and then looking directly into the camera. Does this implicate us in any way in the themes that the film raises? If you were the cardinal, what would you have done?

Selected Additional Resources

Ebert, Roger. Review of *The Mission*. November 14, 1986. http://www.roger ebert.com/reviews/the-mission-1986.

Kempley, Rita. "'The Mission' (PG)." *Washington Post*, November 14, 1986. http://www.washingtonpost.com/wp-srv/style/longterm/movies/videos/the missionpgkempley_a0cad9.htm.

                                                             Kutter Callaway

9

Places in the Heart

US, 1984
111 Minutes, Feature, Color
Actors: Sally Field, Danny Glover, John
  Malkovich, Amy Madigan, Ed Harris,
  Lindsay Crouse, Terry O'Quinn, Lane
  Smith
Director: Robert Benton
Screenwriter: Robert Benton
Rated: PG

Who Is My Neighbor?
The Church, Community,
Forgiveness, Loss,
Prejudice/Oppression,
Reconciliation,
Spirituality of
Everyday Life

Synopsis and Theological Reflection

Many movies seem like worlds unto themselves, with the characters' lives beginning immediately after the opening credits and ending as the closing credits roll across the screen. *Places in the Heart* is not one of those films. The film feels as if its characters have been living their lives since long before the cameras started rolling and will continue long after the cameras stop. Viewers experience *Places in the Heart* as a moment captured out of a much larger story—a slice of life.

The film recounts the lives of a handful of people trying to make ends meet during the Great Depression in Waxahachie, Texas, focusing primarily on sisters Edna Spalding (Sally Field in an Oscar-winning role) and Margaret

51

Edna reunited with her husband, Royce, at Communion

Lomax (Lindsay Crouse) and the people connected to them. Edna is recently widowed, and with the help of an African American drifter named Moses (Danny Glover) and a blind boarder named Mr. Will (John Malkovich), she finds a way to make her mortgage payment and save her family. Margaret's husband, Wayne (Ed Harris), is cheating on her, and when she finds out, she has to decide what to do. The film's authentic texture comes from a host of bit players and background extras that seem like they walked into the film straight from the local Waxahachie High School football game rather than off a Hollywood back lot. *Places in the Heart*'s opening sequence connects them all by showing them in their homes and places of worship as "Blessed Assurance" plays on the sound track. The sequence suggests that whatever else divides the citizens of this community from each other—race and wealth, principally—they are all included in the love of God as exemplified in Christ.

But then *Places in the Heart* adds another item to its list of what divides people from one another: death. In the film's first proper scene, Edna Spalding's husband, the town sheriff, dies after being accidentally shot by a drunk black teenager acting foolishly with a pistol. A lynch mob quickly kills the boy. Later in the film, a tornado claims still more lives. Death, senseless and tragic, claims all, and there's little we can do to escape it.

Given death's closeness to the characters, the question that hangs over this sweet, quiet film is whether the people of Waxahachie, struggling though they are to get by during the Great Depression, will reach out humbly to help one another, to forgive one another, to act justly toward one another, and to love one another. They have every reason and opportunity to let racism, sexism, fear, greed, and bitterness rule their lives. Choosing love instead is an act of great moral courage and social justice. It is only by loving each other across social boundaries that they are able to survive, and still death is there on the doorstep threatening to tear them apart.

Or is it? The final scene of this film suggests otherwise.

Before I write about that scene, I want to assure you that I am not spoiling the film by doing so. There is plenty of narrative tension in *Places in the Heart*, because this is a film full of complex characters with compelling stories. This wealth of characters is part of what makes this film so rewarding and doubt-less what earned writer/director Robert Benton the Academy Award for Best Original Screenplay in 1985.

But back to that last scene. It takes place in a church on a Sunday morning. First we see the town again, and we hear the choir singing "Blessed Assurance," as we did when the film began. We watch one couple drive out of town sadly, and the film cuts to inside the church. The pastor reads Paul's famous chapter on love in 1 Corinthians 13, and then the choir rises to sing as the Communion elements are passed between the parishioners. The choir sings "In the Garden" by C. Austin Miles, a hymn written from the perspective of Mary Magdalene recounting what it was like to meet Jesus the morning of his resurrection.

And what do we see? There in the pews joining in the Communion feast are all the people stolen from this community by death. All the barriers be-tween them—prejudice and economic vulnerability—have been erased. All are welcome at the table. All are included in Christ's mercy. All share in the atoning sacrifice of his body and blood. They pass the peace to each other, male and female, black and white, rich and poor, fair and foul alike. This is what we believe, that in partaking of Christ's body and blood we join with all the saints who have come before us and all the saints who will come after us in partaking of the mercy of God.

In the end, *Places in the Heart* is a picture of the struggles we face in this mortal life and the joy to come in the eternal one. It is a moment captured out of a much larger story—the story of the resurrected life to come that continues long after the final credits roll.

Dialogue Texts

When the hour came, he took his place at the table, and the apostles with him. He said to them, "I have eagerly desired to eat this Passover with you before I suffer; for I tell you, I will not eat it until it is fulfilled in the kingdom of God." Then he took a cup, and after giving thanks he said, "Take this and divide it among yourselves; for I tell you that from now on I will not drink of the fruit of the vine until the kingdom of God comes." Then he took a loaf of bread, and when he had given thanks, he broke it and gave it to them, saying, "This is my body, which is given for you. Do this in remembrance of me." And he did the same with the cup after supper, saying, "This cup that is poured out for you is the new covenant in my blood."

Luke 22:14–20

He has told you, O mortal, what is good;
    and what does the Lord require of you
but to do justice, and to love kindness,
    and to walk humbly with your God?

Micah 6:8

Sing to God, sing praises to his name. . . .
Father of orphans and protector of widows
    is God in his holy habitation.

Psalm 68:4–5

Now concerning love of the brothers and sisters, you do not need to have anyone write to you, for you yourselves have been taught by God to love one another; and indeed you do love all the brothers and sisters throughout Macedonia. But we urge you, beloved, to do so more and more, to aspire to live quietly, to mind your own affairs, and to work with your hands, as we directed you, so that you may behave properly toward outsiders and be dependent on no one.

But we do not want you to be uninformed, brothers and sisters, about those who have died, so that you may not grieve as others do who have no hope. For since we believe that Jesus died and rose again, even so, through Jesus, God will bring with him those who have died. For this we declare to you by the word of the Lord, that we who are alive, who are left until the coming of the Lord, will by no means precede those who have died. For the Lord himself, with a cry of command, with the archangel's call and with the sound of God's trumpet, will descend from heaven, and the dead in Christ will rise first. Then we who are alive, who are left, will be caught up in the clouds together with them to meet the Lord in the air; and so we will be with the Lord forever. Therefore encourage one another with these words.

1 Thessalonians 4:9–18

Discussion Questions and Clip Conversations

All clips are available for viewing at ReelSpirituality.com/Books/God-In-The-Movies. We have also listed the timestamp range of the scenes for your reference.

1. *Places in the Heart* feels authentic, as if this is a movie about real people in a real place dealing with real problems. How does the movie accomplish this feeling of authenticity? How is this film different from other films and even other melodramas? Does anything in this film feel untrue to you? What? Why? How does the film's authenticity lend weight to the impossible presence of deceased community members at the end of the film?

2. "Caught Smoking" [50:54–54:35]. Edna's son Frank gets caught smoking at school. His teacher brings him home for punishment, and Edna prepares to spank him. She's never spanked her son before, because her husband always handled disciplining their children. She has to get one of her late husband's belts still hanging in the closet, and Frank has to talk her through the process. The other members of the household listen outside the door. When we lose someone we love, odd things bring up memories of them for us. Have you ever been reminded of a lost loved one unexpectedly? Is there anything you'll never do again because of how it reminds you of someone you've lost? How do we fill the gaps left in our lives by lost loved ones? Can we?

3. "Passing the Peace" [1:44:07–1:48:22]. The citizens of Waxahachie share Communion with each other at church. The congregation includes both the living and the dead. How does this scene make you feel? Why do you think the people who are present are present? Why do you think the people who are absent are absent? If you could welcome anyone to the Communion table, living or dead, whom would you invite? Where is there the greatest need for reconciliation in your life? How does Christ's body and blood accomplish that reconciliation?

4. The characters in *Places in the Heart* are divided by race, economics, and unfaithfulness. Only tragedy brings them together. In what ways is our time different from the Great Depression? How is our time the same? What separates people in the world today? How can we cross those barriers as a society?

Bonus Material

If *Places in the Heart* feels especially authentic, it's likely because writer/director Robert Benton cares very much about his hometown. Benton was born in Waxahachie, Texas, where *Places in the Heart* is set, in 1932. His first screen credit was as screenwriter of the landmark film *Bonnie and Clyde*, which takes place predominantly around the area in Texas where he grew up. Benton once said, "In America, people rarely stay in the town where they grew up, rarely stay in close proximity to their parents throughout their lives. You rarely find parents in their old age being taken care of by their children."

C. Austin Miles said of his hymn "In the Garden":

I read . . . the story of the greatest morn in history: "The first day of the week cometh Mary Magdalene early, while it was yet very dark, unto the sepulcher." Instantly, completely, there unfolded in my mind the scenes of the garden of Joseph. . . . Out of the mists of the garden comes a form, halting, hesitating, tearful, seeking, turning from side to side in bewildering amazement. Falteringly, bearing grief in every accent, with tear-dimmed eyes, she whispers, "If thou hast borne him hence." . . . "He speaks, and the sound of His voice is so sweet the birds hush their singing." Jesus said to her, "Mary!" Just one word from his lips, and forgotten the heartaches, the long dreary hours . . . all the past blotted out in the presence of the Living Present and the Eternal Future.

Selected Additional Resources

In 2011, the film lovers of the Arts and Faith online community voted *Places in the Heart* fifty-second on their list of the top one hundred films of all time. http://artsandfaith.com/t100/placesintheheart.html.

Elijah Davidson

10

Wings of Desire

Love
Hope, the Nature of the Human, Wonder

Original title: *Der Himmel über Berlin*
Germany, 1987
127 Minutes, Feature, Black and White and Color
Actors: Bruno Ganz, Solveig Dommartin, Otto Sander, Curt Bois, Peter Falk
Director: Wim Wenders
Screenwriters: Wim Wenders, Peter Handke
Rated: PG-13 (brief strong language, violent images, partial nudity, some smoking)

Synopsis and Theological Reflection

Wings of Desire has all the requisite elements of a serious "art house" film. It is in black and white. It has subtitles. It deals with the specter of post–World War II Germany and the Cold War in Berlin. Wim Wenders was honored as best director at the 1987 Cannes Film Festival. All of this screams complexity. And yet *Wings of Desire* is also among the lightest, brightest, most transcendent tales in cinematic history. It dares to approximate an angel's life (or rather, timeless existence). It suggests that almost nothing is as glorious as our complicated, earthly lives full of pain, love, laughter, and a strong cup of coffee.

American audiences almost ignored the film despite rapturous reviews and an amazing sound track. Yet *Wings of Desire* lives on in a sterling, two-disc Criterion Collection edition. It communicates empathy for our plight, sensitivity toward our tangled histories, and hope for a future laden with love. *Wings of Desire* is an immersive experience, more about feelings than actions, perspectives rather than plot. It is a film about listening that rewards careful attention and surrender.

Wings of Desire opens with a poem, "A Song of Childhood" by Peter Handke. It celebrates the purity of children, their vivaciousness, their imagination. The poem echoes the meditation of St. Paul on love in 1 Corinthians 13, which challenges us to put childish ways behind us, to become adult in our understanding. Stanzas from Handke's poem waft throughout *Wings of Desire*. It looks back on childhood with longing, with an appreciation for the simple pleasures of life, and invites us to embrace the beauty of God-given gifts.

The gorgeous cinematography by seventy-seven-year-old Henri Alekan is immediately distinct, as the camera floats above Berlin. Viewers are given an omniscient perspective, soaring into apartment buildings, listening to the private thoughts of the residents. The sound design is sophisticated. The ten-minute post-credit opening of *Wings of Desire* is extraordinary, bravura filmmaking that offers an opportunity to adopt an angel's perspective on humanity.

It is initially tough to figure out the plot in *Wings of Desire*. Who is the hero? Who are we following? We finally settle into the movie in a BMW showroom, where two angels compare notes on the day. Cassiel (Otto Sander) and Damiel (Bruno Ganz) list the moments of human kindness, beauty, and courage they witnessed. Damiel expresses a longing to live the human experience from illness to angst. He wants to move beyond the occasional angelic intervention like wrestling with Jacob in Genesis 32.

Why would Damiel give up an angelic existence? These cherubim look so cool and stylish in their trench coats and ponytails. They hang out at the public library or atop the highest statues in Berlin. They tap into people's interior monologues, offering a comfortable presence amid humans' self-doubt. Children can see these angels; evidently their unjaded eyes are attuned to spiritual realities surrounding us. Yet the wonder of color, of blood, of food, of love continues to tug at Damiel.

The circus is in town, but it is closing down. On the trapeze, Marion (Solveig Dommartin) wears angel wings made of chicken feathers. When she climbs into her lonely trailer, she wonders if she will ever satisfy her "desire to love." Damiel adopts a voyeuristic perch and reaches out to her with sexual longing, a desire for contact. Suddenly, color appears on-screen for the first time. The director clearly wants us to pay attention. These are the *Wings of Desire* that drive Wim Wenders's movie.

An elderly man wanders through leveled sections of Berlin thinking about peace. Images of the Holocaust flash by. He is a storyteller, a living witness who can help his country recover from World War II. But for now, he is confused, disoriented. Where is the Potsdamer Platz, and how do we move forward if we ignore the past he embodies?

An American actor, Peter Falk, appears on a movie set in Berlin. They are re-creating World War II. Extras dressed in Nazi uniforms or wearing badges of shame associated with Judaism spark all kinds of memories on set. Survivors see flashbacks in color. Has God abandoned their city? *Wings of Desire* seeks to heal a divided people, ashamed of their sordid history. Can an American TV star like Columbo help? What about the children at the circus, just seeking to be entertained? How can Berlin get past the borders that divide it into East and West, communist versus capitalist?

The characters in *Wings of Desire* (and the filmmakers) have so much on their mind. It is a weighty movie about taking flight and falling down. Can an angel keep us from committing suicide? What prevents angels from giving up their wings? Damiel takes a dramatic plunge. The story shifts to vibrant color as Damiel dives into the human experience. He revels in the glory of everyday life—a bath, a shave, the morning newspaper, a cup of coffee. Things we take for granted become a precious gift to be savored by Damiel. What about Marion, his greatest reason for eschewing eternity? She wonders, "Who am I with the circus gone?" Will the fallen angel be able to find the flying artist who no longer soars?

Damiel and Marion are brought together by the haunted music of Nick Cave. The Australian musician sings murder ballads of lust, jealousy, and God's judgment. But like Wim Wenders, Cave also believes in the transcendent power of love. While Nick Cave and the Bad Seeds sing "From Her to Eternity," Damiel moves from eternity to her—Marion. *Wings of Desire* climaxes with a paean to love: "There is no greater story than ours, of man and woman." We find home when we find each other. Wim Wenders has crafted a fairy-tale romance that ends with "Once upon a time." Damiel turns out to be the poet, bringing us an eternal perspective on the wonders of childhood and the joy of finding true love.

Wings of Desire grants us the rare opportunity to rise above our limited perspective, to peek into the pain of others, to expand our empathy, and to appreciate the gift of life and love. It is a masterful marriage of sound, image, and insight.

Dialogue Texts

> A spirit glided past my face;
>> the hair of my flesh bristled.
> It stood still,
>> but I could not discern its appearance.
> A form was before my eyes;
>> there was silence, then I heard a voice:
> "Can mortals be righteous before God?
>> Can human beings be pure before their Maker?"
>
> Job 4:15–17

> What is mankind that you are mindful of them,
>> human beings that you care for them?
>
> You have made them a little lower than the angels
>> and crowned them with glory and honor.
> You made them rulers over the works of your hands;
>> you put everything under their feet.
>
> Psalm 8:4–6 (NIV)

> For he will command his angels concerning you
>> to guard you in all your ways.
> On their hands they will bear you up,
>> so that you will not dash your foot against a stone.
>
> Psalm 91:11–12

Go, eat your food with gladness, and drink your wine with a joyful heart, for God has already approved what you do. Always be clothed in white, and always anoint your head with oil. Enjoy life with your wife, whom you love, all the days of this meaningless life that God has given you under the sun—all your meaningless days. For this is your lot in life and in your toilsome labor under the sun.

Ecclesiastes 9:7–9 (NIV)

Take care that you do not despise one of these little ones; for, I tell you, in heaven their angels continually see the face of my Father in heaven.

Matthew 18:10

Are not all angels spirits in the divine service, sent to serve for the sake of those who are to inherit salvation?

Hebrews 1:14

Discussion Questions and Clip Conversations

All clips are available for viewing at ReelSpirituality.com/Books/God-In -The-Movies. We have also listed the timestamp range of the scenes for your reference.

1. "On This Day" [12:40–16:04]. Two stylish angels, Cassiel and Damiel, meet at a BMW dealership to compare notes on their day. What have they seen and noticed? Damiel's admiration for humanity is infectious. It raises questions like: Are there advantages to now versus eternity? What special privileges do we enjoy as humans? What everyday activities do we fail to appreciate or embrace? Damiel also refers to several pretenses when angels and humanity intersected. When have angels intervened in the Bible or even in your life?

2. "An Angel Passes By" [22:23–23:51]. When we are commuting, our minds are often free to wander. Do we consider what others are thinking? What thoughts and prayers surround us at work, at school, on the freeway or bus? What prayers and concerns do you carry with you daily (or even now)? Damiel draws near to one particularly distraught man. How and when have you been comforted by God or even an angel? Would you recognize it, or would you attribute it to something else, as in this scene?

3. "Do You Remember?" [1:01:15–1:05:22]. Cassiel and Damiel reflect on their eternal perspective. How long have angels been around? What have they witnessed? Are humans relatively recent arrivals in terms of global time? What does it mean to enter history or have a story?

4. "My First Day" [1:29:26–1:31:42]. Cassiel and Damiel meet up at the Berlin Wall. Why is that a prime location for this scene? What does the close-up of footsteps reveal? How many basic human activities and gifts do we take for granted? What would you do on your first day as a human? What everyday things can we approach with an attitude of gratitude today?

Bonus Material

I once bumped into Wim Wenders at the Telluride Film Festival. I asked him directly, "Why angels?" He talked about the poetry in Rainer Maria Rilke's *Duino Elegies* as his inspiration. In the decades since *Wings*, Wenders's faith has deepened, but his narrative films have grown less popular, less praised. He has become spiritually attuned to how fear and surveillance are alienating us from each other (*The End of Violence*, 1997), to how strange and colorful the occupants of God's kingdom can be (*The Million Dollar Hotel*, 2000), and to how necessary healing remains after 9/11 when we continue to distrust each other (*Land of Plenty*, 2004). His documentary work has blossomed, from *Buena Vista Social Club* (1999) to *Pina* (2011), and especially *The Salt of the Earth* (2014). Wenders loves art, music, dance, photography, and humanity.

Wings of Desire ends with the words "To Be Continued." Wim Wenders released a sequel, *Faraway, So Close!*, in 1993 after the fall of the Berlin Wall. Damiel and Marion have gotten married, are raising a daughter, and run a pizza shop named Casa dell'angelo. Now Cassiel wrestles with the limitations and challenges of being human. Although it won the Grand Prix at the 1993 Cannes Film Festival, *Faraway, So Close!* earned much less money and enthusiasm than *Wings of Desire*. Watch it and compare the two films.

An American remake of *Wings of Desire*—*City of Angels*—debuted in 1998 starring Nicolas Cage and Meg Ryan. While far from beloved by critics, *City of Angels* made evocative use of Los Angeles by placing angels observing humanity from skyscrapers and gathering at the beach for sunrise. It earned almost $200 million at the box office, with a far larger audience than Wim Wenders's classic source material. What was lost in translation?

Selected Additional Resources

Check out how Wim Wenders answered the question, "Why believe in God?" for *Image Journal*: https://www.imagejournal.org/article/interrogation/.

Craig Detweiler

A BRIDGE DECADE

The 1990s, the last decade both of the century and of the millennium, saw massive changes in the cultural landscape—politically, culturally, and technologically. The Soviet empire, already on its last legs, came crashing down, ending the Cold War, and Germany reunited. This gave the West a respite from the years of military posturing and preoccupation with the threat of communism, allowing Western liberal capitalism to continue its global march virtually unhindered. In its place came the rise of the Far Right, the first of the Iraq wars, and other rumblings of unrest around the globe. But for a brief while, the world breathed a sigh of relief and devoted itself to the excesses of the burgeoning consumer economy.

The nineties proved to be a bridge decade between an age slowly passing away that had culminated in the outrageous eighties and the dawning new century with all its digital and technological possibilities. The decade was marked by the emergence of new media—cable television and, of course, the World Wide Web. In the nineties, we all got "wired" and globally interconnected, which heralded a shift not only to new modes of communication but also to new ways of seeing the world. With new technology came new perspectives and a reframing of the way we see ourselves and each other.

Culturally, the nineties felt as though we were entering a brave new world not only of possibility but also of concern: the demise of the Cold War was replaced by the emergence of new religious fundamentalisms, we were increasingly alarmed by environmental issues, and the HIV/AIDS crisis filled us with anxieties about new global pandemics.

In cinema, the decade saw the continuation of developments from previous decades, as well as new dynamics. The blockbuster continued to reshape film production and marketing, aided by new technologies in filmmaking and production. The development of CGI (computer-generated imagery) allowed for more elaborate and imaginative portrayals of cinematic visions. This was the era of *Jurassic Park*, *Terminator 2*, and of course James Cameron's *Titanic* (the highest-grossing film of all time until it was eclipsed by his next film, *Avatar*). It was also a time that heralded the resurgence of Disney as a major force in cinema with films like *The Lion King* and *The Little Mermaid*. But alongside the blockbuster, the nineties saw the cementing of independent and global cinema. By the end of the decade, most of the major film companies had an independent film division.

Religious films, religiously themed films, and spiritually significant films continued to emerge, though, interestingly, many had an R rating. This seemed a contradiction to many conservative Christians, but perhaps it signaled a willingness on the part of the wider culture to embrace religion and religious themes, even while rejecting the more sanitized approach to those ideas that had characterized Hollywood for decades. *American Beauty*, *Breaking the Waves*, *Shawshank Redemption*, *Dead Man Walking*, and *Magnolia* are all good examples of this trend. In the hands of 1990s filmmakers, religion was no longer handled with kid gloves. Films were often antagonistic to orthodox believers and institutional religion in general, but spiritual themes were explored with an honesty and authenticity that allowed those who were resistant to organized religion an opportunity to rethink what religion might have to offer to their everyday lives.

Barry Taylor

11

American Beauty

US, 1999
122 Minutes, Feature, Color
Actors: Kevin Spacey, Annette Bening, Thora
 Birch, Allison Janney, Mena Suvari, Chris
 Cooper, Wes Bentley
Director: Sam Mendes
Screenwriter: Alan Ball
Rated: R (strong sexuality, language, violence, drug content)

The Meaning of Life
Art/Play Mediating God's
Presence, Beauty,
Idolatry, Life's Vanity

Synopsis and Theological Reflection

When *American Beauty* was released in 1999, it was hailed by many as a
cinematic masterpiece, winning five Academy Awards, including Best Picture. A drama about a suburban family and their inability to connect with
one another, the film focuses primarily on Lester Burnham (Kevin Spacey), a
dispirited father going through a midlife crisis. In 2008, *Entertainment Weekly*
published a story that questioned whether the film should still be considered
a masterpiece. Certainly the film's portrayal of the meaninglessness of life in
suburbia, centering on Lester's sophomoric attempts to escape his humdrum
existence, made some viewers wonder about *American Beauty* (see the bonus
material regarding Chuck Colson).

So what was it about this film that made it such a critical darling for its time? Perhaps it has something to do with the fact that it originally debuted during a time when media was just beginning its dance and consequential love affair with the antihero—the Tony Sopranos, the Omar Littles, and eventually the Walter Whites. Or perhaps it was its presence in the context of the current events of its day, just one year after the Bill Clinton and Monica Lewinsky scandal, and only five months after the Columbine High School mass shooting. The *Guardian* printed an interview with director Sam Mendes around the time of the film's release suggesting that the movie was a reflection of a certain loss in humanity. It concluded, "When the soul becomes a shopping mall, when to live is to own things, it is hardly surprising if kids turn to murder. *American Beauty* manages to be both hilarious and dark about that crisis in spirit." If so, perhaps the appeal of *American Beauty* came from society identifying with Lester's emptiness. Just as we wanted to believe that Lester could be redeemed and find fulfillment in life, we had the same hopes for ourselves, that there would be something more to this life than the ordinary status quo. And perhaps those same desires still make the film relevant today.

The portrayal of the Burnham family in *American Beauty* reminds us that superficial happiness can be costly. Carolyn, the obsessive and lonely mother and wife, tries to find happiness and significance by being a star as a real estate agent, only to fail at landing the sale of a mediocre track house. Lester and Carolyn's reclusive teenage daughter, Jane, goes through the motions of being a "typical" teenage girl, but it is clear that she marches to the beat of a different drummer. Lester tries to connect with his daughter and wife, only to find rejection, which he compensates for in part by fixating on Jane's cheerleader friend, Angela. His emptiness and fantasies combine to cause him to throw caution to the wind—that is, to quit his boring office job, blackmail his boss, begin exercising more, and smoke marijuana with Ricky, the teenager who lives next door.

Lester's story is not chiefly about his sexual appetite or infantile regression, however, but rather about his search for freedom from the superficial. Most likely, if we could have asked Lester and Carolyn Burnham what happiness looked like in the early years of their relationship, they probably would have described the typical American Dream—marriage, a house with a white picket fence in the suburbs, two children, a dog, and a pension plan. The Burnham family have close to all of these things, and yet these things begin to feel stale over time, their everyday preciousness being forgotten, causing a yearning for something else to fulfill their desires. Through it all, Carolyn tries to keep up appearances, while Lester regresses to life as a teenager just to feel alive again. But their joint misery is transparent to all.

In many ways, Lester's and Carolyn's search for something "more" than ordinary, everyday life reflects our society's obsession. In "The New Legalism: Missional, Radical, Narcissistic, and Shamed," Anthony Bradley elaborates on the dangers of shaming millennials for wanting to live ordinary lives. Bradley believes that because Christian leaders continue to push a message of exceptionalism beyond the ordinary, young people are now more resistant to "settling" for marriage, family, and small-town life. He states, "The combination of anti-suburbanism with new categories like 'missional' and 'radical' has positioned a generation of youth and young adults to experience an intense amount of shame for simply being ordinary Christians who desire to love God and love their neighbors." Lester, in a voice-over that ends the movie, tells us that he has discovered life's fullness and depth to be found in the everyday beauty of life, which is a gift. As he speaks, viewers see pictures of events from his life that have brought him joy—Carolyn at the fair, his grandmother's papery hands, lying down in a pile of leaves, his cousin's red Firebird, his boyhood neighborhood.

Here also is the focus of the book of Ecclesiastes. Its teacher warns us that all the riches in this world are fleeting and that the best we can do is enjoy life's simple gifts, which are from God. In a culture in which consumerism entices us to believe that our happiness hinges on having the latest gadget or the best body, and in which "reality TV" provides glass houses for us to peer into the lives of our favorite rich and famous celebrities, *American Beauty* invites us to "look closer," to see that the beauty of our everyday life and relationships is upheld by something or someone greater; here is what really matters. Here is our true freedom.

Dialogue Texts

Compare Lester's voice-over at the end of the movie with this text from Ecclesiastes:

> Go, eat your bread with enjoyment, and drink your wine with a merry heart; for God has long ago approved what you do. Let your garments always be white; do not let oil be lacking on your head. Enjoy life with the wife whom you love, all the days of your vain life that are given you under the sun, because that is your portion in life and in your toil at which you toil under the sun.
>
> Ecclesiastes 9:7–9

I saw all the deeds that are done under the sun; and see, all is vanity and a chasing after wind. . . . Then I considered all that my hands had done and the toil I had spent in doing it, and again, all was vanity and a chasing after wind.

Ecclesiastes 1:14; 2:11

But we urge you, beloved, to do so more and more, to aspire to live quietly, to mind your own affairs, and to work with your hands, as we directed you.

1 Thessalonians 4:10–11

Discussion Questions and Clip Conversations

All clips are available for viewing at ReelSpirituality.com/Books/God-In -The-Movies. We have also listed the timestamp range of the scenes for your reference.

1. "Prisoners in Our Own Home" [39:49–41:20]. Director Sam Mendes says that a common trope used throughout the movie was to visually position people within a frame (e.g., a door or a window) in order to show their mental entrapment. In this clip, we see Lester working out in his garage while being filmed by Ricky's video camera next door. He is filmed through the garage door panes. Can you recall the opening shots of Lester looking out of his house? How do the characters' thoughts and actions in this movie imprison them? Do you sometimes feel imprisoned by the life you lead?

2. The color red figures significantly throughout the film—the red roses that Carolyn cuts in the opening sequence, the red door of the Burnham house, the red rose petals that float through Lester's fantasies about Angela, Lester's red Firebird, blood. Writer Alan Ball identifies the color red with passion, as a life force. Some also say that red in the film symbolizes transcendence, as is the case when Lester dies at peace, even while his blood pools beneath him. What do you think the color red symbolizes in the context of the story?

3. "So Much Beauty in the World" [1:01:52–1:04:57]. Ricky is able to see beauty in the ordinary. According to Sam Mendes, Ricky serves as the film's conscience. One of the signature scenes in the film is when he and Jane watch his video of a chilly fall day when the air was electric and a plastic bag was dancing in the wind. During this scene, Ricky says of the bag, "Sometimes there's so much beauty in the world I feel like I can't take it . . . and my heart is going to cave in." Has there ever been a time

when you have seen beauty in something ordinary and mundane? Was it in any way revelatory? Ricky goes on to say, "That's the day I realized there was this entire life behind things, and this incredibly benevolent force wanted me to know there was no reason to be afraid . . . ever." Have you ever experienced a spirituality in or through everyday life? Was this a life-shaping event, as it was for Ricky?

1. "Where Is Beauty?" [1:52:00–1.55.42]. Ricky sees beauty in death and in the ordinary. How is this similar to or different from what Lester realizes about beauty in the end? Was the journey that he took to get to this realization worth it? How does his mortality play into his revelation about beauty, and how does that relate to Ecclesiastes's commentary on life and death?

Bonus Material

American Beauty, in its critique of the American Dream, follows in the tradition of Mike Nichols's *The Graduate* (1967), Oliver Stone's *Wall Street* (1987), Ang Lee's *The Ice Storm* (1997), and David Fincher's *Fight Club* (1999).

The film's title is a play on a well-known varietal rose that is perfect in its outer shape and color but lacking in any fragrance—any inner beauty. This dichotomy between inner reality and what is on the surface plays out in the film over and over again. It has also served as a lens through which to view this film. Feminist critics, for example, have examined in depth the questionable role that women play in the film. In her 2004 article "Too Close for Comfort: *American Beauty* and the Incest Motif," Kathleen Karlyn raises questions about the sexualization of young women at the expense of unsympathetic mothers. The result, according to Karlyn, is a glamorization of the white, middle-class male (Lester) who is redeemed by a sort of spiritual awakening. Such a reading of the text casts Carolyn as the primary character in the film, someone whose desires are completely neglected. It is interesting to think about the same themes from her vantage point instead of Lester's.

Alan Ball says that the idea for *American Beauty* came about after seeing a comic book featuring Joey Buttafuoco and Amy Fisher. For those unfamiliar with their story, Buttafuoco was a thirty-something auto-shop owner from Long Island, New York, who was having an affair with sixteen-year-old Fisher. They made headlines in 1992 when Fisher drove to the Buttafuoco home and shot Joey's wife in the face. While accusations and conflicting reports circled through media during their very public trial, Joey Buttafuoco eventually pled guilty to statutory rape. Ball says that the comic book featured on one side a "virginal-looking Amy and a predatory, leering Joey," whereas the other side of the comic book portrayed Joey as an innocent husband with a predatory Amy. "I remember thinking, the truth is somewhere between those, and we will never know what it is," says Ball. These events helped spawn the idea for the story. In the original script, Ricky and Jane were part of a big media trial in which their videotape became evidence, and the movie ends with them going to jail for murder.

The inspiration for the plastic bag scene came from Ball's own real-life experience. "I was walking home from brunch," he said in an *Inside Film* interview, "and a plastic bag came out of nowhere and sort of circled me about—literally about 25 times. And, you know, it was a weird unexpected profound moment and I always felt like I was in the presence of something; that always stuck with me."

Chuck Colson initially gave *American Beauty* a scathing review in his weekly online column *Breakpoint*, finding nothing redeeming in the movie. But months later, after receiving hundreds of letters giving testimony to the spiritual illumination and even transformation that had happened to some of his readers while viewing the movie, Colson admitted that he had missed the film's deeper wisdom, simply being disgusted by Lester's futile chasing after wind.

Selected Additional Resources

Davis, Patricia H. "Live Free and Die: The Moral Dilemma of *American Beauty*." *Journal of Pastoral Theology* 11 (2001): 53–67.

Deacy, Christopher. "Integration and Rebirth through Confrontation: *Fight Club* and *American Beauty* as Contemporary Religious Parables." *Journal of Contemporary Religion* 17, no. 4 (2002): 61–74.

Karlyn, Kathleen Rowe. "Too Close for Comfort: *American Beauty* and the Incest Motif." *Cinema Journal* 44, no. 1 (Fall 2004): 69–93.

Avril Z. Speaks

12

Breaking the Waves

Original title: *Amor omnie*
Denmark/Sweden/France/Netherlands/
Norway, 1996
154 Minutes, Feature, Color
Actors: Emily Watson, Stellan Skarsgård, Katrin Cartlidge
Director: Lars von Trier
Screenwriters: Lars von Trier, Peter Asmussen, David Pirie
Rated: R (strong graphic sexuality, nudity, language, some violence)

Faith/Belief
God's Mercy vs. Human Judgment, Love, Redemptive Love

Caveat: This film is not for viewers who find themes of sex juxtaposed with spirituality to be insurmountably difficult. A challenging film, *Breaking the Waves* is unlikely to be judged must-see viewing by conservative audiences, and once seen—as the saying goes—it cannot be unseen. The storyteller, controversial Danish filmmaker Lars von Trier, is indisputably plumbing the depths of Christian faith through film, and so his film belongs firmly in this volume; however, each must determine whether he dives deeper than the viewer's lungs can bear. (If you are undecided, steer away from the director's cut in the Criterion Collection release in favor of a more modest edit for audiences in America, where cultural sensibilities concerning nudity are more tender than in Europe.)

Synopsis and Theological Reflection

Bess McNeill (Emily Watson) is a naive and protected member of a small Scottish fishing village where she lives with her mother and widowed sister-in-law until she becomes engaged to Jan (Stellan Skarsgård), an outsider working on an offshore oil rig. The sexual bliss of their wedded union, and the connection it forges in Bess, is threatened by Jan's return to the rig. Their separation causes Bess to teeter dangerously over the bow of emotional stability, and her despair is cataclysmic. Daily entreaties to God for Jan's permanent return are interrupted (or answered?) by a tragic, crippling accident. Jan returns, paralyzed from the neck down and on his deathbed. The flip side of a faith that allows Bess to fear that her prayers are responsible for Jan's accident is her unwavering confidence in her indispensable role in the accomplishment of a miraculous healing.

On the other hand, Jan, an atheist, is confused and driven by his condition to drug-addled despair. He hatches a disastrous plan to push Bess into going on with her life by suggesting that she take a lover. He rightly assumes that the village religious elders will be just as recalcitrant to grant a divorce as they were to grant the marriage in the first place, and he cannot bear that his accident will deprive her forever. Unable to believe that all Bess wants is to be with him and to love him, he bullies her into seeking out sexual experiences with others by suggesting that it will help him get well. Perhaps he imagines her enjoying something like a romantic interlude with his handsome doctor—who is willing, it turns out, because he has fallen in love with Bess. Instead, she seeks meaningless and humiliating encounters that become more and more sordid and violent.

All along, in her simple faith Bess believes that by being obedient to her husband and faithful to God, she is working to bring about Jan's healing. Bess is devoted to her religious community, formed by the kind of strict patriarchy that bonds congregations through tyranny. Her faith is defined beyond fear of her elders, however: Bess has a soul-level connection with God that evokes Joan of Arc, Teresa of Avila, Hildegard—an unfettered passion bound to elicit suspicion of delusion among some. Many, including husband Jan, are drawn to Bess *because* she is without guile: her maddening single-mindedness carries with it a corresponding charisma that makes her irresistible to some (her beloved sister-in-law, her husband, her husband's doctor) and anathema to others (the elders and those they too-heavily influence). Those elders banish her from the church for the same enmeshment of themes that will tempt some to reject von Trier's film: belief and sex (and love, passion, joy, fear, faith, judgment, cruelty, violence, miracle, and transcendence). Still, for all the elders' intention to protect the purity of their congregation, the surprise will be on all who calculate Bess's odds by something other than Jesus's dictum that it is faith that makes one whole.

Because Bess is excommunicated from the church, the reversal of Jan's incapacitation becomes an issue between her and God alone. She is forced to rely on her unique gift—the gift of, as she informs Jan's sophisticated doctor,

Breaking the Waves © 1996 Zentropa Entertainments ApS and La Sept Cinéma

Bess and Jan's "holy" matrimony

her faith. Though she admits that she has never been clever, "I can believe," she says, recalling one of the highest virtues of the way of Jesus. Religious villagers, including her distressed mother, are shocked and disgusted with the actions she claims her faith prompts her to take. As they shun her for offending their convictions, she is illuminated: "You cannot love words," she tells them. "You cannot be in love with a word. You can only love a human being." She resonates something core to the gospel: it was not enough for the Word to remain Word alone, even though it was powerful enough to speak the planets into being. The Word had to become flesh, had to become embodied, for love to flower into everlasting life.

Bess's love for Jan was permanently cemented upon their (rather un-romantic) physical consummation. Eager for their union, Bess was the one who pressed for sex before they even left the wedding reception hall. She was so innocent that she had to ask her momentarily disbelieving groom, "What am I supposed to do?" Making love did just what it was designed to do according to the Christian faith; it fused the two of them into one person. She no longer belonged in the same way to mother, church, or sister. Love became incarnated for Bess, in a gift for which she thanked God wholeheartedly. More sophisticated minds manage to interpret the marriage union of "oneness" to be symbolic, but Bess was transformed by it at a molecular level. She believed, and it was so for her. When that embodied love was removed from her after her honeymoon and taken far out to sea, she could not bear a retreat from incarnation back to theory any more than one might return from grace back to law. Jan became, for Bess, the earthly incarnation of God's love, and giving her own body for the preservation of that love was, to her, a perfectly reasonable expectation. Giving her own life for Jan's was a martyrdom she happily embraced because it made perfect Christian sense.

A well-constructed film will reflect at its beginning and its end what it is about; this film is a dialogue about love between Bess and God. *Breaking the Waves* starts with Bess trying to convince the church elders of the legitimacy of her love, and it ends with God's harshly won endorsement. Throughout, her faith is unwavering as she lives by the unique gift God has given her—belief. God goes absent, requires absurd things, is unable (or unwilling) to steer the adherents of faith toward mercy, fails to protect her from trouble, and then appears suddenly in her darkest hour to claim, "Of course I am with you, I am *always* with you." In the beginning, God considers her a silly, selfish girl, and in the end, God's transformed opinion resounds from the heavens.

Dialogue Texts

Please read the entire passage (Luke 7:36–50), but note especially the following sections:

> And a woman in the city, who was a sinner, having learned that he was eating in the Pharisee's house, brought an alabaster jar of ointment. She stood behind him at his feet weeping, and began to bathe his feet with her tears, and to dry them with her hair. Then she continued kissing his feet and anointing them with the ointment. Now when the Pharisee who had invited him saw it, he said to himself, "If this man were a prophet, he would have known who and what kind of woman this is who is touching him—that she is a sinner." . . . [Jesus said,] "Therefore, I tell you, her sins, which were many, have been forgiven; hence she has shown great love. But the one to whom little is forgiven, loves little." Then he said to her, "Your sins are forgiven." But those who were at the table with him began to say among themselves, "Who is this who even forgives sins?" And he said to the woman, "Your faith has saved you; go in peace."
>
> Luke 7:37–39, 47–50

Jesus's ministry is characterized by stories of granting healing because of the sincerity (not necessarily the purity) of someone's faith. Notice the repeated refrains that end a number of biblical stories about Jesus the healer:

> He said to her, "Daughter, your faith has made you well; go in peace, and be healed of your disease."
>
> Mark 5:34

> Then he said to him, "Get up and go on your way; your faith has made you well."
>
> Luke 17:19

He said to her, "Daughter, your faith has made you well; go in peace."

Luke 8:48

And to the centurion Jesus said, "Go; let it be done for you according to your faith." And the servant was healed in that hour.

Matthew 8:13

Discussion Questions and Clip Conversations

All clips are available for viewing at ReelSpirituality.com/Books/God-In
-The-Movies. We have also listed the timestamp range of the scenes for your
reference.

1. "Love Is the Greatest Gift" [19:47–22:16]. Just after Jan discovers that Bess remained a virgin for her wedding night, he reflects that waiting must have been lonely. Immediately, the director cuts to the first in a series throughout the movie of Bess's conversations with God. This time in the church, she thanks God for the greatest gift of all: love. Later, as Jan is making love to her, she repeats her thanks. What is the connection between Bess's love for God and her love for Jan?

2. At several key moments in the film, Bess looks directly into the camera. Called "breaking the fourth wall" in theater, this is a very bold choice. Who is she looking at? What do these piercing moments mean taken together? How do you as a viewer feel?

3. "Your Love for Jan Is Being Put to the Test" [58:00–1:00:00]. A core tenet of screenwriting holds that the protagonist is identified as the one who changes through the course of the film and that the antagonist is the agent of change. *Breaking the Waves* might be read as a love story between Bess and God, with Bess as antagonist to God's protagonist. God challenges Bess, "Prove to me that you love him, and I'll let him live." God is the one who is, finally, convinced: Bess changes God's mind about Jan and convinces God to save him. She does this by virtue of living fully into her special gift that God is susceptible to: she believes. What occasions in Scripture underpin the idea that God's mind can be changed by a true believer? What possibilities for you arise from this thought?

4. "God's Absence and Presence" [1:56:00–1:57:00]. Several times Bess calls out to ask if God is still present, only to receive God's assurance. Even when she confesses her sins, God reassures her that "Mary Magdalene

sinned—and she was among my dearly beloved." For periods of time, however, God goes absent—absent when Bess is being shunned by her neighbors and the church, absent when the children torment her. And yet when she is heading toward the ship where she will surely die, she calls out again, and God answers, "Of course I am with you." What is the meaning of God's absence and reappearance in the film? Even the great mystics of the church speak of God's "absence" (e.g., John of the Cross, Mother Teresa). Can you think of such a time in your life? What did you learn from that experience?

Bonus Material

Breaking the Waves is the first film in von Trier's Golden Heart trilogy, which also includes *The Idiots* (1998) and *Dancer in the Dark* (2000)—the latter is worth a view. These films were influenced by a children's book von Trier read as a boy, about a pure-hearted girl sustained through unimaginable terrors by her simple faith. The film's style is influenced by the Dogme 95 movement, of which von Trier was a founding member, that protested overwrought plotlines and the unrealistic imagery and lighting of popular films, swearing instead to "force the truth" out of films.

Lauralee Farrer

13

Dead Man Walking

US, 1995
122 Minutes, Feature, Color
Actors: Susan Sarandon, Sean Penn, Robert
  Prosky
Director: Tim Robbins
Screenwriter: Tim Robbins (based on
  the book with the same title by Helen
  Prejean)
Rated: R (depictions of rape, murder, and an execution)

Who Is My Neighbor?
Christ Figure,
Human Dignity,
Justice/Vengeance,
the Nature of the Human,
Redemptive Love

Synopsis and Theological Reflection

During a recent trip to Alcatraz Island, former home to the notorious high-security federal penitentiary located in the San Francisco Bay, I noticed on a banner the following quote regarding the types of felons that used to be sentenced there: "Alcatraz should be reserved for desperate or irredeemable types of individuals." That quote was from Sanford Bates, the director of the US Bureau of Prisons in 1933, and it stood out to me because I wondered who gets to decide whether someone is redeemable. As Christians, we embrace the concept of redemption when we are on its receiving end. Yet we struggle when God's redeeming grace falls on those we deem unworthy.

Good news in the midst of a long walk: Sister Helen accompanies Matthew

What does it look like to be a model Christian? Is it saying the right things? Is it doing the right things or going to the right places? Is it saying prayers every day? No matter your choice of an answer, *Dead Man Walking* shows us a deeper way. Based on the true story of Sister Helen Prejean, a Catholic nun who dedicated her life to the poor, the film shines light on her experience as a spiritual adviser to death-row inmate Matthew Poncelet in the days before his execution. The premise of the film alone draws contemplation about our convictions when it comes to the death penalty and human life. But this film also shines a light on how our own convictions can hinder us from knowing the truth about Jesus's expectations for real discipleship.

In the first five minutes of the film, we get a glimpse of how the gospel is lived out in the life of Sister Helen (Susan Sarandon). We learn that she lives and serves in a poor African American community, showing care and concern "for the least of these." In an early shot, while Sister Helen reads one of the letters from Matthew (Sean Penn), there is a "March for the Homeless" poster hanging on the wall behind her, which is intercut with flashbacks of a young Helen at her confirmation and eventually becoming a nun. In these moments we are introduced to a woman who looks so happy and optimistic to be fulfilling her calling. But her faith and optimism are challenged from her first encounter with Matthew. His raw candor could have been off-putting for Sister Helen if she weren't a woman of her word and completely insistent on helping someone in need. As their friendship develops throughout the film, the challenges that come with such grace are revealed in more ways than one.

Sister Helen quickly learns the consequences of befriending a convicted killer in a world in which people would rather pick sides than listen and empathize. She draws contempt from many, but most importantly from the parents of the victims who cannot seem to understand how she could side with Matthew. Sister Helen knows that perfect Christianity is nonexistent, even in the case of a nun. Through various flashbacks, we learn that Sister Helen has demons of her own (for example, killing a rabbit when she was a young child). Although the event may seem trivial compared to Matthew's crime, it haunts Sister Helen. Yet it also humanizes her; as Paul writes, we have all sinned and fallen short of God's expectations.

Yet it is not their common humanity that unites Sister Helen and Matthew but rather the real presence of a gospel that invites us all to come as we are. Matthew begins the film as a coldhearted, racist criminal who probably believes himself to be irredeemable. But Sister Helen introduces him, not to a God who condemns or shuts people out or who deems them hopeless, but to a God who loves, who forgives, and who is boundless in grace—even toward a killer. Through their relationship, Matthew learns that salvation is available and that it transcends this earthly world.

When Matthew makes one last attempt to appeal his case before execution, the media frenzy around the murders grows. As is so often the case, people are crucified in the court of public opinion. Sister Helen tries to be a peacemaker between the victims' grieving families and Matthew. For both sides, she provides something that the media cannot—a listening ear for full stories instead of sound bites. In Matthew, she hears a man with a strong work ethic and a need to belong. In Earl Delacroix (the murdered boy's father), she hears of the devastating loss of a son and subsequently a marriage. In the Percy family, she hears copious amounts of bitterness and grief over their daughter's death. While everyone else chooses to silo themselves in their own pain, Sister Helen decides to give dignity to all points of view.

Just before his lethal injection, Matthew makes a final plea to God for forgiveness as he accepts his fate, while the parents of the victims watch, hoping this act will make them feel that a modicum of justice has been served. As Matthew is strapped into the chair, he calls on the name of God in his own way, much like the criminal on the cross next to Jesus. Even in that moment, Jesus offers redemption, whether or not Matthew lived a life that deserved it. That is the challenge and irony of grace. That is the challenge of an inverted gospel in which the poor inherit the kingdom and the prisoners are set free.

Sister Helen's act of courage serves as a reminder of Jesus's example of loving those whom society deems irredeemable. Normally, someone like Matthew Poncelet would fit into that category. But there is an element in all of us that is also "irredeemable," as seen in the characters of Sister Helen and in the parents of both victims. This film forces us to face the audacity of a grace that is not a respecter of persons. All can be forgiven by God, but that forgiveness comes only through faith.

Dialogue Texts

> The LORD sets the prisoners free;
>   the LORD opens the eyes of the blind.
> The LORD lifts up those who are bowed down;
>   the LORD loves the righteous.
> The LORD watches over the strangers;
>   he upholds the orphan and the widow,
>   but the way of the wicked he brings to ruin.
>
> Psalm 146:7–9

Blessed are the peacemakers, for they will be called children of God.

Matthew 5:9

Then they also will answer, "Lord, when was it that we saw you hungry or thirsty or a stranger or naked or sick or in prison, and did not take care of you?" Then he will answer them, "Truly I tell you, just as you did not do it to one of the least of these, you did not do it to me." And these will go away into eternal punishment, but the righteous into eternal life.

Matthew 25:44–46

"And we indeed have been condemned justly, for we are getting what we deserve for our deeds, but this man has done nothing wrong." Then he said, "Jesus, remember me when you come into your kingdom." He replied, "Truly I tell you, today you will be with me in Paradise."

Luke 23:41–43

Discussion Questions and Clip Conversations

All clips are available for viewing at ReelSpirituality.com/Books/God-In-The -Movies. We have also listed the timestamp range of the scenes for your reference.

1. "I'm Just Trying to Follow the Way of Jesus" [45:59–53:57]. In this scene, Sister Helen visits the parents of Hope Percy, the young girl who

was killed by Matthew Poncelet. Since Helen is there, they assume that she has changed her mind and shifted her allegiance to their side. They become angry with Sister Helen when they learn this is not the case, telling her she cannot be friends with him and be friends with them as well. What would justice look like for the Percy family? What does justice look like for Matthew, according to Sister Helen? The Percys and Sister Helen both see themselves as Christians. How do we account for their two vastly different viewpoints about justice? Do you think it is unfair of the Percys to demand that Sister Helen make a choice between being friends with them or Matthew? Do you think that the Percys would have felt differently if Matthew had issued a public apology for the murders?

2. At what point does it sink in for Matthew what redemption really is? Is it fair that someone like Matthew could receive forgiveness in the last hours of his life? Why are we inclined to rank our sins? Do you think if we saw all of our sins as grievous to God that it might change the way we think about justice and compassion?

3. "You Are a Son of God" [1:30:30–1:40:29]. Sister Helen spends the last few moments with Matthew, and he thanks her for loving him, stating that he never had anyone to love him before. He also confesses to the murders right before his execution. Do you think Matthew's confession was authentic? Do you think Matthew is capable of remorse? Do you feel any sympathy for Matthew at the end of this scene? Why or why not? What do you think social media platforms today would say about someone like Matthew Poncelet? What would be your response?

4. Think about the quote from Sanford Bates at the beginning of this chapter. Is there a way to tell whether someone is irredeemable? Why or why not? Does someone like Matthew deserve to die? What are we to make of the Percys hating Sister Helen because she took a stand and befriended Matthew? Do you think Jesus would have taken the same stand? Do you think the Percys would have hated Jesus if he had done the same thing Helen did? In terms of people being irredeemable, what is significant about the film ending with Sister Helen and Earl Delacroix being the ones on their knees praying in church?

Bonus Material

The film *Dead Man Walking* is based on a book by the real Sister Helen Prejean, who has a long history of leading the fight to end the death penalty. The book focused on two prisoners—one whose guilt or innocence was unclear and one whose guilt was more definitive. Director Tim Robbins decided to focus the film on the man who was clearly guilty because he didn't want the audience to be manipulated in any way by making him innocent in the end. Robbins also wanted to give voice to the victims and their feelings in order to show the complexity of emotions associated with murder. In an interview with the *Guardian*, Robbins reflected: "You have to respect the other side; there is a great deal of anger and rightful anger in the victims' families, and I didn't ever want to portray them as crazy or irrational. I wanted that to be given its dignity."

According to Sister Helen, the concern is not so much the guilt or innocence of prisoners. Instead, she chooses to focus on showing them the love of God. She says, "It's easy to forgive the innocent. It's the guilty who test our morality." Sister Helen's love for the worst of humanity is due to her belief in restoring life and treating every person with dignity and respect, regardless of what they have done. She thus has been vocal about her disapproval of the entire criminal justice system, not just of capital punishment. Everything from arrest, to trial, to conviction through execution is flawed, she says, with minorities and the poor often disproportionately targeted.

Sister Helen remains active in her fight against capital punishment, most recently standing up for death-row inmate Richard Glossip, a prisoner in Oklahoma whom she believes to have been wrongfully convicted. Susan Sarandon says that by the time she finished filming the movie, she also believed that the death penalty was wrong, being moved by Sister Helen loving someone beyond his worst act.

Selected Additional Resources

"*Dead Man Walking*: Extended Interview with Sister Helen Prejean." June 19, 2013. http://www.youtube.com/watch?v=QZYMgn2oiks.

Prejean, Sister Helen. "Would Jesus Pull the Switch?" *Salt of the Earth*, March/April 1997. http://dioscg.org/index.php/would-jesus-pull-the-switch/.

Avril Z. Speaks

14

Groundhog Day

The Meaning of Life
Life's Vanity, Love

US, 1993
101 Minutes, Feature, Color
Actors: Bill Murray, Andie McDowell, Chris
    Elliott, Stephen Tobolowski
Director: Harold Ramis
Screenwriters: Danny Rubin, Harold Ramis
Rated: PG

Synopsis and Theological Reflection

PHIL: What would you do if you were stuck in one place and every day was
    exactly the same, and nothing you did mattered?
(RALPH *and* GUS, *two bowling-alley drunks, look at their beers.*)
RALPH (*drunkenly*): That about sums it up for me.

The above exchange serves both as a succinct summation of *Groundhog
Day*'s plot and as an explanation of the film's appeal. Jerk weatherman Phil
Connors is stuck in Punxsutawney, Pennsylvania, reliving the same day for
what he fears is all eternity, and there is nothing he can do about it. Though
none of us are living through that same fantastic circumstance, we are all

living lives that sometimes seem repetitive and pointless. *Groundhog Day* is one man's very odd story, but it is also the very ordinary story of everyone in the world.

Groundhog Day begins as a comedy, briefly turns into an existential nightmare, and ends as a romance. It carries itself lightly throughout, and because of this, though it was reviewed positively when it was released in theaters in 1993—reviewers called it "breezy" and "lovable"—no one gave it serious thought. *Groundhog Day* was seen as a good Bill Murray vehicle and not much more.

Casting Murray as the lead is certainly key to the film's charm. Murray always seems to have one foot in the movie and one foot out. Moreover, he moves between these spaces effortlessly. Murray's characters feel like they are participating in the events of the story and commenting on them at the same time. *Groundhog Day* allows Murray to do this within the story explicitly. Because Phil has lived through February 2 countless times before, he knows what's going to happen in every moment and anticipates it, sometimes cynically, sometimes sentimentally, but always humorously. Murray makes this movie "breezy" and "lovable." He never takes what's happening too seriously, so the audience doesn't either. This lightness allows *Groundhog Day* to offer a perspective on life without ever feeling preachy.

But that doesn't mean preachers from many faiths haven't noticed *Groundhog Day*'s profundity and appropriated it for their own purposes. Alex Kuczynski covered the film's interreligious appeal in-depth in an article titled "Groundhog Almighty" for the *New York Times* in 2003. Kuczynski quotes Buddhist, Jewish, Christian (Catholic and evangelical), Falun Dafa, and even Wiccan adherents who point to *Groundhog Day* to support their spiritual practice. (For what it's worth, neither writer Danny Rubin nor writer/director Harold Ramis have publicly identified with any religion.)

Much of the film's broad appeal is due to its lack of specificity as to what causes Phil's internment in February 2. Is God behind it? Is it karma? Is it witchcraft? The film never says. The film does show us how Phil escapes his temporal prison cell—he learns to appreciate the life he's living. This allows him to care about others for the first time. Here's a message most religions can get behind. But we are getting ahead of the story.

What *Groundhog Day* does so well is found not in the movie's comedic or romantic ends but in the existential nightmare that fills out its middle. "Vanity of vanities! All is vanity!" the author (who describes himself as the Teacher) cries as Ecclesiastes begins. That sounds very much like Phil Connors in the bowling alley. Phil, like the Teacher, gains all knowledge, amasses great wealth, seduces any woman he wants, and indulges in every kind of food and drink.

Bowling-alley "wisdom": "That about sums it up for me."

Then, importantly, in trying and failing to save an old man, Phil learns that death is inescapable. At the end of this scene, he even looks up toward the heavens as if to acknowledge God's authority. Even if he could escape February 2, death would find and claim him—it finds everyone, good and evil alike. But Phil also learns that it is better to be loved than to be despised, for being loved makes his meaningless day more pleasant. He learns that it is better to enjoy oneself than to be miserable, an invaluable lesson for a cynic like Phil. It's better to enjoy a meaningless life and to make the most of it than to wallow in misery.

Eventually, Phil learns how to love Rita (Andie McDowell). As Roger Ebert wrote in 2005 to commemorate *Groundhog Day*'s inclusion in his book *Great Movies*, "There is a moment when Phil tells Rita, 'When you stand in the snow, you look like an angel.'" The point is not that Phil has fallen in love with Rita, though he has, Ebert tells us. Rather, it is "that he has learned to see the angel." Phil learns how to love, and in learning how to love, Phil finds peace. But this is part of a larger insight: Phil learns to live in the moment. He says to Rita, "No matter what happens tomorrow or for the rest of my life, I'm happy now, because I love you." Then a magical sound plays on the film's sound track, which Phil reacts to (in characteristic "one foot in the film, one foot out" Bill Murray fashion). Phil is free.

Phil's escape from February 2 is not because of what some critics believe—that he's learned to be a better person; he learns that much earlier in the film. No, Phil's ability to move on with his life is rooted in his learning to appreciate the life he's living. He's found peace even though life remains imperfect and death will come one day. By the end of the film, one can imagine Phil quoting the writer of Ecclesiastes:

> Go, eat your bread with enjoyment, and drink your wine with a merry heart; for God has long ago approved what you do. Let your garments always be white; do not let oil be lacking on your head. Enjoy life with the wife whom you love, all the days of your vain life that are given you under the sun, because that is your portion in life and in your toil at which you toil under the sun. Whatever your hand finds to do, do with your might; for there is no work or thought or knowledge or wisdom in Sheol, to which you are going. (Ecclesiastes 9:7–10)

Dialogue Texts

In addition to Ecclesiastes 9:7–10, readers will want to read the first two chapters of the book. In particular,

> What has been is what will be,
>   and what has been done is what will be done;
>   there is nothing new under the sun.
>
> Ecclesiastes 1:9

> I said to myself, "Come now, I will make a test of pleasure; enjoy yourself." But again, this also was vanity. I said of laughter, "It is mad," and of pleasure, "What use is it?"
>
> Ecclesiastes 2:1–2

> How can the wise die just like fools? So I hated life, because what is done under the sun was grievous to me; for all is vanity and a chasing after wind.
>
> Ecclesiastes 2:16–17

> There is nothing better for mortals than to eat and drink, and find enjoyment in their toil. This also, I saw, is from the hand of God.
>
> Ecclesiastes 2:24

> You were dead through the trespasses and sins in which you once lived, following the course of this world, following the ruler of the power of the air, the spirit that is now at work among those who are disobedient. All of us once lived among them in the passions of our flesh, following the desires of flesh and senses, and we were by nature children of wrath, like everyone else. But God, who is rich in mercy, out of the great love with which he loved us even when we were dead through our trespasses, made us alive together with Christ—by

grace you have been saved—and raised us up with him and seated us with him in the heavenly places in Christ Jesus, so that in the ages to come he might show the immeasurable riches of his grace in kindness toward us in Christ Jesus. For by grace you have been saved through faith, and this is not your own doing; it is the gift of God—not the result of works, so that no one may boast. For we are what he has made us, created in Christ Jesus for good works, which God prepared beforehand to be our way of life.

Ephesians 2:1–10

Discussion Questions and Clip Conversations

All clips are available for viewing at ReelSpirituality.com/Books/God-In -The-Movies. We have also listed the timestamp range of the scenes for your reference.

1. *Groundhog Day* has become a contemporary classic and is frequently shown on television. How many times have you seen the film? What's your favorite scene? Why? If *Groundhog Day* isn't one of your favorite comedies, what are your favorite comedies? What do comedies do for us emotionally that dramas do not? How does laughter help us deal with the meaninglessness (and meaningfulness!) of life?

2. "Bad Phil" [34:30–40:01]. After his existential crisis in the bowling alley and his subsequent run-in with the cops, Phil wakes up resolved to take advantage of his life without consequence. He does what he wants, indulges in whatever he wants, and manipulates women without conscience. Is Phil's response to his life's meaninglessness typical? If you found yourself in his position, what would be your response? How are Phil's actions similar to those described in Ecclesiastes 1 and 2?

3. "Good Phil" [1:21:56–1:24:37]. After trying and failing to save the old man, Phil approaches life differently. He begins to do good for others instead of only for himself. Why do you think he decides to spend his day helping people rather than only helping himself? If you had found yourself in his position, what do you think you would have done? Is there any sense that Phil is responding to what he thinks God wants? Why or why not?

4. Eventually, Phil finds peace and learns to enjoy the life he is living whatever comes, including his love for Rita. Ecclesiastes counsels us similarly to find our enjoyment as we eat, drink, and love happily, even though life's ultimate meaning evades us. Such a life is what we all would want,

even though it remains out of our reach for many. Why do you think this is? What have you found to be true in your own life?

Bonus Material

Harold Ramis said that their original idea was to have Phil live February 2 for ten thousand years. In the film, fortunately, we see only thirty-eight different iterations of Phil's day.

Image Journal's Arts and Faith community named *Groundhog Day* the number one "Divine Comedy" of all time on their 2014 list, likening it to a modern telling of Dante's *Inferno*.

Selected Additional Resources

Alex Kuczynski's "Groundhog Almighty" (December 7, 2003) is worth reading in its entirety: http://www.nytimes.com/2003/12/07/style/groundhog-almighty .html.

Janet Maslin's review of *Groundhog Day* (February 12, 1993) is typical of the way the film was first reviewed after its 1993 release: http://www.nytimes.com /movie/review?res=9F0CEED6123EF931A25751C0A965958260.

Roger Ebert's "Great Movies" review of *Groundhog Day* (January 30, 2005) perfectly captures the film's enduring appeal: http://www.rogerebert.com /reviews/great-movie-groundhog-day-1993.

Elijah Davidson

15

To Live

Original title: *Huo zhe*
China, 1994
132 Minutes, Feature, Color
Actors: Ge You, Gong Li, Jiang Wu, Tao Guo,
    Niu Ben
Director: Zhang Yimou
Screenwriter: Lu Wei (adapted from a novel by Yu Hua)
Rated: Unrated (mature thematic material)

*Spirituality of
Everyday Life
Human Dignity,
the Meaning of Life, the
Nature of the Human*

Synopsis and Theological Reflection

Chinese director Zhang Yimou has long been considered a leading international filmmaker. To Western audiences, he is perhaps best known for directing the spectacular opening and closing ceremonies of the 2008 Beijing Summer Olympics and for popular martial arts epics like *Hero* (2002), an Oscar nominee for Best Foreign Language Film, and *House of Flying Daggers* (2004). In his early days, though, he and his fellow Fifth Generation filmmakers—a group of like-minded Chinese artists that began making movies in the aftermath of Mao Zedong's Cultural Revolution—were known for a string of powerful dramas about the reality of life in China that sensitively dealt with marginal characters and stories rarely acknowledged by official history. His 1994 film *To*

Live, which is from this period, is a must-see, a deeply moving and engrossing drama that is also a stirring ode to life. Viewers will be compelled by its power, inspired by its wisdom, and moved by its beauty.

On paper, *To Live* could sound hopelessly depressing: Zhang follows the life of an ordinary couple as they live through four of the most turbulent decades in modern Chinese history, from the mid-1940s to the 1970s, a period that in turn witnessed the Chinese Civil War between the Nationalists and the Communists, Mao's Great Leap Forward, and the Cultural Revolution. This was a time when millions of Chinese people perished, when the lives of countless families were forever changed by poverty, gender inequality, political persecution, and other forms of degradation and hardship. But remarkably, *To Live* is not a relentlessly downbeat portrayal of the reality of human suffering. Instead, it is a profoundly compassionate and life-affirming testimony to human resilience and the dignity and grace with which ordinary people face life's unexpected twists and turns.

When the story opens in the 1940s, the protagonist, Fugui, is a lazy but well-to-do young man who spends his days wasting away at a gambling den. His family regards his aimless existence with dismay and despair. When, overnight, Fugui loses his entire fortune and family estate to a scheming acquaintance, the destitution Fugui faces brings him to his senses. He resolves to lead a responsible life with his two children and wife, Jiazhen. He begins to make a living as a traveling shadow puppeteer, but when the Chinese Civil War breaks out, he finds himself caught up between the Nationalists and the Communists, trying to stay alive against impossible odds. In an ironic twist, Fugui's unwitting participation in the war on the Communist side helps to legitimize his proletariat credentials, while the scheming acquaintance who took over his family estate before the war is now branded a counterrevolutionary landowner and swiftly executed. This unexpected development is just one of several significant events that occur over the course of the film.

As the story progresses into the 1950s, the 1960s, and the 1970s, we see Fugui and Jiazhen going through seasons of sorrow and joy, defeat and triumph, as they attempt to raise their family in the midst of dramatic social upheavals. A great pleasure of the movie comes from journeying with them throughout the years. The movie masterfully conveys the passage of time and a sense of life as it is lived.

To Live has the historical sweep of a David Lean epic (e.g., *Lawrence of Arabia*, 1962), but it is also resolutely intimate in detail. It is not about heroes or revolutionaries but about everyday people and the way their fortunes are shaped by the changing tides of history. Fugui and Jiazhen are decent, unassuming individuals who simply yearn for a quiet life with their children. But forces beyond their control intervene at every juncture in the movie—their son and daughter each suffer a tragic fate that is simultaneously the result of bureaucratic ineptitude and life's terrible coincidences; family friends and acquaintances are successively branded capitalists and enemies of the people, depending on the shifting winds of ideology.

But despite the movie's rich political subtexts (it unsettled the Communist government enough that the movie was banned in China), Zhang's artistic aim is ultimately a spiritual and existential one. In *To Live*, the filmmaker gives his viewers a sense of what it means to be human and to deal with the slings and arrows of fortune, to exist in a broken, sometimes absurd world (the movie has striking moments of comedy) that is nonetheless beautiful and worthwhile. Throughout the many hardships and tragedies that Fugui and Jiazhen face, their hunger for life persists. This is the film's inherent power.

To Live possesses not only great power but also great humor and poignancy. Like the best of movies, it deepens our understanding and gratitude for life as it is given. The lead performances by Chinese actor Ge You and iconic actress Gong Li are magnificent and indescribably touching. They effortlessly convey their characters' decency, dignity, and mutual devotion over the span of thirty years. The score by Zhao Jiping, featuring the erhu (a kind of violin with two strings), is also exceptional, helping viewers interpret the story's meaning. This is a movie where the story, acting, and craft all come together to create a compelling cinematic experience. When the movie premiered at the Cannes Film Festival in 1994, it won the prestigious Grand Jury Prize, the Best Actor award for Ge You, and the Ecumenical Jury Prize (given by a Christian jury for films with strong spiritual significance). It further won the BAFTA Award for Best Foreign Language Film and received a Golden Globe nomination in the same category. *To Live* is a world cinema classic that deserves to be seen and experienced.

Dialogue Texts

For everything there is a season, and a time for every matter under heaven:

a time to be born, a time to die.

Ecclesiastes 3:1–2

For who knows what is good for mortals while they live the few days of their vain life, which they pass like a shadow? For who can tell them what will be after them under the sun? . . . In the day of prosperity be joyful, and in the day of adversity consider; God has made the one as well as the other, so that mortals may not find out anything that will come after them.

Ecclesiastes 6:12; 7:14

Go, eat your bread with enjoyment, and drink your wine with a merry heart; for God has long ago approved what you do. Let your garments always be white; do not let oil be lacking on your head. Enjoy life with the wife whom you love, all the days of your vain life that are given you under the sun, because that is your portion in life and in your toil at which you toil under the sun. Whatever your hand finds to do, do with your might; for there is no work or thought or knowledge or wisdom in Sheol, to which you are going.

Ecclesiastes 9:7–10

However that may be, let each of you lead the life that the Lord has assigned, to which God called you.

1 Corinthians 7:17

Discussion Questions and Clip Conversations

All clips are available for viewing at ReelSpirituality.com/Books/God-In -The-Movies. We have also listed the timestamp range of the scenes for your reference.

1. When director Zhang Yimou set out to make *To Live*, he was unhappy with the way movies often fail to reflect the lives of ordinary people. Indeed, even though major historical events happen throughout the movie—the Chinese Civil War, the Great Leap Forward, the Cultural Revolution—Zhang chooses to focus on the minute details in the life of Fugui and Jiazhen. What is the significance of approaching the story this way? Why do you think Fugui's and Jiazhen's lives attracted the film-maker's attention? What might be the spiritual significance of keeping viewers' attention on the mundane and the ordinary?

2. "You Owe Us a Life" [1:15:27–1:21:16]. Near the beginning of the movie, Jiazhen tells Fugui, "I'm not asking much, only to live a quiet life to-gether." This simple wish proves elusive throughout the story. One of the most striking incidents in their life together is the accidental death of their son, Youqing, at the hands of Chunsheng, the region's new district chief who, in a surprising twist, turns out to be Fugui's closest friend from the war. What is the importance of this ironic turn of events? What

are some of the other major events in the movie that disrupt Fugui and Jiazhen's life? Why do you think the filmmakers chose to include them, and what do they tell us about the film's view on life?

3. "Fengxia's Wedding" [1:32:42–1:37:20]. The occasion of their daughter Fengxia's marriage is one of the most joyous and moving sequences in the movie. Here, we see the love between parents and children, as well as the inevitable separation that comes in the life of a family. What are some of the happiest moments in your life, and what are some of the most joyous memories you have of your own family? How have these experiences shaped your identity?

4. "You Just Have to Live" [1:43:43–1:48:00]. In this powerful scene, Chunsheng comes knocking on the door in the middle of the night, not long after having been publicly tried and denounced as a "capitalist" in the heat of the Cultural Revolution. Chunsheng's wife has just committed suicide, and he himself is also contemplating death. At this point, Fugui reminds him that during the war they both came out of the valley of death and that it is important to go on living. What are some of the biggest challenges and hardships you have had to face in your own life? How did you overcome them? Who were some of the people, or what were some of the things, that gave you support and kept you going during times of trial and difficulty?

5. "And Life Will Get Better and Better" [2:07:46–2:12:10]. The last scene in the film shows Fugui and Jiazhen, now both in their old age, having a meal with their grandson, Little Bun, and son-in-law, Erxi. Why do you think the film ends this way?

Bonus Material

To Live is adapted from a novel by the Chinese writer Yu Hua. When Zhang Yimou first came across the source material, he was moved by its depiction of an ordinary Chinese family's evolution through life. He also injected elements of humor and levity into the movie as a reaction to what he regarded as excessively somber treatments of the same historical period by other Chinese movies.

Despite its international renown, the movie's critical depiction of the Communist government's campaigns and policies caused it to be banned in its native China when it was completed in 1994. (However, pirated copies of the movie remain in wide circulation in China.) Director Zhang Yimou was also banned from receiving foreign financing for his work for two years.

The actress Gong Li, who plays Jiazhen, is one of the icons of Chinese cinema and has starred in such American movies as *Miami Vice* and *Memoirs of a Geisha*. In the 1980s and the 1990s, she was director Zhang Yimou's main creative partner (they were also romantically involved). Together, they made some of the best-known Chinese movies in the world today, including *Raise the Red Lantern* and *Ju Dou* (both nominated for the Best Foreign Language Film Oscar), together with *Red Sorghum* (winner of the Golden Bear at the Berlin International Film Festival).

Less known to Western audiences is the actor Ge You, who plays Fugui. Ge is one of the most popular actors in China today and is largely known for his comedic roles. His performance in *To Live* shows his remarkable depth and made him the first Chinese actor to win the Best Actor award at Cannes.

Selected Additional Resources

Ebert, Roger. Review of *To Live*. December 23, 1994. http://www.rogerebert .com/reviews/to-live-1994.

The Film Sufi (blog). "*To Live*." April 5, 2010. http://www.filmsufi.com/2010/04 /to-live-zhang-yimou-1994.html.

Thomas, Kevin. "*To Live*: A Sweeping Saga of Modern China." *Los Angeles Times*, December 14, 1994. http://articles.latimes.com/1994-12-14/entertain ment/ca-8647_1_director-zhang-yimou.

Eugene Suen

16

Magnolia

The Meaning of Life
*Human Suffering, Life's
Mystery, Life's Vanity,
Redemptive Love, Sin
and Its Consequences*

US, 1999
188 Minutes, Feature, Color
Actors: Jason Robards, Julianne Moore, Tom
Cruise, Philip Seymour Hoffman, John C.
Reilly, William H. Macy, Philip Baker Hall,
Melora Walters, Jeremy Blackman
Director: Paul Thomas Anderson
Screenwriter: Paul Thomas Anderson
Rated: R (strong language, drug usage, sexuality, some violence)

Synopsis and Theological Reflection

> I put my heart—every embarrassing thing that I wanted to say—in
> *Magnolia*.
>
> Paul Thomas Anderson

On the surface, *Magnolia* is a melodrama about larger-than-life characters
whose parallel lives intersect through coincidence, death, ambition, and
dreams. It is filled with frailty, betrayal, and turmoil. And yet the movie is
paradoxically lyrical and hopeful. Viewers sense a profound wisdom, even

95

if events don't always "make sense." The movie is not only honest about the human condition with its mystery, amorality, and death; it also recognizes that life is a gift to be cherished. As John C. Reilly, who plays the well-meaning but bungling cop, Jim Kurring, comments about the script: "I think Paul has a remarkable ability for capturing the little human details of life and at the same time presenting a very big perspective on humanity at large. It's the perfect kind of millennial movie, I think, an intense investigation into what really drives us and the distance between who we think we are and who we really are."

Magnolia is set on Magnolia Boulevard in the San Fernando Valley and takes place during one twenty-four-hour period in 1999. In rapid-fire, frenetic succession we dip into the lives of nine individuals in the opening montage. As we watch, overlaid is the music, "One is the loneliest number that you'll ever do." The music unifies the scene. All of the characters are searching for meaning in life, or at least some happiness, given their lack of loving relationships. At the center of the seemingly diverse but interconnected group is an elderly TV producer, Earl Partridge (Jason Robards), who is dying of cancer. There is a deeper cancer, however: he has earlier abandoned his wife and let his teenage son care for her alone as she too died of cancer. His trophy wife, Linda (Julianne Moore), has married him for his money but now realizes as he is dying that she has come to love him. Phil Parma (Philip Seymour Hoffman), Earl's nurse, is trying to help his patient reconnect with his estranged son, Frank T. J. Mackey (Tom Cruise), a disgustingly chauvinistic self-help guru.

A second constellation of characters revolves around Jimmy Gator (Philip Baker Hall). He has been host of one of Earl Partridge's programs, *What Do Kids Know?*, for over thirty years. Jimmy is estranged from his daughter, Claudia Wilson Gator (Melora Walters), a drug addict devoid of self-worth, who is struggling in the aftermath of sexual abuse by her father. Jim Kurring meets her while answering a routine domestic disturbance call—her music is too loud. A Christian who prays, Jim knows his job is tough, but he is happy if he can even occasionally help someone. Meanwhile, we see Stanley Spector (Jeremy Blackman), the current whiz kid, being browbeaten by his father, who is hoping for riches. We are also introduced to Donny Smith (William H. Macy), a former winner on the show and now a mediocre appliance salesman, lonely and bitter toward his parents, who stole his quiz show earnings.

If such a listing of the main characters is hard to keep straight, it is no less so for the viewer of *Magnolia*. Much of the movie seems a mélange of intersecting stories that connect only through chance and coincidence, and whose full nature is not evident until much of the way through the movie.

But as the movie cuts in and out of the lives of these nine individuals and other supporting cast, viewers discover relationships between the vignettes that point to a greater interconnectedness in all our lives.

As the writer of Ecclesiastes observes, "time and chance" happen to us all (Eccles. 9:11). But in *Magnolia* Anderson has woven a tapestry that suggest that meaning can emerge from what otherwise would seem mere coincidence and loss. As the lives of his characters are presented to us much like a collage, it is clear, as in the biblical book, that neither power nor money nor fame nor wisdom brings meaning and satisfaction to life. Earl Partridge might have once been a powerful, rich TV executive, but when we see him, he is a shell of a man who is dying of cancer, alone with his regrets. Similarly, Jimmy Gator might seem a model of wholesomeness and wisdom to his public, but his ego, infidelities, and child abuse betray a darker story.

Anticipating America's fascination with *Who Wants to Be a Millionaire?* (or mirroring the long-running *Jeopardy*), the plot weaves in and out of the television game show *What Do Kids Know?*, which pits brainy kids against adults. And the kids are often more knowledgeable. But the movie's larger concern is for wisdom of a different sort, one that goes beyond our dominant cultural values. Just as Anderson's initial introduction of his nine lead characters played out to the accompaniment of an Aimee Mann song, two hours and twenty minutes into the movie, after the tragedies of the characters' lives have become all too apparent, Anderson makes use of another Mann song, "Wise Up," to express his convictions.

In an audacious move that serves as the emotional heart of the movie, Anderson weaves together the lives of these characters by having them sing along with Aimee Mann's vocals, which they are hearing on their radios. As the film cuts to their diverse settings, we hear each of them sing of their need to wise up. Though they each remain isolated, the fact that they are all singing along with this song makes theirs a corporate voice. With rain falling outside and most of the characters at the end of their rope, we see Claudia sitting alone in her apartment as she softly joins Mann. Then we cut to Jim Kurring, the inept, lonely cop, who picks up the lyrics. And on it goes. First Jimmy Gator, then Donnie, then Phil and Earl, then Linda in her car, then Frank, and finally Stanley—each singing along with Mann in succession. The lyrics we hear the characters sing match their particular situation—Donnie's drinking, Claudia's drugs, Jimmy's cancer, Linda's need to make things right, Stanley's resignation. But they also are all singing, "It's not going to stop / Till you wise up."

Magnolia invites viewers to wise up by looking deeper—by finding a wisdom that defies our traditional human agendas, whether power, fame, pleasure, or knowledge. But this proves difficult. Even after we hear the cast of characters singing of the need to wise up, we see them all still trying to save themselves by their own efforts. Jimmy destroys what little is left of his relationship with his wife, Rose, with his brutal, self-serving honesty. Donnie tries to steal money for braces. Claudia sniffs coke in order to gain the courage to see Jim. Frank lashes out angrily at Earl. But though each of these characters might continue to try to manage their fate, these are but last gasps. These characters sense (and we the audience know) the futility of all attempts to produce meaning by our own work. As the writer of Ecclesiastes states, "It is useless, useless" (1:2 GNT).

The foregrounding of music continues in *Magnolia* with a third Mann song, "Save Me," that ends the movie and continues into the credits. No one in the movie is able to redeem himself or herself. They need a friend. As the movie ends, Claudia is seen sitting disconsolate on the edge of her bed. Jim is talking to her as we hear Aimee Mann sing in the foreground, "You look like the perfect fit, / a girl in need of a tourniquet." And Jim offers just that. "Can you save me / come on and save me," the song pleads, giving words to Claudia's suffering silence. As the song continues, "If you could save me / from the ranks of the freaks / who suspect they could never love anyone," Jim's voice is barely audible over the music as he says, "You are a good and beautiful person." The camera focuses on Claudia and stays there as she struggles to accept his gift of love. Miraculously, she smiles briefly for the first time, and the movie ends.

No individualistic agendas will suffice. Our rationalistic assumptions simply prove hollow. Nowhere is this clearer than in the scenes leading up to the movie's climax, where a prolonged shower of frogs(!) stops people in their tracks. The rain of frogs, however absurd, actually becomes a catalyst for community. The falling frogs awaken Earl from his coma/stupor long enough for him to acknowledge the presence of his son, Frank. It proves redemptive. Jim, the LAPD cop, is able to assist Donnie after he is knocked off a building by the pelting frogs. The frogs even bring Claudia and her mother together once again. The frogs defy logic, to be sure, but then so does life. As Stanley comments, "It happens. This is something that happens." Viewers have been set up for this miraculous shower of frogs by the film's opening, which shows three amazing coincidences. *Magnolia*'s characters and viewers alike are forced to confront a reality beyond their ability to control. And the result is salvific.

Rather than being simply a series of vignettes, *Magnolia*'s nine stories ultimately play out as one voice, much like the nine petals of a magnolia flower. Unified by the Aimee Mann music that initially inspired it, the story moves painfully from "One Is the Loneliest Number" to a recognition of the need to "Wise Up" to a fragile acceptance of the sacred gift of another's care—"Save Me." Like Simon and Garfunkel's music in *The Graduate* or Cat Stevens's in *Harold and Maude*, Mann's music offers the movie's point of view. It becomes the built-in voice of the movie. Through music, reinforced by image and dialogue, the movie presents a coherent understanding of life, one rooted in others and quickened by the reality of death. Dark yet hopeful, *Magnolia* helps viewers confront their pasts and live into an uncertain future with hope.

Dialogue Texts

Someone may rise from poverty to become king of his country, or go from prison to the throne, but if in his old age he is too foolish to take advice, he is not as well off as a young man who is poor but intelligent.

Ecclesiastes 4:13–14 (GNT)

No matter how much you dream, how much useless work you do, or how much you talk, you must still stand in awe of God.

Ecclesiastes 5:7 (GNT)

We leave this world just as we entered it—with nothing. In spite of all our work there is nothing we can take with us.

Ecclesiastes 5:15 (GNT)

Only the wise know what things really mean. Wisdom makes them smile and makes their frowns disappear.

Ecclesiastes 8:1 (GNT)

Again I saw that under the sun the race is not to the swift, nor the battle to the strong, nor bread to the wise, nor riches to the intelligent, nor favor to the skillful; but time and chance happen to them all.

Ecclesiastes 9:11

Discussion Questions and Clip Conversations

All clips are available for viewing at ReelSpirituality.com/Books/God-In -The-Movies. We have also listed the timestamp range of the scenes for your reference.

1. "Prologue" [00:01–06:25]. Anderson opens the film with footage from old newsreels purporting to show three examples of mind-boggling coincidences, all of which involve death. How do these set the stage for all that happens, providing the movie its interpretive framework? What did you make of these?

2. "Wise Up" [2:18:55–2:22:30]. What is the nature of wisdom for Anderson and his characters? Who in the movie can be said to have "wised up" by the time the movie ends? Who is still in process, and who has failed to change? Go through the nine characters. What evidence can you muster from the film itself to support your conclusions? The clip ends with one of the several written weather forecasts that divides chapters of the story. How do these weather forecasts function within the story?

3. "Save Me" [2:58:30–3:02:00]. What is the reason for this music to be foregrounded and the conversation by Jim Kurring made so soft as to be almost unintelligible? Who else in the movie are agents of transformation who "save" others?

Bonus Material

Anderson says he got the idea for the frogs, not from the book of Exodus (though references to Exodus 8:2 are playfully scattered throughout the movie—can you recall them?), but from reading the best-selling books of Charles Fort. Those watching carefully will note that Stanley is reading one of Fort's books in the library as he prepares for the quiz show. Fort lived from 1874 to 1932 and spent his adult life collecting accounts of mysterious incidents that he hoped would undermine our confidence in science and engineering as the be-all and end-all. Sea monsters, ghosts, mysterious lights, live creatures falling from the sky—all these were a fascination to Fort. But showers of frogs were his favorite. Fort (and Anderson) sensed that modernity has feigned control and understanding only by ignoring what it can't figure out, and the price has been our soul.

Robert K. Johnston

17

The Piano

New Zealand/Australia/France, 1993
117 Minutes, Feature, Color
Actors: Holly Hunter, Harvey Keitel, Sam
  Neill, Anna Paquin
Director: Jane Campion
Screenwriter: Jane Campion
Rated: R (moments of graphic sexuality)

Human Agency
Beauty, Freedom,
Human Dignity,
Human Suffering,
Prejudice/Oppression,
Sin and Its Consequences

Synopsis and Theological Reflection

When *The Piano* was released in 1993, it was considered by many to be a masterpiece—including the Academy of Motion Picture Arts and Sciences, which gifted it with three Academy Awards—and by others as too offensive for Christian viewing. Like many films that inspire controversy, it is set firmly on the border crossing between suffering and love, cultural expectation and personal freedom.

The Piano is an achingly beautiful film about a woman's voice. Written, directed, edited, produced, and starring women, it tells of strong-willed Scotswoman Ada McGrath (Holly Hunter) who lives in an era of jealous male oppression. From the age of six, Ada controls her destiny in one of few ways available to her, thereby infuriating the men who expect her obedience: she chooses to be mute. Though her boundaries of self are contained within her

101

skin, boundaries she allows none to cross with the exception of daughter Flora (Anna Paquin), she is not silent, she says, "because of my piano."

In the opening shot, we see dimly the new shore on which Ada has been abandoned—sold by her father to lonely bachelor-landowner Alisdair Stewart (Sam Neill) and shipped to the coast of New Zealand. Her eyes covered with her hands, we view the brutal shoreline through fingers that appear remarkably like a keyboard.

We know within two minutes, through flashbacks and the narration we hear from the "voice of [her] mind," that she will live her own life at whatever cost. "The day I take it into my head to stop breathing will be my last." Hers is an indomitable will. Imagine, then, the cruelty of her belongings—including her piano—left to the elements as she is deposited on the shore with her daughter, unmet by husband-owner Stewart until the following day. Even when he does retrieve her and her daughter, he chooses to leave her piano because he considers the overland trek to his cabin too treacherous. Circling, he assesses her as though she were a packhorse at auction, remarking that she is shorter, duller, different than he hoped. He cannot see her as a woman, cannot hear the things that she is telegraphing. But another man in their company will— George Baines, Stewart's property manager, whose untamed imagination will first threaten and ultimately invite Ada into a new freedom.

Jane Campion's masterpiece has, as one of its key image systems, hands: hands that play, hands that strike, hands that caress, hands that force, hands that are mutilated and repaired. Ada's sensitive interior life is put into the hands of a man so insular and fearful that he can manage the harsh outback but is wholly flummoxed by the humans around him, misreading all their cues, hiding all his emotions—and his obsessively combed hair—under his useless hat. Ada communicates to the world through an elaborate pad and pencil case that hangs around her neck and through her tiny alter ego, Flora, who is as mouthy as her mother is mute. Stewart is deaf to it all.

Ada's story has been compared to a retelling of *The Robber Bridegroom* (aka *Bluebeard*), the tale of a woman sold/traded to a murderous husband with a hair-trigger temper, capable of rape and violence, by sisters who are falsely pious. Even Stewart's own relatives, who presumably live under his provision and protection, in spite of circumstances inhospitable to their lace pantaloons and china teacups, stage an absurd Christmas pageant that includes the Bluebeard story. This causes a near-riot among locals who presume the onstage carnage to be literal. Unknown to them, however, the same story is being played out in real life among their neighbors in the audience. Stewart's passions roil beneath the surface of a repressive cultural religion mocked by the unfettered humanity around him. When his anger emerges, as it is bound

Ada and Flora await their new home

to do, it is volcanic like Bluebeard's: the rules of polite society and religious conservatism are broken as he is shamed by Ada's affair with the low-born Baines, and his frozen patience erupts into brutality.

We are given many insights about Baines early on: he wears Maori facial tattoos that are, when closely observed, much like a musical note on his nose and the lines of a keyboard on his forehead. We see that the door of his hut has a string of un-wished-upon wishbones. This is the first hint that he is a romantic with yearnings too deep to be spoken. Upon his hesitant reception of Ada, who has come to his door with an urgent handwritten request to be taken to see about her abandoned piano, we learn that he is illiterate. Now our triangle is complete: a woman who cannot speak, a man who cannot hear, and another who cannot read. Of them all, Baines is the most permeable and the most influenced by the upcoming cataclysm between passion and restraint. He reluctantly takes a worried Ada and Flora back to the shore where the piano has been left to the disastrous effects of wind, salt air, and rain.

Upon her reunion with her "voice"—loud enough to overcome the ocean roar—Ada is in ecstasy. Baines is transfixed by Ada's transformation—a transformation he, too, wishes for. Not long after, he barters for the piano to be brought to his shack, where it will draw Ada like a beating heart removed from the chest of its owner. A confrontation between Baines, possessor of Ada's heart, and Stewart, rightful owner of her body, cannot be far behind. Ada travels the muddy terrain between her personhood and the life to which she has been unwillingly obligated, and it is Flora's curiosity that changes the tides of all their lives.

Baines has procured the piano not for his own interest in music but because he is drawn to *who* Ada becomes when she plays, and presumably to the possibility of the same transformation in himself. Through his own tortured journey, he is changed. He starts as a man capable of blackmailing Ada for intimacy. This was the rule of the day among men, it seems, and it is at least a little consolation that Baines bargains as an equal with Ada. As he realizes that their bargain is not transcendent and that she has no romantic feelings for him, he gives up and returns the piano to Ada, saying that their arrangement "is making you a whore, and me wretched." He has discovered love, and he longs for her willing affection in return. "My mind has seized on you," he confesses, "and I can think of nothing else. I don't eat. I don't sleep. I am sick with longing."

Concurrently, upon hearing of her infidelity, Stewart devolves into animal instincts, attempting to rape her and finally brutalizing her in the most profane way imaginable—all along blaming her for his actions: "Why do you make me hurt you? You make me angry!" In a remarkable cinematic sequence, we see Ada, stubborn as the horse from her childhood, falling to the ground in the mud, quiet, unmoving, in shock. Flora, as the embodiment of Ada's spirit, flees screaming from the scene as Ada's body appears to dissolve into the mud before our eyes. She races to Baines, taking, at Stewart's command, the symbol of Ada's defeat.

Yet, in a dream, Stewart hears the voice of Ada's mind begging for release, and he concedes, urging them all to leave him in the peace of his solitude. As Baines, Ada, and Flora leave the shoreline and go out to sea, Ada insists that the piano be pushed overboard, to sink to the bottom of the ocean. At first she chooses to go overboard with it, as some part of her must die with the piano before she can be fully free. Eventually, however, Ada floats to the surface, deciding to live. (Campion later regretted the decision to let Ada live. Both endings are viable.) The coda of the film tells of that "death" and the lullaby that is her life fiercely won: "At night I think of my piano in its sunken grave and sometimes of myself floating above it. Down there everything is so still and silent that it lulls me to sleep. It is a weird lullaby. And so it is. It is mine."

Dialogue Texts

The spirits of prophets are subject to the control of prophets. For God is not a God of disorder but of peace—as in all the congregations of the Lord's people.

Women should remain silent in the churches. They are not allowed to speak, but must be in submission, as the law says. If they want to inquire about something, they should ask their own husbands at home; for it is disgraceful for a woman to speak in the church.

1 Corinthians 14:32–35 (NIV)

Then the Lord said,

> "Because this people draw near with their words
> And honor Me with their lip service,
> But they remove their hearts far from Me,
> And their reverence for Me consists of tradition learned by rote."
>
> Isaiah 29:13 (NASB)

For all of you who were baptized into Christ have clothed yourselves with Christ. There is neither Jew nor Greek, there is neither slave nor free man, there is neither male nor female; for you are all one in Christ Jesus. And if you belong to Christ, then you are Abraham's descendants, heirs according to promise.

Galatians 3:27–29

If I speak in the tongues of mortals and of angels, but do not have love, I am a noisy gong or a clanging cymbal. And if I have prophetic powers, and understand all mysteries and all knowledge, and if I have all faith, so as to remove mountains, but do not have love, I am nothing. If I give away all my possessions, and if I hand over my body so that I may boast, but do not have love, I gain nothing.

Love is patient; love is kind; love is not envious or boastful or arrogant or rude. It does not insist on its own way; it is not irritable or resentful; it does not rejoice in wrongdoing, but rejoices in the truth. It bears all things, believes all things, hopes all things, endures all things.

Love never ends. But as for prophecies, they will come to an end; as for tongues, they will cease; as for knowledge, it will come to an end. For we know only in part, and we prophesy only in part; but when the complete comes, the partial will come to an end. When I was a child, I spoke like a child, I thought like a child, I reasoned like a child; when I became an adult, I put an end to childish ways. For now we see in a mirror, dimly, but then we will see face to face. Now I know only in part; then I will know fully, even as I have been fully known. And now faith, hope, and love abide, these three; and the greatest of these is love.

1 Corinthians 13:1–13

Discussion Questions and Clip Conversations

All clips are available for viewing at ReelSpirituality.com/Books/God-In-The-Movies. We have also listed the timestamp range of the scenes for your reference.

1. "This Is the Sound of My Mind" [01:46–03:30]. Ada says, "The voice you hear is not my speaking voice, but my mind's voice." She explains that no one knows why she stopped talking at the age of six, "not even

me." What might have locked up Ada's voice, and what, in the end, unlocked it?

2. "George Strives for Betterment" [30:13–34:00]. This is signified by the fact that he hires a piano tuner to care for the piano, and he drinks his tea in a china cup. What is the arc of George's transformation, and how will that eventually transform Ada? Where do they both stumble along the way?

3. "Baines and Ada Negotiate" [52:39–54:37]. They proceed into territory far from learning scales on the piano. What is going on in Ada? What is going on in Baines?

4. "Stewart and Intimacy" [1:04:00–1:06:00]. As Flora and other local children mimic the sounds and rhythms of sex against the forest trees, a horrified Stewart says, "You have shamed these trunks!" What does this say about his attitude toward intimacy? Later, he will turn away in shame from Ada, who attempts to create intimacy between them, even though it is the thing he has been longing for. What motivates Stewart?

5. "Why Won't She Play?" [1:08:00–1:13:00]. Ada's piano has been relinquished by Baines and moved to Stewart's cabin, but she won't play it. Why?

6. "Ada as 'Other'" [1:27:00–1:30:00]. Stewart's relatives say of Ada that "she does not play the piano as we do." Truer words were never spoken. What are the many ways in which this is true?

Selected Additional Resources

The film sound track by Michael Nyman is achingly beautiful.

Roger Ebert's review (November 4, 1993) is insightful: http://www.roger ebert.com/rogers-journal/the-piano-plays-on-the-inner-voice.

This profile of director Jane Campion from the *Guardian* is illuminating: http:// www.theguardian.com/film/2014/may/12/jane-campion-interview-cannes -the-piano.

Lauralee Farrer

18

The Shawshank Redemption

US, 1994
142 Minutes, Feature, Color
Actors: Tim Robbins, Morgan Freeman,
   James Whitmore
Director: Frank Darabont
Screenwriter: Frank Darabont (based on
   Stephen King's short story "Rita Hayworth and Shawshank Redemption")
Rated: R (language, prison violence)

Hope
Beauty, Friendship,
Human Identity,
the Nature of the Human

Synopsis and Theological Reflection

The Shawshank Redemption did poorly at the box office when it was released, though by Oscar time it garnered seven nominations. However, as this essay is being written, the movie continues to be number one on the Internet Movie Database (IMDb) list of all-time best movies as voted by viewers. The fact that *Shawshank* is a prison movie (a place most people know little about but nevertheless fear) about someone unjustly sent to prison (what if I were unjustly incarcerated?) might explain why audiences failed initially to embrace it. But the movie's narrative arc, revealing a hard-won freedom rooted in hope and friendship, has ultimately proved decisive for audiences. As Bobette Buster, a friend of Fuller's Reel Spirituality Institute and a leading

107

The Shawshank Redemption © 1994 Castle Rock Entertainment

A friendship develops on the roof: Red and Andy

script adviser in Hollywood, repeatedly tells her clients, a redemptive arc in a screenplay sells more tickets. It is what people desire. Certainly *Shawshank* would support her claim.

The film celebrates human possibility within the impossibility of Shawshank Prison's corrupt and inhuman domain. In particular, the movie is a story of hope rooted in human friendship—the friendship of Andrew Dufresne (Tim Robbins) and Ellis Redding (Morgan Freeman). "Red" has been sent to prison for a crime committed in his youth twenty years earlier. Andy was formerly a bank vice president and has been recently and wrongly convicted of the murder of his wife, who was found in the arms of her lover. Red is African American; Andy is white. Red has little formal education but lots of street smarts (he can get anything smuggled into prison). Andy has lots of education but lacks prison savvy (he is beaten to within an inch of his life by the prison "sisters").

The movie begins by showing Andy's wife's murder while a radio plays, "If I didn't care more than words can say. . . . If this isn't love, then why do I thrill? . . . Is it love beyond compare?" And viewers understand the full irony. No, it is not love that Andy's wife and her lover have. It is a vulgar, desperate, mutually self-centered affair that ends in a double murder. But even by its absence, the question of what constitutes true love is thus established in viewers' minds. As the movie proceeds, here will become the movie's theme as Andy and Red come to care deeply for each other and as their friendship becomes, in fact, a love beyond compare.

Most of the story is narrated by Red. A violent and corrupt world, Shawshank Prison allows for little humanity among the inmates. But two moments of joy Red remembers. Both have their genesis in Andy. When prisoners are conscripted to tar a roof, Andy literally risks his life bargaining with the worst of the guards. He interrupts a conversation between the guards and offers to help the chief guard save money with his taxes if the prisoner-workers are each given cold beers to drink at the end of their work day. The guard reluctantly agrees. As Red describes the experience, "We sat with the sun on our shoulders and drank like free men."

Later, when Andy has gained the confidence of the warden because of his financial expertise, Andy is left alone in the office where the prison-wide microphone is housed. While playing an aria from a Mozart opera on the record player, he chooses again to act on behalf of his fellow inmates, broadcasting the music on speakers throughout the prison. In a voice-over, Red reflects on his friend's generous act: "I have no idea to this day what those two Italian ladies were singing about. . . . I like to think they were singing about something so beautiful it can't be expressed in words, and makes your heart ache because of it. . . . It was like some beautiful bird flapped into our drab little cage and made those walls dissolve away. And for the briefest of moments, every man in Shawshank felt free."

When later asked by his inmate friends how he endured his lockup in solitary confinement that resulted from this insubordination, Andy responds that the "hole" was easy because the beauty of that music kept him company. "You need music so you don't forget." When asked what he meant, Andy replied, "Hope. . . . There is something inside that they can't get to, that they can't touch. It's yours."

But *Shawshank* shows that hope can be dangerous as well. When the old prison librarian, Brooks (James Whitmore), is released after fifty years in prison so the government can save money, he is afraid. Trying to live as a free man, he finds himself alone. Finally he writes a note back to the prison ("I don't like it here. I've decided not to stay.") and then hangs himself in his rooming house. With no friends, he cannot cope. "Woe to one who is alone and falls and does not have another to help" (Eccles. 4:10).

As Red grows older, he too becomes fearful that he has become "institutionalized." He is scared that he too will be let out of the prison when he is too old to readjust on the outside. Wanting to give hope to his friend, Andy shares with him a dream he has. When Andy gets out of prison, he wants to go to a little town in Mexico on the edge of the Pacific Ocean—Zihuatanejo. He will buy a little hotel and an old boat that needs fixing up. Andy says to Red, "A place like that could use a man who knew how to get things." Red fears he is too old for such dreams, but Andy persists with his friend: "Red, if you ever get out of here, do me a favor. Go to a hayfield near Baxton . . .

[Andy describes the place] . . . and look for a black rock and find what is buried there." Red agrees.

These two friends do get out (the title, *The Shawshank Redemption*, is already a spoiler), Andy first and Red sometime later. Like Brooks, Red at first almost despairs of fitting back into society. But there is an important difference. Red has promised his friend to go to the field in Baxton. So as a final act of desperate courage, Red goes and finds money that Andy has left for him and a note that reads: "Remember, hope is a good thing." The film ends with Red traveling south to Zihuatanejo, where he finds his friend on the beach repairing an old boat.

"If I didn't care, more than words can say . . . is it love, beyond compare?" The shallow words of the radio song that opens the movie have been replaced by the profound actions of two men whose friendship proves life-giving and life-sustaining. As the writer of Ecclesiastes recognizes, "Two are better than one, because they have a good reward for their toil. For if they fall, one will lift up the other. . . . Though one might prevail against another, two will withstand one" (Eccles. 4:9–10, 12).

Dialogue Texts

> Hope deferred makes the heart sick,
> but a desire fulfilled is a tree of life.

Proverbs 13:12 (cf. Prov. 10:28; 23:18)

And now faith, hope, and love abide, these three; and the greatest of these is love.

1 Corinthians 13:13

If resident aliens among you prosper, and if any of your kin fall into difficulty with one of them and sell themselves to an alien . . . they shall have the right of redemption; one of their brothers may redeem them.

Leviticus 25:47–48 (cf. Lev. 25:49–55)

> Some friends play at friendship
> but a true friend sticks closer than one's nearest kin.

Proverbs 18:24 (cf. Prov. 27:6)

Discussion Questions and Clip Conversations

All clips are available for viewing at ReelSpirituality.com/Books/God-In-The -Movies. We have also listed the timestamp range of the scenes for your reference.

1. "Time for Mozart" [1:07:00–1:12:42]. One of the two scenes most commonly referenced in the movie is Andy's decision to play Mozart over the prison's public-address system. Why did Andy turn on the microphone? What is there about music, or art more generally, that helps humanize a person? Why would a harmonica be important for Red to have? How does music help sustain hope while Andy is in solitary confinement?

2. "Beer on the Roof" [33:18–38:35]. The other transformative scene in *Shawshank* is the crew of prisoners working to tar a roof and then being able to relax and drink beer together. What is the value of work in a human's life? Of play? What was the value of work for Andy, both authorized and clandestine (e.g., carving chess figures, getting new books, being the warden's accountant, digging a tunnel)? And what about the beer and the music? What about for Red?

3. "Certain Hayfield" [1:42:30–1:47:04]. Andy, Red, and Brooks each have differing perspectives concerning "hope." Perhaps Andy sums up his understanding best when he says to Red after the warden has killed the one person who could exonerate Andy: "I guess it comes down to a simple choice, really. Get busy living, or get busy dying." What was the basis for Andy's hope, and how was it more robust than Red's? How many examples can you give where Andy's actions give hope to others? And how are we to understand Andy's use of deceit and illegal practices as one basis for his hope? What was the difference in the lives of Red and Brooks that motivated Red to get busy living while Brooks committed suicide? For Red, what turned fantasy into hope? How did Red help Andy? How did Andy help Red?

4. James Hogan, in his book *Reel Parables*, suggests that *Shawshank* asks the difficult question, "When bad things happen to good people, what should good people do?" Do you agree? What possible responses does the movie show?

5. In what way does Shawshank Prison function in the movie as a metaphor?

6. "He [God] has rescued us from the power of darkness and transferred us into the kingdom of his beloved Son, in whom we have redemption, the forgiveness of sins" (Col. 1:13–14). In what way might you understand Andy to be a Christ figure, an innocent man wrongly convicted of a crime who sets others free? Does such a redemptive interpretation of the story add depth to the film's meaning, or is it a distraction from the story's core themes?

Bonus Material

On November 18, 2014, the Academy of Motion Picture Arts and Sciences (which awards the Oscars each year) held a twentieth anniversary screening of *Shawshank*, followed by a Q&A with Frank Darabont, Morgan Freeman, and Tim Robbins. The sold-out crowd, diverse in age and gender, gave the film a standing ovation. When asked why they signed on to do the movie, both actors mentioned the incredible script, which changed little during the story's filming. One change suggested by the studio executives was the ending. While the script ended with Red on the bus, the studio wanted there to be a reunion in Mexico. It was added.

When asked when they knew that they had produced a classic, Freeman mentioned the poll in Britain in which *Shawshank* was voted one of the ten best films of all time. Darabont spoke more personally, citing mail he received in which one man wrote that the movie stopped him from committing suicide, while for another it inspired him to lose two hundred and fifty pounds. The person said the movie changed his life. "It got me out of my depression. Something in the film transformed me." Tim Robbins spoke of the movie as a world phenomenon. He was in rural China and people had seen it. Nelson Mandela saw it. Said Robbins, "The movie taps into a basic human need. People laugh and cry during the movie in every culture. The story is timeless and borderless."

Selected Additional Resources

Stevenson, Bryan. *Just Mercy: A Story of Justice and Redemption*. New York: Spiegel & Grau, 2015.

Robert K. Johnston

19

Three Colors: Blue

Original title: *Trois couleurs: Bleu*
France/Poland, 1993
98 Minutes, Feature, Color
Actors: Juliette Binoche, Benoît Régent
Director: Krzysztof Kieślowski
Screenwriters: Krzysztof Piesiewicz,
    Krzysztof Kieślowski, Agnieszka Holland,
    Edward Żebrowski, Stawomir Idziak
Rated: R (some sexuality)

Human Agency
Art/Play Mediating
God's Mercy, Freedom,
Human Identity, Human
Suffering, Loss, Love

Synopsis and Theological Reflection

Blue is the first film in a trilogy by Polish master filmmaker Krzysztof Kieślowski using the colors of the French flag and their concomitant concepts of liberty, equality, and fraternity to contemplate the themes of the Ten Commandments. Following his 1989 television miniseries *Dekalog* (*The Decalogue*), it was the brainchild of screenwriting partner Krzysztof Piesiewicz "to make a film where the commanding dictums of the Decalogue are understood in a wider context." Why not "see how the Ten Commandments function today—what our attitude toward them is, and how the three words 'liberty,' 'equality,' and 'fraternity' function on a very human, intimate, and personal plane?"

Blue uses "liberty" to consider the wider themes of idolatry, hypocrisy, murder, adultery, deceit, and covetousness, all put within a set of complicated relationships with mother, neighbor, and God.

By the first sound of this masterpiece—the whistling of the wind, heard even before the first image appears—we know that change is imminent for someone in the car we have joined on the road at sundown. Three brief minutes in, and we know who will live and who will die: the car crashes, a ball floats away from the scene (the daughter's soul?), papers are scattered to the wind from the thrown-open door (the composer-husband's soul?), and a lone woman's screams are heard. A young passerby, witnessing the accident, flings a toy he is playing with into the air as he races to the grisly scene that we are left to imagine from a distance. Later we will discover that he takes from the scene a necklace belonging to heroine Julie Vignon de Courcy (Juliette Binoche). His wooden cup and ball have been exchanged for a cross, and his innocence, too, is gone. So much loss is communicated in a moment of brilliant, wordless implication.

The next shot is an extreme close-up, directly into Julie's eye, opening onto a new world that will—after some tortured pain—bring with it a love that is true, a generosity that is deep, and a new birth that is rich and visceral. This world, by fire, trauma, blood, and shape-shifting pain, will right itself as the truth of Julie's life is revealed to her. This is the truth that the New Testament tells us is the beginning of freedom.

Julie, tucked safely under hospital blankets like a child, watches on a tiny screen as the memorial service for her husband and daughter unfolds with all the earnestness and pomp of a royal wake. Her husband, a famous composer commissioned to create a concerto to commemorate the reunification of Europe, is lauded and mourned. "No one," says his eulogist, "can accept that he is gone." Julie, unmentioned in the myopic ceremony, strokes with one finger the tiny casket that appears on the screen next to her husband's. She looks into the camera. *There is more to this story*, that look says, *than is being told here*. Turns out, there's more to the story than Julie knows, too.

The film is an exploration of the choice to feel or not to feel, of coming alive after death. A reporter who violates Julie's privacy says, when she is rightly rebuffed, "You have changed." Exactly. Julie is alone with her fractured heart. Later she will say, from the depth of her grief, "I don't want any more friends, belongings, love. They are all traps." But that is not where she is meant to finish. "All the films I make," Kieślowski says, "are about the need to open up."

Julie returns to the villa she shared with her famous husband and gives instructions to sell everything. She takes only a cheap beaded mobile hanging in her daughter's bedroom and a scribbled musical idea left on the piano that, when she looks at it, plays the unfinished concerto in her head. All assets are designated to provide for the housekeepers and the gardeners and her invalid mother, and she has her own account to live on. She allows a brief moment of passion with Olivier, her husband's colleague who has loved her from afar for years. She intends to disenchant him, thereby breaking the last bond connecting her to her old life. It doesn't go that way for him, however.

She retakes her maiden name and moves away from everyone she knows to an apartment in the center of a lively arrondissement of Paris. Life blossoms all around this space—an indication of her will to live. A long climb to her new perch on the top floor reveals windows that overlook a market where a street performer plays a tune Julie recognizes as her own. The new living space is empty except for a few mirrors left behind. She is forced to face herself and to see what she is composed of. She hangs her daughter's beads, she buys a plant, she creates a nesting place.

Her neighborly friendships, her daily espresso at the nearby café, her attempts to create a new and calm life are interrupted by interlopers small and large who require her attention—her stripper neighbor, an unwelcome litter of mice, a visit from Olivier who, rebuffed by her, says, "I have seen you. It's enough." In each case she must choose between feeling and not feeling, between love and solitude, between life and death. One day she is contacted by the young boy who witnessed her accident. He has searched her out to return her necklace, her cross. A beautifully framed moment shows the boy as icon, with streams of light emanating around his head. She gives him the cross, a gift from her husband, and lets go of one more memory in the process.

Later, together, we will learn that her husband, Patrice, was having an affair, and that his mistress, Lucille, wears the very same cross. He gave the same gifts to both women, represented by the necklace and by the child that Lucille carries. Suddenly, Julie knows what to do with a legacy that feels no longer hers: she gives Lucille the villa and all the wealth necessary to raise the child; she even grants her husband's last name. By walking away from all that she thought she shared with her husband (now lost to her), she is free to truly live on her own account. She cannot, however, leave everything behind—she must still admit that the music he was writing was, in fact, her own to accept and to complete.

At Olivier's house, where he is trying to complete the unfinished concerto left behind by Patrice, she pulls a Bible from his wall of books and opens to the Scripture that provides the text for the concerto's choir: 1 Corinthians 13. "If I speak in the tongues of men and of angels and have not love, I am like a noisy gong or a clanging cymbal." She will learn, finally, that even after fully embracing the music as her own, it isn't until she returns Olivier's true love for her that she finds rest and possibility for a future.

One of Kieślowski's last shots is a close-up of Olivier's eye—reminiscent of the extreme close-up of Julie's eye in the hospital—but this time she is reflected in it. She is seen. She is real. Now she can exist in a way more fully formed and honest than just as the wife of a famous composer. As a soloist and choir sing St. Paul's praise of love from the concerto, the rising sun catches her in its glow and she allows a faint smile of hope. (For a similar faint smile of hope, see the ending of *Magnolia*, chap. 16.)

Dialogue Texts

The text of the concerto, sung by a choir, is from 1 Corinthians 13:1–2:

> Though I speak with the tongues of men and of angels, but have not love, I have become sounding brass or a clanging cymbal. And though I have the gift of prophecy, and understand all mysteries and all knowledge, and though I have all faith, so that I could remove mountains, but have not love, I am nothing.
>
> 1 Corinthians 13:1–2 (NKJV)

> O sing to the LORD a new song;
>   sing to the LORD, all the earth.
> Sing to the LORD, bless his name;
>   tell of his salvation from day to day.
>   Psalm 96:1–2

> Then the LORD God said, "It is not good that the man should be alone; I will make him a helper as his partner."
>
> Genesis 2:18

> Two are better than one, because they have a good reward for their toil. For if they fall, one will lift up the other; but woe to one who is alone and falls and does not have another to help.
>
> Ecclesiastes 4:9–10

Discussion Questions and Clip Conversations

All clips are available for viewing at ReelSpirituality.com/Books/God-In-The-Movies. We have also listed the timestamp range of the scenes for your reference.

1. "I Broke the Window" [05:22–07:40]. Julie breaks the hospital window to create a diversion so she can access the narcotics with which to kill herself. Once she has them in her mouth, however, she cannot continue. This is the first indication of her nascent will to live. She spits them into her hand, and as the night nurse finds her, she confesses the obvious. What follows is a beautiful moment of absolution between her and the nurse: "I broke the window," she confesses. Her nurse, not breaking eye contact, replies, "It doesn't matter." Julie continues, "I'm sorry." And the nurse replies, "We'll replace it." What is the subtext beneath the surface of this benign conversation? What does this opening vignette tell us about how Julie's story is likely to end?

2. "The Color Blue" [11:18–12:05; 16:04–17:00; 30:54–32:42; cf. 34:00–39:44; 1:26:26–1:30:10]. What does it mean when the music interrupts Julie's reverie? Why does the blue reflection cross her face at those times? Later we discover her in the blue room that reminds her of her daughter. The plastic beads hanging from the ceiling reflect on her face, and these are the only thing she takes with her from the house and hangs in her new home. What do these beads suggest? Their reflection appears again later, when Julie is locked out from her new apartment. They play out across her closed eyes as the ethereal music suggests itself to her consciousness. How are the beads, the music, the blue reflection, and Julie's sorrow intertwined? Whose concerto is it?

3. "Causing Herself Pain" [19:37–21:00; 27:27–29:05]. Julie drops the lid of the piano on her fingers and shortly thereafter, as she is walking away from their home, scrapes her fingers on the rough stone wall as she passes. What is this inclination to cause herself pain? Is she trying to feel or perhaps to stop feeling? What other examples of this are to be found in the film? Have you ever felt numb to life? How could you finally move on?

4. "A Diorama" [1:34:08–1:38:00]. At the end, a beautiful diorama of all the movie's characters plays out before the final note. What is the purpose of revisiting each of them in their place on that night? As the movie ends, how has Julie chosen to sing the new song? And is she now singing St. Paul's ode to love (1 Cor. 13)?

Selected Additional Resources

Investigation into this masterpiece of Kieślowski's should include, of course, the other two films in the trilogy: *White* (1994), starring Zbigniew

Zamachowski and Julie Delpy, and *Red* (1994), starring Irène Jacob. It is also worth watching Kieślowski's series *Dekalog* (interrogating the Decalogue) to fully understand the deeper themes of his work on this trilogy.

Joe Kickasola's *The Films of Krzysztof Kieślowski: The Liminal Image* (New York: Continuum, 2004) is illuminating for anyone interested in understanding the filmmaker behind the films and the influences of a unique convergence of Communist, Catholic, and Polish cultural influences of his time.

Available DVD features on the Criterion Collection edition are a veritable film school of extras, including three cinema lessons with director Krzysztof Kieślowski; interviews with *Blue*'s composer, writer, and three actors; selected-scene commentary with Juliette Binoche; video essays by three leading Kieślowski scholars; Kieślowski's student short *The Tram* (1966) and a fellow student's short featuring Kieślowski as the solo actor; two short early documentaries by Kieślowski; *Krzysztof Kieślowski: I'm So-So . . .* (1995), a feature-length documentary in which the filmmaker discusses his life and work; two multi-interview programs called *Reflections on "Blue"* and *Kieślowski: The Early Years*; a booklet featuring essays by critics; an excerpt from *Kieślowski on Kieślowski*; interviews with three cinematographers; and, believe it or not, more.

Lauralee Farrer

20

Unforgiven

Forgiveness
Human Identity

US, 1992
131 Minutes, Feature, Color
Actors: Clint Eastwood, Gene Hackman,
Morgan Freeman, Jaimz Woolvett, Richard
Harris, Saul Rubinek, Frances Fisher, Anna Levine
Director: Clint Eastwood
Screenwriter: David Webb Peoples
Rated: R (language, violence, a scene of sexuality)

Synopsis and Theological Reflection

England has King Arthur and his knights; the Middle East has Ali Baba and the forty thieves; and the United States of America has the gunslingers, lawmen, farmers, prostitutes with hearts of gold, railroad men, and cowpokes who settled the Western frontier. These Western tales are the stories we tell to form our national identity (even when they aren't accurate or exclude facts or focus on that which makes us feel uncomfortable—consider the Native Americans!). They tell us who we are, where we've come from, and what it takes to secure a future in this world.

Unforgiven is one of those stories, and it feels like the last one of those stories that ever needs to be told. It's not, of course. We never stop needing to discern our national identity, but *Unforgiven* has an air of finality about it, as if this is all that ever again needs to be said about the American frontier myth and what its inherent violence means for us, the American people.

This air of finality has as much to do with the director and star of the film as it does with the film's story. Clint Eastwood had been a movie star for over thirty years when he made this film, and at the time, he claimed it would be his last—as both an actor and director. Time has not proven that claim to be true, though time has proven *Unforgiven* to be Eastwood's last Western. It denotes the final screen appearance of an American icon—Clint Eastwood with shark-dead eyes staring down the barrel of a rifle, enacting morally ambiguous justice on a morally ambiguous world.

Clint Eastwood is as tied to the Western mythos as any other actor save, perhaps, John Wayne. Wayne's characters (primarily in the films of John Ford) are men of character who, in the end, always do what is right and on whose shoulders the honorable foundation of the nation was built. Clint Eastwood's characters (primarily in the films of Sergio Leone), on the other hand, are nameless characters of dubious reputation who vie with men and women of similarly questionable moral quality. Eastwood's West is morally bankrupt. Mercy is the exception, not the rule. Clint Eastwood's career calls into question the stories we tell ourselves about the West and, therefore, the stories we tell ourselves about who we are, where we've come from, and what it takes to secure a future in this world.

Unforgiven is a movie principally about the stories we tell and the ways those stories shape us. Most often, the characters' stories turn out not to be true, as we see with "English" Bob and the "Schofield Kid." Their personal stories are full of exaggerations and lies. "Little" Bill may tell the truth about his past and the kind of man he is, but he's lying to himself about his ability to be anything else, as shown by his treatment of the prostitutes, English Bob, Will Munny, and Ned Logan—and symbolized by his leaky roof and out-of-level house. English Bob, the Schofield Kid, and Little Bill define themselves by false myths. One by one, these fabrications betray them.

The stories about the murderous exploits of William Munny turn out to be more than true; the truth is more terrible and more thrilling than anyone could have imagined. Will Munny doesn't remember any of it though, because he was drunk during his days as a "vicious and intemperate" man. He drank to escape the horrible reality of his violent life, but eventually he found a better escape than whiskey—a wife. She helped him sober up, and they lived peacefully together for almost a decade. The story of their shared love is the story he chooses to define his life, or at least he tries to until the events of the film force him to pick up a gun and a bottle again. When he does, all hell breaks loose in his life and in the lives of everyone who wronged him.

In *Unforgiven*, Clint Eastwood and screenwriter David Webb Peoples give us the myth of the American West replete with symbol and stereotype. Then, moment by moment, they pick apart that myth and show us both the cowardly and the terrible truth behind it. *Unforgiven* suggests that if this is how we want to define ourselves as a people, we had better own up to the terror of it. The movie suggests we'd be much better off finding a more peaceful story to govern our lives.

We Christians are a people defined by stories as well. Our Bible is full of them. We repeat them constantly and make claims about what the stories say about who we are, where we've come from, and what it takes to secure a future in this world. Sometimes those stories conflict with the American myth. Sometimes they don't. Too often, we take these stories—both the ones in the Bible and the ones on our movie screens—for granted and don't thoughtfully consider their ramifications. *Unforgiven* reminds us how important it is to take seriously the stories we tell ourselves.

We often treat the Bible as if it is a dime-store novel like the one W. W. Beauchamp writes about English Bob in *Unforgiven*. The heroes and villains are easy to distinguish, the heroes' causes are always righteous, and the villains end up getting what they deserve. The Bible's stories are more complicated than that. The characters in them are closer to what Little Bill divulges and what Will Munny exemplifies. The Bible's characters are often cowards. They barely scrape by. When they do triumph over their enemies, the violence is often horrific, and "deserve's got nothin' to do with it."

But in the end, the Bible is different from *Unforgiven*, because while *Unforgiven* is a retelling of the American myth, the Bible is not ultimately about who we are, where we've come from, or what it takes to secure a future in this world. The stories in the Bible aren't about us. They are about God. They exist to define us in relation to God and spur us toward worship of God. So we should not anesthetize or simplify them. When they confuse us or trouble us, we should accept that confusion, because they are about a God beyond our comprehension. When they comfort us or encourage us, we should accept that too, because they are about a God who loved us enough to reveal Godself to us and rescue us from the cycle of bloodshed that is our only identity without Christ. When we treat the stories in the Bible appropriately, they prove more terrible and thrilling than we ever could have imagined.

Dialogue Texts

Rather than provide biblical texts for this film, we want to encourage you to talk with others about biblical passages that confuse, trouble, comfort, or encourage you. What do those passages reveal about God? What do they suggest about how you should think about and respond to God?

Discussion Questions and Clip Conversations

All clips are available for viewing at ReelSpirituality.com/Books/God-In-The-Movies. We have also listed the timestamp range of the scenes for your reference.

1. The stories *Unforgiven*'s gunslingers tell about themselves and about each other are sometimes false, sometimes true, and sometimes less terrifying than they ought to be. Nevertheless, these stories determine how these people treat each other and what they hope to accomplish with their lives. Which of the stories shared in *Unforgiven* are true? Which are false? When we finally see Will Munny "uncloaked" at the end of the film, is he better or worse than we've heard? What stories do we tell about ourselves and about others (particularly on social media)? Are these stories true? How do these stories define our lives?

2. "The Duck of Death" [53:44–58:05]. Beauchamp has written a dime-store novel about the exploits of English Bob, but Little Bill knows the truth behind the story, and the facts upset Beauchamp's opinion of his hero. Which story—the book's or Little Bill's—is the one we typically see in Westerns? How is Little Bill's story more disheartening? How does Beauchamp respond to learning the truth? Have you ever experienced something similar—you thought you knew the truth of a person or situation, but when you learned the truth, it changed your perspective entirely? How did you respond? Are you ever hesitant to learn the truth because it might upset your understanding of the world?

3. "The Death of Davy Boy" [1:29:40–1:34:27]. Will, Ned, and the Schofield Kid ambush one of the cowboys responsible for disfiguring Delilah and kill him from afar. If this were a scene in a typical Western, when would it have ended? Why do you think the filmmakers allow it to continue? What do you feel as the scene goes on and we watch and listen to Davy die? What does this suggest to you about *Unforgiven*'s aims? What does this scene suggest about violence? Do any biblical stories make you feel similarly? Do any biblical stories go on longer than you anticipate and reveal more details than you expect? How do those stories make you feel?

4. The Western myth is essential to the American identity. How does what we see in *Unforgiven* challenge that identity? How should Americans view themselves in light of what we see in *Unforgiven*? Which biblical

stories are essential to your identity as a Christian? Do you think about those stories as being "about" you? If you think of them as being primarily about God, how does that change the way you understand them? Are there any stories in the Bible that you don't like thinking about? Why? If you think about those stories as being "about God," does that make you more or less eager to think about them? Why or why not?

Bonus Material

As a celebrity, Clint Eastwood's politics have always been a matter of public interest, and his films are always combed through for hints of political ideologies. Eastwood has frequently endorsed Republican candidates for office, going back as far as Dwight D. Eisenhower in 1952 and as recently as 2012, when he endorsed Mitt Romney. He has also, however, campaigned for same-sex marriage and stricter gun control laws. Eastwood calls himself a Libertarian, and he registered as such in 2009. Ultimately, this means Eastwood is an individual, he'd like to keep it that way, and his movies aren't the place to look for insight into his political beliefs.

Unforgiven was remade in Japan in 2013 by director Lee Sang-il as a samurai film starring Ken Watanabe. There is a fun irony in this as Clint Eastwood became famous in Sergio Leone's *A Fistful of Dollars*, a Western remake of Akira Kurosawa's samurai classic *Yojimbo*.

Selected Additional Resources

Keith Phipp's review of the tenth-anniversary DVD release of *Unforgiven* is graced by the perspective that only time can give: http://www.avclub.com/review/unforgiven-10th-anniversary-edition-dvd-12335.

On the 525th episode of *Filmspotting*, Adam Kempanar, Josh Larsen, and Michael Phillips had a heated discussion about *Unforgiven* in recognition of the release of *American Sniper*, Eastwood's 2015 film about another American hero with a penchant for killing. Their discussion gets at all the controversy surrounding both films: http://filmspotting.net/reviews/show-archive/43-2015-shows/1274-525-oscar-picks-sacred-cow-unforgiven.html.

Elijah Davidson

A **DECADE** OF THE **UNEXPECTED**

The two thousands, the double ohs, the aughts, the noughties—it's hard to name a decade that ends in zeroes and even harder perhaps to capture all that happened in this period at the turn of the millennium. Calling it "a decade of the unexpected" points to how the dawn of the new century brought with it a host of unexpected tragedies and possibilities.

While the panic and fear generated around the possibility of the total global collapse of the internet and subsequent economic meltdown failed to materialize, we were not long into the decade before another event reshaped the world we live in. Y2K may have fizzled, but the attacks on the World Trade Center on September 11, 2001, led to both the War on Terror and the invasion of Afghanistan and Iraq, ushering in more than a decade of global concerns about terrorism and religious fundamentalism, concerns still central today. While the rise of digital technology and new media connected us in ways we had never experienced before, they also made us more aware of differences and tensions across the world. It is difficult to characterize the '00s beyond these early and tragic events, for all other developments happened in the shadow of them. In many ways, the '00s were a sobering and transitional time.

Perhaps the most significant development during the decade was our exponentially expanded connectivity. For instance, between 2000 and 2010 the number of mobile phone users in the United States went from 97 million to 293 million. Everyone was increasingly mobile and online, and as a result, we now swim in a sea of Wi-Fi. Not only did technology connect us via our mobile phones (which very quickly became mobile devices), but we used technology to connect in other ways—Facebook and other social media tools allowed us to redefine and reinscribe everything from friendships to what it means to "go to church."

In cinema, the '00s were the decade in which global cinema, already emerging in the nineties, became a significant force. The "world" found its way onto our movie theater screens in unprecedented ways, and with it came stories of the particular and the universal—movies like *The Son, Water, Secret Sunshine, Spirited Away, Motorcycle Diaries, Departures, The Sea Inside,* and *The Story of a Weeping Camel*. These, and others like them, presented an opportunity for Christians involved in the movies to engage in significant theological dialogue with the world and its myriad voices.

We can't talk about film in this decade without making mention of one additional movie—*The Passion of the Christ*, Mel Gibson's controversial story of Christ's passion. Singled out by some not for its religious theme but for its graphic violence, the film was a huge hit, grossing in excess of $600 million during its theatrical release. It was also an R-rated film (the highest-grossing R-rated film of all time, apparently) that Christians wanted to see. Despite decades of arguing against graphic violence in movies, many evangelicals defended its use in the *Passion* as realistic and necessary, rather than being merely entertainment. The discussion once again highlighted the folly of using movie ratings as a sign of spiritual depth or acceptability.

Barry Taylor

21

Children of Men

UK/US/Japan, 2006
109 Minutes, Feature, Color
Actors: Clive Owen, Julianne Moore, Michael
Caine, Chiwetel Ejiofor, Clare-Hope
Ashitey
Director: Alfonso Cuarón
Screenwriters: Alfonso Cuarón, Timothy J. Sexton, David Arata, Mark Fergus, Hawk
Ostby (based on the novel *The Children of Men* by P. D. James)
Rated: R (strong violence, language, some drug use, brief nudity)

Hope
Destiny and Chance,
Faith/Belief,
the Incarnation, the
Meaning of Life

Synopsis and Theological Reflection

A woman swaddles her baby in a bundle of rags. A man lays a protective arm around the mother. They slowly walk out of a rundown building sheltering countless distraught refugees. A belligerent soldier notices the child and suddenly comes to a halt.

"Cease fire," he screams. The groaning and moaning in the building suddenly abate. The refugees crawl out of their holes, trying to get a glimpse of the child. They bow down, as if to worship the child; some venture to reach out and touch its tiny legs. Their grim faces are now lit with awe and wonder.

Who is this child? The symbolism is obvious for a film released on Christmas Day. But let us not get carried away. *Children of Men* is much darker and more sinister than the Nativity story, though it is refreshingly redeeming, like the Gospels themselves.

The film is set in 2027. A mysterious disease has ravaged the planet, making humanity infertile for almost eighteen years. The nation-states have collapsed, and the sectarian violence that ensued has torn the world apart. Britain is the only country that still holds any semblance of civilization. The country is on a permanent lockdown, closing its door to all "fugees," or illegal aliens. The immigrants are rounded up on street corners and are penned in animal cages. The rebel fighters, called "fishes," deploy guerrilla warfare on the establishment, ambushing soldiers and civilians alike. Worst of all, the absence of children has drained the world of the one thing that is absolutely essential for the survival of humanity—hope.

The plot revolves around Theodore "Theo" Faron (Clive Owen, his character's name seemingly derived from *Theos*, the Greek word for God), a former radical protester who has now settled for the mediocre life of a bureaucrat. His estranged wife (Julianne Moore), the leader of the rebel group, forcefully enlists him for a dangerous mission. He has to smuggle out a precious human cargo, Kee (Clare-Hope Ashitey), from the middle of the war-torn city. Kee, as her name seems to suggest, is the key to the future. She carries in her womb embryonic hope for humanity—the first child to be born on planet earth after nearly two decades. Theo has to deliver Kee to a mysterious entity called "the Human Project," which has pledged the safekeeping of her child. But a faction of the "fishes" who are assigned to protect the child now want to use it for their own ends, putting its very life in danger. The heartbeat of this miracle child sets the pulse that drives the action in *Children of Men*, which some critics describe as "a thinking person's action movie."

Cuarón's ultra-visceral depiction of this chaotic future world makes it both magical and realistic at once. Right from the opening scene, Cuarón draws us into the middle of ferociously choreographed action sequences flooded with flying bullets, shattering structures, and exploding body parts. Using groundbreaking technical sophistication that boasts a combination of handheld cameras, cutaway scenes, and lengthy single-camera shots, he creates the ultimate sensory experience, where each frame is scented with fear and death. The raw emotional power of the actors and the sheer brutality of their environment are elegantly captured in every scene. Emmanuel Lubezki's cinematography is dark and savagely unstable. With a carbon-blue palette, he

Theo, Kee, and her baby girl

captures the hopelessness of the characters, making their emotional turmoil palpable to human eyes.

Children of Men is rated R for foul language, violence, and a brief scene of nudity. However, the film does not promote violence or nudity for the sake of voyeurism; rather, it portrays the grim reality of a world that has entrapped its inhabitants. Moreover, if we look closer, the future world portrayed in the film is not much different from our own. The narrative bears troubling resemblance to many atrocities we have witnessed, including the Holocaust of World War II, radical Islamic terrorism, and the continued unjust treatment of illegal immigrants. In that sense, Cuarón's screen acts as a two-way mirror, reflecting current social issues such as border policing, homeland security, and our war on terrorism, while it portrays similar events that unfold in his future world.

Although it's not given much screen time, the film also alludes to the presence of many religious cults in the dystopian world. We hear rumors about factions such as the Repenters ("those who kneel down for a month for salvation") and the Renouncers ("those who flagellate themselves for the forgiveness of humanity"). We witness political protests pronouncing doomsday declarations ("Infertility is God's judgment!") in religious tents. Miriam (Pam Ferris), the midwife who accompanies Kee, exhibits a spectrum of eclectic spirituality. She not only recites prayers addressed to blessed Mary and angel Gabriel but also quotes the Taoist "ying-yang" and Hindu "Shiva/Shakti," and even performs bits and pieces of Buddhist and aboriginal rituals. Jasper (Michael Caine), Theo's eccentric mentor, looks and sounds like a product of the hippie movement of the seventies, with his yogi-like hairstyle and habitual use of pot. He intermixes quotes from sacred texts and popular music, reciting Shanti mantras and Lennon/McCartney tunes in the same conversation.

The film's Christian symbolism is all-pervasive. So too is its basic Christian shape. Its allusion to the Nativity story is both intentional and obvious. However, *Children of Men* also delves deeply into universal themes where the Christ story converges with the human quest for meaning, purpose, and hope. As in the Christ story, the overarching theological theme that emerges from the core of the narrative is one of hope (or the lack of it). In the original novel, P. D. James wrote, "Man is diminished if he lives without knowledge of his past; without hope of a future he becomes a beast." The absence of children is used by James mainly as a metaphorical device to communicate the lack of hope that plagues the human race. Theo positions himself as a representative of all humankind when he remarks, "I can't really remember when I last had any hope, and I certainly can't remember when anyone else did either. Because really, since women stopped being able to have babies, what's left to hope for?" The same sentiment is collectively echoed in the television commercials: "No children. No future. No hope. The last one to die please turn out the light."

In order to regain hope, Theo needs to have faith in that which he cannot be certain of. He is unsure of his calling as the protector of a child that is not his own. He has no proof to believe that a secret society of the world's best minds, the Human Project, really exists. Neither does he know for sure that a ship called *Tomorrow* is coming to their rescue. It is Theo's faith in this greater reality that enables him to trust his calling to embark on the journey with the child. It is hope that drives him to the redemption that is waiting for him and the viewer in the final act.

Children of Men is a story of the triumph of human spirit over chaos, violence, and evil through actions based on faith. The ultimate hope in this spiritual journey comes in the form of a child given to a dark, desolate, and dying world. In Jasper's words, this child is "the miracle the whole world has been waiting for." For those who believe in this greater reality, *Tomorrow* is going to emerge out of the blinding mist. It is this redemptive promise that *Children of Men* offers to its viewers.

Dialogue Texts

For in hope we were saved. Now hope that is seen is not hope. For who hopes for what is seen? But if we hope for what we do not see, we wait for it with patience.

Romans 8:24–25

But when the fullness of time had come, God sent his Son, born of a woman, born under the law, in order to redeem those who were under the law, so that we might receive adoption as children.

Galatians 4:4–5

For a child has been born for us,
   a son given to us;
authority rests upon his shoulders;
   and he is named
Wonderful Counselor, Mighty God,
   Everlasting Father, Prince of Peace.

Isaiah 9:6

And Mary said,
"My soul magnifies the Lord,
   and my spirit rejoices in God my Savior,
for he has looked with favor on the lowliness of his servant.
   Surely, from now on all generations will call me blessed;
for the Mighty One has done great things for me,
   and holy is his name.
His mercy is for those who fear him
   from generation to generation.
He has shown strength with his arm;
   he has scattered the proud in the thoughts of their hearts.
He has brought down the powerful from their thrones,
   and lifted up the lowly;
he has filled the hungry with good things,
   and sent the rich away empty.
He has helped his servant Israel,
   in remembrance of his mercy,
according to the promise he made to our ancestors,
   to Abraham and to his descendants forever."

Luke 1:46–55 (Mary's Magnificat)

Discussion Questions and Clip Conversations

All clips are available for viewing at ReelSpirituality.com/Books/God-In-The-Movies. We have also listed the timestamp range of the scenes for your reference.

1. Do you think that the future world is going to be as dark and grim as that portrayed in the film? What do you think of the government policies depicted in the film? Would you have joined the resistance movement if you were present in this world? Why, or why not?

2. "Everything Is a Mythical, Cosmic Battle between Faith and Chance" [53:30–55:30]. In this clip, Jasper delivers a profound speech on the interplay between faith and chance in the working of the universe. Do you agree with his quasi-religious rhetoric? In the subsequent discussion Miriam stands to represent "faith" ("everything happens for a reason") and Jasper speaks for "chance" ("Theo's faith lost out to chance"). Which side would you pick? Why? Is there a third option? How would you respond to Jasper's argument: "Why bother if life is going to make its own choices?"

3. "Theo and Kee Carry the Child Out of the Building" [1:31:00–1:34:00]. Watch this clip with the sound track on mute. Read or sing the Magnificat (Luke 1:46–55) as the scene plays out. Do you feel the Scripture resonating with the images? What are some of the themes common to the film and Mary's Magnificat?

4. Theo Faron is an unlikely action hero for a Hollywood movie, one who wears sandals into a combat zone. How is this image of a hero different from the one that is in your perception? Does he surprise you at any point? Do you think his name, Theo, has any significance?

5. The reluctant protagonist's journey to protect a child that is not his own is familiar to the Western audience, and it brings immediate association to the Nativity story. How do you think the rest of the world, which is not accustomed to this cultural archetype, would respond to this allusion?

Bonus Material

P. D. James, author of the novel *Children of Men* (1992), was a professing Christian. Alfonso Cuarón hired himself and four other writers to revise her story and reassign character roles for the screenplay. In the book, for example, Julian is the pregnant woman, and the miracle child is a boy. Kee's character as a black woman and her child's gender as a girl were devised for the film, perhaps to raise minority voices.

On a personal note, *Children of Men* reminds me of one of my favorite Christmas songs, "Labor of Love" by Randy Travis, which includes these words:

And little Mary full of grace with tears upon her face had no mother's
   hand to hold.
It was a labor of pain; it was a cold sky above.
But for the girl on the ground in the dark with every beat of her beau-
   tiful heart,
It was a labor of love.

Mathew P. John

22

Lars and the Real Girl

Redemptive Love
The Church, Community

US/Canada, 2007
106 Minutes, Feature, Color
Actors: Ryan Gosling, Patricia Clarkson, Emily
    Mortimer, Paul Schneider
Director: Craig Gillespie
Screenwriter: Nancy Oliver
Rated: PG-13 (some sex-related content)

> The men and women who are going to be most valuable to us
> in spiritual formation-by-resurrection are most likely going to be
> people at the edge of respectability: the poor, minorities, the suf-
> fering, the rejected, poets and children.
>
> Eugene H. Peterson, *Living the Resurrection:*
> *The Risen Christ in Everyday Life*

Synopsis and Theological Reflection

Advent 2007 was a season marked by several special moments that I continue
to remember. One of these came at the ever-so-familiar Christmas Eve service
at our church. We had so many of our little ones dressed up as animals, shep-
herds, kings—the usual suspects in a Christmas pageant. As many of them
made their grand entry, a voice behind us seemed to be especially excited as

she explained the characters to the person next to her. Could this have been a proud young mother sharing her enthusiasm with another mother? No, in fact, it was an older woman in our congregation who has for years given her creativity and leadership to our church in the area of the arts and worship. She was like a kid again, explaining the pageant to her husband, who at one time was a key actor in all our church's dramatic presentations. Now Gene, not so advanced in years, is living with the effects of a stroke. Together they were thoroughly enjoying the children's story as if it were the first time they had ever seen it come to life.

But this was not the end of the pageant dynamics surrounding us. For suddenly, near our seats, the angels bounded into view. They were lovely—their flowing white dresses, their feathery wings, their glittering halos. But one little angel was feeling a bit uncomfortable in her heavenly attire, so she began to disrobe right there in the midst of the angelic choir. This particular angel's mom was sitting right in front of us. She leaned back and impishly whispered to us, "We might have our first nude angel!" If there are any real angels, nude or otherwise, in our congregation, Molly is probably one of them. And Molly has Down syndrome.

That night those dear ones in our congregation made me think of an experience I had earlier during Advent. One night after grading term papers, my husband and I headed to the movies. We went to our neighborhood theater. We really hadn't thought about what movie we wanted to see; we just showed up and went to the one that was about to begin—*Lars and the Real Girl*. It was a small, low-budget US/Canadian film. There were no big Hollywood stars (at the time), no car chases, guns, or sex. Rather, it was a study of illness, treatment through caring therapy, and community.

Actually, *Lars and the Real Girl* is hilariously funny while also poignantly transparent—equal parts comedy and pathos. The premise is simple: a pathologically shy—to the point of fearing human touch—but dear young man named Lars Lindstrom (Ryan Gosling is phenomenal), whose friends and family try to encourage him to "get out more," buys a life-size sex doll on the internet and truly falls in love with it, or rather "her." He endows the anatomically correct doll with a colorful biography—her name is Bianca and she's a paraplegic (Lars takes her everywhere in a wheelchair) missionary from a Brazilian-Danish family. In one scene Lars sings Nat King Cole's classic song "L-O-V-E" to Bianca with all the joy of a love that is true:

> L is for the way you look at me . . .

And of course their love is chaste—she sleeps in his brother's home, not his.

As a viewer I found myself moving from uncontrollable laughter (OK, I'll go along with the gag) to gentle tears (oh, it's not a gag). And I wasn't the only one. Lars's brother (Paul Schneider) and sister-in-law (Emily Mortimer), the town doctor (Patricia Clarkson), the local church, and finally the whole town end up going along with Lars too, as they find themselves a part of what is not only raucously ludicrous but also quietly momentous. And as the town journeys with Lars, hoping that he will be healed of his emotional problems, they are changed. They come to realize that Lars is not a "nutcase" but rather a soul in distress. Because Bianca is real to Lars, she becomes real to the community. Lars's love humanizes Bianca and a whole community. Soon Bianca is treated with the same respect and love that they hold for Lars. She is taken to the local women's book club, invited to join the volunteers at the hospital and to help out at church, and so on. Soon her "dance card" is full and we see kindness in full bloom!

In the film, the local pastor preaches a sermon on the church's "only one law"—"love one another." He ends by proclaiming that "love is God in action." In a time and space filled with cynical manipulation, *Lars and the Real Girl* shows us a picture of lived religion. It is like the medieval miracle and morality plays. These portrayals of biblical stories and ethical tales were staples of village life in preliterate Europe and the Middle East. Believers and nonbelievers alike saw biblical parables and miraculous events reenacted before their very eyes by traveling minstrels and actors. These plays spread the teachings of the Bible far and wide, often serving as sparks or catalysts for experiences of religious and spiritual conversion.

Lars and the Real Girl functioned similarly for me, helping me to see ever more clearly what we as the body of Christ are called to be. For in our midst are Lars, Gene, Molly, and others, calling us to be a community that extends the loving arms of God.

Dialogue Texts

If there is among you anyone in need, a member of your community in any of your towns within the land that the LORD your God is giving you, do not be hard-hearted or tight-fisted toward your needy neighbor.

Deuteronomy 15:7

Two are better than one, because they have a good reward for their toil. For if they fall, one will lift up the other; but woe to one who is alone and falls and does not have another to help. Again, if two lie together, they keep warm; but how can one keep warm alone? And though one might prevail against another, two will withstand one. A threefold cord is not quickly broken.

Ecclesiastes 4:9–12

I give you a new commandment, that you love one another. Just as I have loved you, you also should love one another. By this everyone will know that you are my disciples, if you have love for one another.

John 13:34–35

And let us consider how to provoke one another to love and good deeds, not neglecting to meet together, as is the habit of some, but encouraging one another, and all the more as you see the Day approaching.

Hebrews 10:24–25

For this is the message you have heard from the beginning, that we should love one another. . . . We know love by this, that he laid down his life for us—and we ought to lay down our lives for one another. How does God's love abide in anyone who has the world's goods and sees a brother or sister in need and yet refuses help?

1 John 3:11, 16–17

Discussion Questions and Clip Conversations

All clips are available for viewing at ReelSpirituality.com/Books/God-In -The-Movies. We have also listed the timestamp range of the scenes for your reference.

1. "The One True Law—Love One Another" [03:40–05:30]. The opening frames of the film show Lars through a paned window. What does that visual remind you of? Then we see him awkwardly interact with his sister-in-law, Karin. Now think about Reverend Bock's sermon. How do these opening moments of the film frame what this story/film is about?

2. "What Would Jesus Do?" [36:25–39:48]. After a hilarious introduction of Bianca to Lars's family and after word spreads to the townspeople, we find ourselves in the church council meeting. What strikes you about members' responses to Lars and Bianca? How would you answer Reverend Bock's question in this case?

3. "Is Love Delusional?" [42:35–49:50]. In this sequence we see Lars expressing his love for Bianca—taking her to the lake where he played as

a child, telling her about his childhood, singing her a love song. What is true and deep about his "delusional" love for Bianca? And how is Bianca helping him learn to love himself and others?

4. "We Love You; We Do It for You" [1:04:24–1:08:52]. Lars has had his first fight with Bianca and feels abandoned as she is often off doing things with townsfolk. He makes the comment that nobody cares about him, to which Karin responds that they spend time with Bianca because they love him. How do you show love to those you care about? Could you do what the townsfolk in the film are doing? Why or why not?

5. "A Lesson in Love" [1:38:31–1:40:05]. After learning that Bianca is dying, we the viewers are given a beautiful and poignant look [1:28:20–1:34:42] at how the whole town is mourning with Lars (from paramedics to nurses to church members to work colleagues to local merchants). At the funeral, Reverend Bock says that Bianca was a lesson in courage and that she loved everyone, but especially Lars (note that the film is bookended with sermons). How is Bianca also a lesson in love? How have Lars, his family, and the townspeople been transformed? What lessons about love is the film speaking to you, the viewer?

Bonus Material

Lars and the Real Girl didn't do well at the box office (maybe too many people were put off by the conceit), but it was critically acclaimed. The film received an Academy Award nomination for Best Writing (Original Screenplay), while Ryan Gosling received two nominations—for a Golden Globe (Best Actor in a Motion Picture Comedy) and a Screen Actors Guild Award (Outstanding Performance by a Male Actor in a Leading Role).

Like Bianca in the film, the real doll was treated like an actual person on set to help Ryan Gosling stay in character. She had her own trailer with wardrobe, and she was present only for her scenes. The real doll had nine unique faces, which were used to show a sort of development of the character. She started with a face with heavy makeup, but then later had a face without makeup. Finally, the doll's face becomes slightly green to reflect her "failing health."

Ryan Gosling improvised several scenes, including when Lars and Bianca are outside the party and when he performed CPR on Margo's teddy bear. In the scene where Lars is reading to Bianca, he is reading from *Don Quixote*—Cervantes's story of an ingenious, chivalrous man with great delusions, who wants to undo wrongs and bring justice to the world.

Selected Additional Resources

Check out Roger Ebert's review (October 18, 2007) at http://www.rogerebert
.com/reviews/lars-and-the-real-girl-2007.

While I love Ryan Gosling's rendition of the song "L-O-V-E" in the film, try
listening to Nat King Cole's original version from 1965 (https://youtu.be/qJBg
QfnRFus). It was composed by Bert Kaempfert, with lyrics by Milt Gabler.

Catherine M. Barsotti

23

Munyurangabo

Rwanda/US, 2008
97 Minutes, Feature, Color
Actors: Jeff Rutagengwa, Eric
Ndorunkundiye, Edouard Uwayo
Director: Lee Isaac Chung
Screenwriters: Samuel Gray Anderson, Lee
Isaac Chung
Rated: Unrated (mature thematic material)

*Forgiveness
Father/Son Relationships,
Friendship, Human
Suffering, Justice,
Loss, Reconciliation,
Who Is My Neighbor?*

Synopsis and Theological Reflection

Over a period of one hundred days in 1994, the majority tribe in Rwanda, the Hutus (85 percent), killed upwards of eight hundred thousand Tutsis (12 percent) and their sympathizers in a government-sponsored genocide. The roots of this atrocity go back to colonial days, when Germans and then Belgians favored the lighter-skinned Tutsi minority. When the battle for national independence broke out in the late 1950s, it naturally also became a war for Hutu control. Coming to power in 1962, the Hutus sporadically persecuted the Tutsis, and Tutsi rebels fought back.

140

After Tutsi rebels invaded Rwanda in 1990, Hutu Power was called for—with its slogan "The Hutu should stop having mercy on the Tutsi"—and over the next three years, perhaps two thousand Tutsi people were murdered. Even more ominously, armed militia, or killing groups (Interahamwe, "those who fight/kill together"), were formed, and over five hundred thousand machetes were imported by businessmen close to President Habyarimana.

When the president's plane was shot down in 1994, all hell broke loose in Kigali, Rwanda's capital. The Interahamwe set out to kill all Tutsis. Age or gender did not matter. Neighbors killed neighbors and fellow villagers. The machete was the weapon of choice. Besides the killings, four hundred thousand children were left orphaned, and perhaps half a million women were raped and mutilated. This is the horrendous background of the movie *Munyurangabo*.

Directed, cowritten, and filmed by a young Korean-American graduate of Yale, Lee Isaac Chung, *Munyurangabo* is a fictional story that weaves together the testimony of many he encountered during a summer in Rwanda. Shot in eleven days by a young crew with no experience except what Chung taught them on the spot, with nonactors in all the leading roles (speaking in Kinyarwanda, which Chung did not speak), the movie had a micro-budget that Chung himself financed. Nevertheless, the movie became a surprise winner on the festival circuit when it was accepted to the Cannes Film Festival in 2007 in the Un Certain Regard section, and later played in Berlin, Toronto, and the AFI Film Festival in Los Angeles, where it won the Grand Jury Prize.

The impetus for Chung to make this movie was a Christian humanitarian mission trip sponsored by the organization Youth With A Mission (YWAM). Chung's wife, Valerie, had already been to Rwanda and had decided to return the next summer with YWAM to again help those affected by the genocide by offering art therapy. She encouraged Chung to come along and teach youth in the slums of Kigali how to make movies. As he prepared in the United States for the assignment with Samuel Anderson, a screenwriting friend, they decided that the only way to effectively teach these youth filmmaking was to actually make a film with them. *Munyurangabo* was the result, a movie that used his students as crew, friends of students and locals as actors, and a class assignment on poetry inserted as the climactic heart of the movie.

To help make their nine-week class work, Chung and Anderson developed a ten-page outline of a story about two teenage boys from Kigali, one a Hutu and the other a Tutsi, who set out on the road with a stolen machete to confront the killer of one of the boys' fathers during the genocide. But

Chung also held to his commitment that the movie would be made by, for, and about Rwandans themselves. Chung commented, "I tried to make *Mun-yurangabo* a cinema of listening rather than self-expression." He said he wanted the movie to almost have the feel of a documentary, though it would be a fictional narrative. To facilitate this, Chung refused to storyboard or even to write a complete script, for both would impose his judgments on the project. Instead, he chose to trust the crew and actors both to flesh out the narrative skeleton and to add to it, using their own intuition and experience as guides.

Particularly important in rooting his movie in Rwandan soil was Chung's decision to cast two teenagers from the Kigali slums in the lead roles. Discovered in a soccer league run by one of the students in Chung's class, they were best of friends, though one was a Hutu and the other a Tutsi. In the movie, Jeff Rutagengwa plays Ngabo, the Tutsi whose father has been butchered, and Eric Ndorunkundiye plays Sangwa, his Hutu friend, who agrees to go with Ngabo to find his father's killer if they will first stop off briefly at his family farm along the way. Both young actors had come to Kigali after losing their fathers, and neither had acted before. The friendship and yet strain in relationship that is portrayed on the screen mirrored their very lives together. Here, art matched life—or was it life matching art?

Having seen other Rwandan films about the genocide, Chung noted that most were centered in the past atrocity, rather than focusing on how Rwandans might go on with their lives today (e.g., *Hotel Rwanda*, d. George, 2004). These other movies seemed to him more colonial in their orientation, focusing politically on the guilt of the West for its nonaction and usually having an outside observer/participant in the story to help make the connection to the West clear. What became lost in the process was anything memorable about the Rwandan people themselves. Chung sought in his film to change this orientation, focusing instead on what *New York Times* critic A. O. Scott labeled "the bruised tranquility of ordinary life" that followed the slaughter. Chung's resultant footage is compelling.

The movie follows the teen boys on their long trek across Rwanda to Sangwa's parents' rural farm, where his family has continued to work the soil after Sangwa ran away to the city, and then on to the film's final confrontation with the killer of Ngabo's father. As the story proceeds, Chung rarely "tells." Instead, he is content to lovingly "show," allowing scenes to play out slowly and naturally. Viewers find themselves walking through Rwanda with the boys. The images of poor rural life allow for a certain dignity to emerge, even among broken plastic jugs and mud huts. Particularly compelling is a scene where the boys come to Sangwa's village, and his estranged father tries to reconnect with his long-absent son by teaching him the rhythm of hoeing the soil. With Ndorunkundiye being a city orphan unused to working the field and the actor playing Sangwa's father a poor, rural farmer who in real life prepares his soil by hand, the scene has a natural authenticity. Hoeing comes easily for the father, but Sangwa's efforts lack grace. The event is both believable and poignant.

Chung also uses Rwandan music and poetry to strong effect. Particularly compelling is a poem read to Ngabo at a roadside café as he comes near to his father's killer's house. It is read by the young poet himself (Edouard B. Uwayo), a member of Chung's filmmaking class. (Interestingly, his poem was added to the movie only after he read it for a class assignment.) Uwayo, in the movie, tells Ngabo he needs to practice his recitation for a public gathering where he is to read his poem. In one single, long close-up as the camera follows the movement of the artist, the movie's informing vision is given voice. We hear the poet passionately call for a new Rwanda, one where reconciliation is projected to go beyond simply a cessation of violence or the ending of poverty to embrace a land characterized by unity, freedom, and equality.

The poem, together with Ngabo ending his journey by entering into the Hutu murderer's hut alone, only to find him dying of AIDS and asking for a drink of water, produces the context for the movie's surprising ending. With no dialogue, but rather relying on two powerful images of reconciliation, the movie again leaves the viewer to decide how realistically the scene is meant to be taken. Are peace and reconciliation really possible?

In an interview in *The Other Journal*, Chung comments, "We wanted to highlight the desire for reconciliation and offer a scenario for it that could even be regarded as a fantasy. Perhaps faith is a lot like this, requiring the act of imagination. . . . Part of me understands the impossibility of this reconciliation on earth, but the other part believes and hopes that it will [happen]. In the meantime, the work is important."

Dialogue Texts

The kingdom of heaven may be compared to a king who wished to settle accounts with his slaves. . . . "Should you not have mercy on your fellow slave, as I had mercy on you?" . . . So my heavenly Father will also do to every one of you, if you do not forgive your brother or sister from your heart.

Matthew 18:23, 33, 35 (see vv. 23–35)

Forgive, and you will be forgiven; give, and it will be given to you . . . for the
measure you give will be the measure you get back.

                                                                    Luke 6:37–38

And now, therefore, let the power of the LORD be great in the way that you
promised when you spoke, saying,

> "The LORD is slow to anger,
>   and abounding in steadfast love,
>   forgiving iniquity and transgression,
>   but by no means clearing the guilty,
>   visiting the iniquity of the parents
>   upon the children
>   to the third and fourth generation."

Forgive the iniquity of this people according to the greatness of your steadfast
love.

                                                                    Numbers 14:17–19

Cain rose up against his brother Abel, and killed him. Then the LORD said
to Cain, "Where is your brother Abel?" He said, "I do not know; am I my
brother's keeper?"

                                                                    Genesis 4:8–9

> The wolf shall live with the lamb,
>   the leopard shall lie down with the kid,
>   the calf and the lion and the fatling together,
>   and a little child shall lead them.

                                                                    Isaiah 11:6

Discussion Questions and Clip Conversations

All clips are available for viewing at ReelSpirituality.com/Books/God-In
-The-Movies. We have also listed the timestamp range of the scenes for your
reference.

1. Observers have noted that in Rwanda, you're no longer officially allowed
   to say "Hutu" or "Tutsi." It's taboo. You are simply Rwandan. Yet, on
   the personal level, as in other parts of the world, racism lingers. How is
   this also depicted in the film? In *Munyurangabo*, is racial reconciliation

a future hope or a present reality, or both? Does the movie give us any helpful models of ethnic differentiation?

2. "The Machete" [00:01–01:14]. In the opening scene, we see Ngabo stealing a machete from an open market and then sitting down to reflect on what he is to do. As he does, we see the machete's blade with dried blood on the end of it. Yet a short time later, the blade is clean, with no blood showing. Do you think this change was intentional, an example of magical realism, or a filmmaker's "mistake"? What could it suggest about the movie's meaning? About Rwanda itself?

3. "Sangwa Banished for Befriending Ngabo" [57:07–1:00:44; 1:03:14–1:07:55]. The movie wrestles with the difficulty both of repentance and of forgiveness. Juxtaposed are love and hate, forgiveness and vengeance, life and death, estrangement and reconciliation. Is this presentation of Rwandan life believable? Understandable? Does life always present us with choices? Or is reconciliation sometimes impossible?

4. "Final Poem" [1:14:40–1:22:34]. The poem that is recited near the end of the movie was written by a member of Chung's filmmaking class and only added to the film after it was read as a class assignment. How does the poem help interpret the movie?

5. Chung has said he did not want the movie to end with a "message" of reconciliation but rather with an "image" of reconciliation. Does he succeed? Is this ending more an eschatological hope than a present reality, or is it meant to be thought possible here and now? Certainly the movie does not presume to give simple answers to how reconciliation can happen, but does it offer hope? What takeaway is there for viewers, if any?

Bonus Material

When the human slaughter started in Rwanda, it proved almost incomprehensible to the outsider in its speed, scope, and brutality. The only response of the United Nations was to reduce their peacekeeping force because it became too dangerous, and the United States declined all involvement, declaring it a "local conflict." President Clinton came to believe he made a mistake and that as few as five thousand US peacekeepers could have perhaps prevented the death of five hundred thousand Rwandans.

In 2010 the Arts and Faith online community voted *Munyurangabo* nineteenth on its list of the top one hundred films of all time (http://artsandfaith .com/t100).

Selected Additional Resources

Overstreet, Jeffrey. "A Cinema of Listening and Looking: A Filmwell Conversation with Lee Isaac Chung, Part One." *The Other Journal*, June 8, 2009. http://theotherjournal.com/filmwell/2009/06/08/a-cinema-of-listening-and -looking-a-filmwell-conversation-with-lee-isaac-chung/.

Robert K. Johnston

24

Secret Sunshine

Original title: *Milyang*
South Korea, 2007
142 Minutes, Feature, Color
Actors: Jeon Do-yeon, Song Kang-ho
Director: Lee Chang-dong
Screenwriter: Lee Chang-dong (based on
    the novella *Story of Insects* by Lee Chung-Joon)
Rated: Unrated (brief violence, brief sexuality, mature thematic material)

The Meaning of Life
*Human Suffering, Justice,
Loss, Spirituality of
Everyday Life*

Synopsis and Theological Reflection

Many great directors have made a name for themselves by making powerful films about spiritual matters: Ingmar Bergman, Robert Bresson, Carl Theodor Dreyer, Andrei Tarkovsky, and Martin Scorsese are only a few of the filmmakers who have looked deeply into the reality of human suffering and depicted our common struggle for redemption with rigor and sensitivity. Now we can add South Korea's Lee Chang-dong to that list. His acclaimed 2007 film *Secret Sunshine* is a searing spiritual drama about an ordinary woman's search for meaning and solace in the aftermath of a devastating tragedy. Without offering an easy solution or simplistic judgment, it takes the viewers through her grief, her conversion, and eventually her rebellion against God. Lee's

Shin-ae grieves the loss of her son

treatment of the story is visceral and uncompromising, but *Secret Sunshine* is not merely harrowing. Like a great novel, the film is engrossing and full of unexpected developments, and it has a richness, depth, and captivating power (even humor) that demand thoughtful Christian engagement and reflection. Many critics have hailed it as one of the great films of the 2000s. We agree.

The basic story of *Secret Sunshine* concerns a woman named Shin-ae (played by Jeon Do-yeon in an intensely emotional, Cannes-winning performance). At the start of the film, she is a widow from Seoul on her way to her deceased husband's hometown of Miryang, a provincial city whose name means "secret sunshine." The place is seemingly unremarkable, but Shin-ae has nonetheless decided to start a new life here with her son, Jun. She meets a host of characters from the town, including a bumbling car mechanic, Jong-chan, who ends up having a crush on her. In this early part of the film, *Secret Sunshine* unfolds like a domestic drama that patiently observes the mundane details of Shin-ae's existence. Just like life itself, however, tragedies can strike at any time. In a shocking turn of events, Jun is kidnapped and senselessly murdered, and Shin-ae's life falls apart. The perpetrator turns out to be Jun's kindergarten teacher, and he is subsequently arrested and sent to prison. However, this punishment does nothing to quell Shin-ae's profound grief. In a state of near-hysteria, Shin-ae wanders into a revival service. There, she wails alongside others who are also crying out for healing and restoration, and she experiences a moment of intense emotional catharsis. Soon after, she converts to Christianity and becomes an active member at a local church. She happily and firmly professes her faith in God's benevolent will before other believers. She seems content and at peace.

A more conventional movie might be inclined to end at this point, but Lee is interested in exploring Shin-ae's faith and raising serious questions about our conception of God and its implication. In the movie's central twist, Shin-ae prematurely decides to visit Jun's killer in prison and offers him God's forgiveness, only to discover that the man has already repented of his sins, welcomed God into his heart, and attained inner peace. She is appalled that God has granted her son's killer such undeserved serenity, and she becomes enraged by the suffering she's had to endure. She lashes out at the Almighty and begins rebelling against him through a series of destructive acts. Throughout all of this, Jong-chan, the car mechanic, faithfully cares for her and stands by her side.

Secret Sunshine is a remarkably visceral and thought-provoking film. Shin-ae's actions, however extreme, echo every human being's innate desire for justice and deliverance in times of trials and tribulations. How could a good and merciful God permit so much suffering? Why do tragedies and misfortunes strike us so suddenly and arbitrarily? Will there ever be an end to our present pain and sorrow? Lee Chang-dong's story powerfully dramatizes the human anguish behind these timeless questions, and it presents Shin-ae as a complex, multidimensional character whose battle with God is both unsettling and sympathetic. Her transformation serves as a provocative response to Job. Unlike the faithful biblical character, Shin-ae rebels against what she perceives to be a malevolent God, but however futile or misguided her effort might be, we empathize with her because we are intimately acquainted with her angst and aches.

Among its many virtues, *Secret Sunshine* offers a rare and realistic portrait of the complicated relationship between religious faith and its practitioners. Opening with a shot of the blue sky and ending with a shot of a rough patch of earth, it is also a striking invitation for us to ask ourselves: Who is God to us? Is the meaning of God and of life to be found in the transcendent heaven above, or is it already here in the immanent reality of the world around us? From where can we receive the answer, restoration, and healing that we seek? Lee Chang-dong's powerful film provides Christian viewers a wonderful opportunity to reflect on these questions and on how we should then live.

Dialogue Texts

When I say, "My bed will comfort me,
    my couch will ease my complaint,"
then you scare me with dreams
    and terrify me with visions,
so that I would choose strangling
    and death rather than this body.

I loathe my life; I would not live forever.
    Let me alone, for my days are a breath.
What are human beings, that you make so much of them,
    that you set your mind on them,
visit them every morning,
    test them every moment?

Job 7:13–18

What is the way to the abode of light?
    And where does darkness reside?
Can you take them to their places?
    Do you know the paths to their dwellings?

Job 38:19–20 (NIV)

One of the criminals who were hanged there kept deriding him and saying, "Are you not the Messiah? Save yourself and us!" But the other rebuked him, saying, "Do you not fear God, since you are under the same sentence of condemnation? And we indeed have been condemned justly, for we are getting what we deserve for our deeds, but this man has done nothing wrong." Then he said, "Jesus, remember me when you come into your kingdom." He replied, "Truly I tell you, today you will be with me in Paradise."

Luke 23:39–43

Discussion Questions and Clip Conversations

All clips are available for viewing at ReelSpirituality.com/Books/God-In-The-Movies. We have also listed the timestamp range of the scenes for your reference.

1. What might be the significance of the title *Secret Sunshine*? Why do you think director Lee Chang-dong chose it?

2. The car mechanic, Jong-chan, played by famed South Korean actor Song Kang-ho, is a pivotal character in *Secret Sunshine*. Despite Shin-ae's resistance and frequent condescension toward him, he is an unconditional presence of support to her in times of need. How would you describe Jong-chan? What are some of the ways he shows his care for Shin-ae? In what ways are they similar and different? What do you think is his significance in the story?

3. "Prayer Meeting for the Wounded Soul" [1:06:10–1:11:44]. Shin-ae is a woman of constant sorrow. After the murder of Jun, she finds herself in

a state of near-hysterical grief and ends up going to the church service recommended by the Christian pharmacist in town. This becomes a turning point for her. Reflect on the catharsis Shin-ae experiences here. Have you ever had similarly emotional experiences with church in your life? What were the circumstances that led to those experiences? Were you able to sustain the epiphany, restoration, or passion from those moments? Why or why not?

4. "The Prison Visit" [1:29:47–1:35:44]. In what is perhaps the central sequence of the film, Shin-ae goes to prison to meet with the man responsible for murdering her son, Jun. She had decided that she would offer God's forgiveness to her enemy. Ironically, Shin-ae discovers that not only has the man already become a Christian, but he is also now living with profound inner peace after repenting of his sins. He is thankful to God for Shin-ae's visit and even vows to pray for her until the day he dies. She is, however, unable to accept that the man who so cruelly robbed her of everything is now living with such serenity. This is the beginning of her rage toward God. Reflect on this sequence and on Shin-ae's subsequent transformation. What do you think was behind her motivation for wanting to offer forgiveness? In what ways was she not ready for this? If you were in Shin-ae's position, how would you have reacted? What do you think director Lee Chang-dong wanted to accomplish with this unexpected development? Reflect also on the theology of grace. Does Christ make unreasonable demands of us when he tells us to forgive?

5. "Lies, Lies, Lies" [1:45:10–1:48:56]. After Shin-ae turns against God, she starts to engage in a series of destructive acts. In this sequence, for example, she goes to an outdoor church service and, during a time of public prayer, replaces the background worship music with a hard-hitting song that screams "lies, lies, lies." Have there been times in your life when you were similarly angry at God? How did you resolve it?

6. "The Haircut" [2:16:58–2:19:40]. In the film's final sequence, Shin-ae is once again trying to start life anew. After a decisive mental breakdown, she is now on the road to recovery and normalcy. She cuts her own hair, with Jong-chan holding up the mirror for her. The camera follows the locks of hair that have fallen to the ground and fixes its gaze on an unremarkable patch of earth. Compare this shot to the opening shot of the blue sky. Why do you think the film is constantly inviting us to focus on the mundane and the ordinary? In the film there is a strong dichotomy between that which is in the heaven above and that which is on the ground below. What are some other examples of this distinction

being reinforced in the film? What is the film communicating through this?

7. *Secret Sunshine* presents a realistic and plausible portrait of religious psychology. As Christians and ministers, how do you make sense of Shin-ae's spiritual journey? How would you walk with and console someone like her?

Bonus Material

Secret Sunshine is based on South Korean writer Lee Chung-Joon's 1985 novella *Story of Insects*, which deals with the dehumanization and helplessness of a human being before an almighty, impassive God. And Miryang, the setting of the film, is a real midsized city located in southeastern Korea. Director Lee Chang-dong deliberately chose the town for its perceived plainness. In the film's original press kit, Lee states that he wanted to show that salvation and meaning can be found in a place as ordinary as Miryang.

South Korea has one of the largest and fastest-growing Christian populations in the world, with over 30 percent of Koreans professing faith in Christ. *Secret Sunshine* has received positive responses for its realistic depiction of the way Christianity is practiced in the country. When the film was released there, it was also widely discussed in the media and among Korean Christians.

In Korean, Shin-ae's name means "faith" (Shin) and "love" (Ae).

Lee Chang-dong is a major cultural figure in South Korea. He was an acclaimed novelist before joining the film industry, and *Secret Sunshine* marks his return to filmmaking after he had served as the country's minister of culture and tourism.

Secret Sunshine was nominated for the Palme d'Or at the Cannes Film Festival, and it swept major Asian film awards when it was released in 2007. Jeon Do-yeon won the Best Actress award at Cannes for her performance as Shin-ae, and she remains the only Korean actor to have won the prestigious prize.

If you want to view more of Lee Chang-dong's work, the more recent *Poetry* is also extraordinary in its portrayal of ordinary people and the challenges and joys they encounter in life.

Selected Additional Resources

Danks, Adrian. "Between Innocence and Experience: Lee Chang-Dong's *Secret Sunshine*." Senses of Cinema (website), June 2012. http://sensesofcinema

.com/2012/cteq/between-innocence-and-experience-lee-chang-dongs-secret
-sunshine/.

Lim, Dennis. "*Secret Sunshine*: A Cinema of Lucidity." The Criterion Collection website, August 24, 2011. https://www.critcrion.com/current/posts
/1964-secret-sunshine-a-cinema-of-lucidity.

Scott, A. O. "Fierce Tests of Endurance and the Resilience of the Spirit." *New
York Times*, December 21, 2010. http://www.nytimes.com/2010/12/22/movies
/22secret.html.

Eugene Suen

25

A Serious Man

US, 2009
106 Minutes, Feature, Color
Actors: Michael Stuhlbarg, Richard Kind,
    Sari Lennick, Fred Melamed, Aaron Wolff,
    Jessica McManus, David Kang, George Wyner, Steve Park, Simon Helberg
Directors: Ethan Coen, Joel Coen
Screenwriters: Joel Coen, Ethan Coen
Rated: R (language, some sexuality/nudity, brief violence)

The Meaning of Life
Life's Mystery,
Life's Vanity,
Loss

Synopsis and Theological Reflection

Can we be sure that God is benevolent? Larry Gopnik, the patriarch in the Coen brothers' film *A Serious Man*, wishes he knew the answer. A perfectly ordinary man whose only desire is to lead a perfectly ordinary life, Larry has it all—a house in a pleasant, if bland, 1960s suburban Minnesotan community; a nuclear family of four with a son who is about to have his bar mitzvah; and a respectable job as a physics professor at a local college, where he is currently under review for tenure. All is well until suddenly and inexplicably a series of troubles begin to pile up, escalating until Larry sees his life falling completely apart. The desperate Larry is confused and helpless, his fate mirroring that of his many forebears in the faith who, in times of great calamity, struggle to comprehend God's will and the meaning of it all.

The Coen brothers' style in this film and others is rigidly controlled. Every frame feels meticulously crafted. Each actor and camera moves perfectly choreographed. Every edit feels necessary. This contrasts with the world of their stories, which seems decidedly lacking in a controlling order. This combination of intentional filmmaking and a haphazard movie-world is profoundly unsettling. The Coens masterfully articulate a universe ruled by chaos, where clueless people run around like laboratory rats trying to make sense of their predicament when there is no sense to be made. Tracing back through their filmography, that sense of dread about a universe gone awry is found in all of their films. Yet while the Coens have hovered consistently around that same theme of finding meaning in a meaningless world, they've also typically settled on either the pessimistic or the optimistic side of that theme in alternating films. *True Grit*, their follow-up to *A Serious Man*, has them in a hopeful mode (as Kutter Callaway discusses in chap. 38 below). *A Serious Man* gives us the Coens at their most hopeless.

Yet there is also something strangely cathartic about *A Serious Man*. Having spent their careers playing with different genres and geographical settings, the Coens, who grew up in suburban Minneapolis in the 1960s, have finally come home, making a film that is not only sociologically faithful to the environment of their childhood but also firmly rooted in the Jewish tradition of their upbringing—a tradition that has evidently shaped their sensibility in fundamental ways. *A Serious Man*, like the works of Jewish filmmaker Woody Allen, thrives on a sense of wry, self-deprecating humor, its worldview unmistakably that of a people who have been outsiders, who know what it feels like to be in exile and persecuted (by others and, seemingly, by God).

A Serious Man's plot bears resemblance to the biblical book of Job, but its theme seems lifted from Ecclesiastes. Unlike those ultimately hopeful stories, though, *A Serious Man* offers no consolation concerning God's sovereignty, no hope for a better future, and scant comfort about the intrinsic purpose of human existence. Despite its appearance as an absurdist comedy (yes, it is often very funny), this Coen tale is bleak through and through.

Fittingly, this story, which intends only to impress upon us that there is no meaning in it, is filled with stories that are also without meaning. The Coens have said that the opening scene about the dybbuk is included only to put the audience in the right mood and that it has no other meaning. Larry and his student, Clive, argue over their respective understandings of the stories Larry uses to illustrate concepts in his physics class, stories that

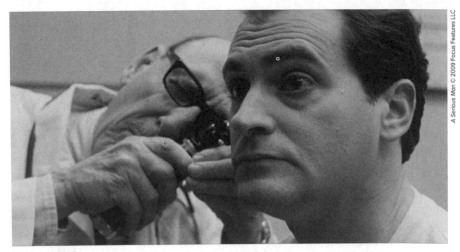

In good health?

Larry claims are ultimately meaningless and incomprehensible. This conflict climaxes when Clive's father tells Larry to "accept the mystery" rather than try to make sense of what's happening. Larry's conversations with Rabbi Scott and Rabbi Nachtner center on meaningless stories about parking lots and a goy's (gentile's) teeth. Larry's wife is having an affair with a neighbor, rendering meaningless the years of marriage she and Larry have shared.

A *Serious Man*'s supporting characters are implicated in the meaningless as well. Larry's brother, Arthur, is working on *The Mentaculus*, a supposed "probability map of the universe" that turns out to be nothing more than a worthless, incomprehensible gambling scheme. Larry's daughter, Sarah, is stealing from him to pay for a nose job, obscuring her Jewish identity and rendering meaningless the familial story she has inherited. Larry's son, Danny, just wants to smoke marijuana and watch *F Troop*, a satirical television show about a fictitious post–Civil War army outpost where the soldiers are inept and nothing they do matters. Everywhere Larry turns, he finds reminders that there is no meaning in anything. If only he could hear the film's sound track—maybe his son will lend him his transistor radio—so he could hear Jefferson Airplane sing that finding "someone to love" might be the only thing worth anything in this meaningless world.

If there is any consolation in *A Serious Man*, it is best summarized by its opening quotation from Jewish biblical commentator Rashi: "Accept with simplicity everything that happens to you." *A Serious Man* points people of faith not toward a fatalistic resignation to the ostensibly arbitrary course of life but toward an acceptance of our finitude. As both Job and Ecclesiastes affirm, God's ways are higher than our ways. Some things are simply beyond our comprehension. We live and move and have our being in God. God gives, God takes away, and the name of the Lord is still to be praised. This does not mean one's suffering will be eased in the meantime, however. *A Serious Man* is compelling in its ability to evoke a sense of helplessness that all of us have surely experienced at some point in life. Larry's guttural cry for answers issuing out of his desire to comprehend his circumstance resonates in a world filled with mysteries and injustice.

Accept with simplicity everything that happens to you. Accept the mystery. Consider the parking lot. Helping others couldn't hurt. If you can, find somebody to love. And maybe take life a little less seriously.

Dialogue Texts

And the LORD said to Job:

> "Shall a faultfinder contend with the Almighty?
> Anyone who argues with God must respond."

Then Job answered the LORD:

> "See, I am of small account; what shall I answer you?
>   I lay my hand on my mouth.
> I have spoken once, and I will not answer;
>   twice, but will proceed no further."

Then the LORD answered Job out of the whirlwind:

> "Gird up your loins like a man;
>   I will question you, and you declare to me.
> Will you even put me in the wrong?
>   Will you condemn me that you may be justified?
> Have you an arm like God,
>   and can you thunder with a voice like his?

> "Deck yourself with majesty and dignity;
>   clothe yourself with glory and splendor.
> Pour out the overflowings of your anger,
>   and look on all who are proud, and abase them.
> Look on all who are proud, and bring them low;
>   tread down the wicked where they stand.
> Hide them all in the dust together;
>   bind their faces in the world below.

Then I will also acknowledge to you
    that your own right hand can give you victory. . . ."

Then Job answered the LORD:

"I know that you can do all things,
    and that no purpose of yours can be thwarted.
'Who is this that hides counsel without knowledge?'
Therefore I have uttered what I did not understand,
    things too wonderful for me, which I did not know.
'Hear, and I will speak;
    I will question you, and you declare to me.'
I had heard of you by the hearing of the ear,
    but now my eye sees you;
therefore I despise myself,
    and repent in dust and ashes."

                               Job 40:1–14; 42:1–6

The words of the Teacher, the son of David, king in Jerusalem.

Vanity of vanities, says the Teacher,
    vanity of vanities! All is vanity.
What do people gain from all the toil
    at which they toil under the sun?
A generation goes, and a generation comes,
    but the earth remains forever.
The sun rises and the sun goes down,
    and hurries to the place where it rises.
The wind blows to the south,
    and goes around to the north;
round and round goes the wind,
    and on its circuits the wind returns.
All streams run to the sea,
    but the sea is not full;
to the place where the streams flow,
    there they continue to flow.
All things are wearisome;
    more than one can express;
the eye is not satisfied with seeing,
    or the ear filled with hearing.
What has been is what will be,
    and what has been done is what will be done;
    there is nothing new under the sun.

                               Ecclesiastes 1:1–9

Discussion Questions and Clip Conversations

All clips are available for viewing at ReelSpirituality.com/Books/God-In
-The-Movies. We have also listed the timestamp range of the scenes for your
reference.

1. Do you think *A Serious Man* is funny? Is it tragic? Why or why not?
   Have you ever felt like Larry? When things have gone wrong in your life,
   where did you turn for consolation? Was there any meaning in those
   bad circumstances? Do you feel like God owes you answers? Do you
   think everything in your life will ever make sense? Should it? How best
   should we react to times in life when nothing makes sense?

2. "The Second Rabbi" [55:48–1:03:10]. Larry goes to see Rabbi Nachtner
   for advice on his current predicament and what it all means. Rabbi
   Nachtner offers only a mysterious story about a goy's teeth. Do you
   find the rabbi's story helpful? Does Larry? Are we supposed to find
   meaning in this story, or, like the fable about the dybbuk that opens
   the film, does it only create a mood instead? How is Rabbi Nachtner's
   story like the stories Jesus told? Rabbi Nachtner doesn't care what
   happened to the goy. Should Larry? Should we? Why is Dr. Sussman
   able to go on to live a happy life after the incident with the goy's teeth?
   Why can't Larry?

3. "Arthur's Escape" [1:23:05–1:27:28]. Arthur has a breakdown in the
   middle of the night, and then Larry has a dream about helping him
   escape, which ends in Arthur's death. Why is Arthur upset in this scene?
   How does Arthur's complaint mirror Larry's from the earlier scene? In
   the dream, why do Larry's neighbors shoot Arthur?

4. Consider both scenes above and think about the rest of the film. Rabbi
   Nachtner tells Larry, "Hashem doesn't owe us anything. The obligation
   goes the other way." Larry's neighbor shoots Arthur not because he is
   escaping but because he's a Jew. In Larry's interactions with gentiles
   throughout this film, how are the gentiles free in a way Larry isn't?
   Larry's son, Danny, smokes marijuana throughout the movie when he's
   supposed to be studying for his bar mitzvah and then right before his
   bar mitzvah. Why does he do this? How is being Jewish a burden in *A
   Serious Man*? As Christians who have been adopted into the promise
   God gave the Jewish people, are we saddled with the same obligation
   to God Larry feels? Why or why not? (Consider what the rabbi exclaims
   as he tries to lift the Torah during Danny's bar mitzvah.)

Bonus Material

During his bar mitzvah, Danny reads the Behar (Lev. 25:1–26:2), in which God promises a year of Jubilee free from suffering in which everyone's land will be returned to them. This reading will be followed by Bechukotai (Lev. 26:3–27:34), in which God warns the Jewish people that they will be punished for disobedience. The film takes place in 1967, which was a Jewish leap year, so the reading of the Bechukotai had been pushed back a month. Punishment had been postponed, but it will come, as Larry and Danny soon learn.

The album Larry refuses from the Columbia Record Company is Santana's *Abraxas*. "Abraxas" is a gnostic term for the god who encompasses all things, good and evil alike. Larry rejects any god other than the Jewish God.

Selected Additional Resources

I love A. O. Scott's review of *A Serious Man* for the *New York Times*, headlined as "Calls to God: Always a Busy Signal" (October 1, 2009). In it, he gets to the troubled heart of the Coens' particular Jewish vision: http://www.nytimes.com/2009/10/02/movies/02serious.html.

Elijah Davidson

26

The Son

Original title: *Le fils*
Belgium/France, 2002
104 Minutes, Feature, Color
Actors: Olivier Gourmet, Morgan Marinne,
Isabella Soupart
Directors: Jean-Pierre Dardenne, Luc
Dardenne
Screenwriters: Jean-Pierre Dardenne, Luc
Dardenne
Rated: Unrated (brief language, mature thematic material)

Father/Son Relationships
Forgiveness, Loss,
Morality/Amorality,
Redemptive Love,
Spirituality of
Everyday Life

Synopsis and Theological Reflection

We have grown accustomed to movies that more or less tell us how we are supposed to be thinking and feeling at every turn (think of the way Hollywood movies use music, editing, and camera compositions). Such movies often have precise expositions and clear epiphanies so we know what the characters are going through and if they have transformed and learned any "lessons" along the way. This is the convention of popular filmmaking in the West. *The Son* does no such thing. With a documentary-like rigor, it simply throws us into the middle of the action, putting us in front of characters and situations that feel as tangible and immediate as anything in real life. As the story unfolds, oftentimes we do not know what is driving the characters or what is going on in their minds, and the film's relentless handheld camera often directs us to spend long stretches of time on what seem like mundane activities. Yet the film is tense and riveting, at once exceedingly simple and indescribably profound, conveying a world of internal drama, conflicts, and human emotions through the characters' actions and interactions. This gives rise to an unexpected grace that, because of its modesty, seems both moving and true. Just like in real life.

This remarkable quality—to usher viewers into the life of another—marks the works of the movie's directors, Jean-Pierre and Luc Dardenne. And it is the main reason why the filmmaking siblings from Belgium—popularly known as the Dardenne brothers—are highly regarded by critics (their films are frequently listed among the best of the past few decades), filmmakers (directors like Darren Aronofsky identify them as artistic heroes), and festivals alike (they belong to a rarefied group of two-time Palme d'Or winners at Cannes). It is why they are also celebrated by Christian writers and critics, who see in their works a spirituality and moral rigor that are uncommon in contemporary cinema.

Like all of the brothers' movies, *The Son* is set in the working-class milieu of their native Belgium, and it is deceptively simple. Here, the focus is on Olivier, a middle-aged man who spends his days teaching carpentry to a group of troubled youth at a training facility, and on the relationship he begins to develop with Francis, his new apprentice. Francis is a troubled teenager trying to start a new life. At first, Olivier flat out refuses to take him on. But he then develops a peculiar fixation on the boy, quickly telling the social worker about his change of heart. The central intrigue of the story, along with its mounting suspense, comes from the viewers not knowing what drives Olivier's action or what he plans to do to Francis. It is only through a carefully crafted revelation over the course of the movie (it is impossible to talk about *The Son* without giving away its premise) that we learn that Francis is responsible for killing Olivier's son several years earlier. Francis is unaware of this connection, and while he comes to see Olivier as a mentor and father figure, we wonder if the older man will succumb to his hatred and what he might do if that happens.

The late critic Roger Ebert once famously said, "It's not what a movie is about; it's how it is about it." What makes a movie compelling is not merely its story but the way it tells its story. *The Son* looks simple enough, but its power and mystery come from the way it captures and renders the banal activities presented before us. The Dardennes are relentlessly fixated on the physical, the visible, and the material. Their camera captures in minute detail Olivier's woodwork, his precise training of the students, his conversation with his ex-wife, and his obsession with Francis. There is no music, no narration, and no overt exposition. We know what we know only from what is shown, from the characters' bodily expressions, gestures, and interactions. This is what makes the movie so engrossing and enigmatic at first, and so suspenseful and gripping as it takes hold.

More importantly, this detached, ostensibly minimalist approach is also the Dardennes' way of underscoring the mystery of how moral choices and even redemption emerge from the concrete reality of everyday life. We walk with the characters; we see how their experiences throughout the film give rise to an ending that is as simple and inevitable as it is moving and true. The movie shows us that grace does not happen in a disembodied vacuum, nor does it arrive with pomp and circumstance. Instead, grace is often imparted and embodied by incidents and people in mundane, often bleak, situations.

In this way, *The Son* is also a startlingly pure and effective religious parable. It is also infused with ample Christian metaphors, from Olivier's profession as a carpenter, to the loss of his only son (the father/son relationship is key), to the way he and Francis carry wooden planks around as if they were bearing crosses. This is a movie where form, content, and symbols all combine to create a uniquely spiritual moviegoing experience. *The Son* demands our attention and patience, and the reward is plentiful.

Dialogue Texts

> Sons are indeed a heritage from the LORD,
>   the fruit of the womb a reward.
> Like arrows in the hand of a warrior
>   are the sons of one's youth.
> Happy is the man who has
>   his quiver full of them.
> He shall not be put to shame
>   when he speaks with his enemies in the gate.
>
> Psalm 127:3–5

As God's chosen ones, holy and beloved, clothe yourselves with compassion, kindness, humility, meekness, and patience. Bear with one another and, if anyone has a complaint against another, forgive each other; just as the Lord has forgiven you, so you also must forgive.

Colossians 3:12–13

Put away from you all bitterness and wrath and anger and wrangling and slander, together with all malice, and be kind to one another, tenderhearted, forgiving one another, as God in Christ has forgiven you.

Ephesians 4:31–32

Discussion Questions and Clip Conversations

All clips are available for viewing at ReelSpirituality.com/Books/God-In -The-Movies. We have also listed the timestamp range of the scenes for your reference.

1. Why is the movie called *The Son*? What does it refer to? How does understanding the title's significance help us better understand the movie?

2. The movie is made in an unconventional way. It uses a shaky, handheld camera to follow its characters around, features no music on the sound track, and spends a significant amount of time on ordinary details (e.g., driving, smoking, eating, woodworking). How did these aesthetic choices affect your viewing experience? How did they help tell the story?

3. Critics like Jeffrey Overstreet and A. O. Scott have described *The Son* as a religious parable. In what ways does the movie fit that label? What are some of the elements, imageries, symbols, and plot turns that might justify this claim? What biblical stories or passages does the movie remind you of?

4. "New Apprentice" [22:08–26:25]. In this scene, we see Olivier take on Francis as his apprentice, and we witness his supervision of the students under his tutelage. There are several scenes in the film that similarly detail the way Olivier interacts with the youth. How is he as a teacher? What does he care about? What do these scenes reveal about his character? What do you make of his interaction with Francis?

5. "Gas Station Conversation with Ex-Wife" [30:51–33:43]. In this scene, Olivier goes to see his ex-wife and talk to her about Francis. This is the moment when Francis's identity is definitively revealed. The ex-wife's anger and grief about what happened in the past is still palpable. What does this scene reveal about Olivier's relationship with her? Have there been times in your life when you have been similarly grief-stricken and angered?

6. "Guardian" [1:09:47–1:14:55]. In this scene, Francis asks Olivier to consider being his guardian. The boy has clearly come to see Olivier

as a mentor and father figure. How did their relationship evolve to this point? What are some of the things that happened during the movie that anticipated this moment?

7. "Letting Go" [1:31:31–1:36:34]. The ending of *The Son* is at once simple and profound. Like the rest of the movie, it is presented in an unobtrusive, matter-of-fact manner. How did the last shot strike you? What does it communicate? What does it tell us about Olivier and Francis? Reflect on the idea of forgiveness. What are some examples from your own life where you received or practiced grace and forgiveness? How did that change you? And how has this film added to your understanding of grace, forgiveness, and the way we relate to one another?

Bonus Material

The Dardenne brothers come from the industrial town of Seraing in eastern Belgium. They continue to live and work in the city. Their films are often about working-class characters from the area. For example, *Rosetta* (1999), the first film that won them the prestigious Palme d'Or at Cannes, is about an unemployed woman's attempt to secure a job. *L'Enfant* (2005), their second Palme d'Or winner, focuses on characters on welfare who engage in petty crimes and black market adoption to make a living. *Two Days, One Night* (2014), starring Marion Cotillard, is about a factory worker's effort to retain employment, which entails convincing her colleagues to give up their much-needed annual bonuses. In fact, before turning to narrative filmmaking, the Dardennes spent years making documentaries about a wide range of political and social issues facing Belgium and Europe. This background is reflected in the aesthetics and subject matters of their narrative films.

It is tempting, then, to think of the Dardennes as political filmmakers in the social-realist tradition, but unlike other directors who focus on similar issues and milieus, the Dardenne brothers are primarily preoccupied with their characters' moral lives and the way circumstances affect people's ethical and spiritual development. Beyond the immediate social relevance, their films are about larger spiritual and moral issues. For this reason, scholars and film critics have often compared them to the likes of Krzysztof Kieślowski and Robert Bresson.

Belgian actor Olivier Gourmet plays Olivier in *The Son*. A longtime collaborator who makes frequent appearances in Dardenne brothers' movies, Gourmet is a master of understatement and concealed emotions, and his mysterious, inscrutable quality stood out to the Dardennes. The film was created specifically with him in mind. For this performance, Gourmet ended up winning the Best Actor award at the 2002 Cannes Film Festival.

Selected Additional Resources

Ebert, Roger. Review of *The Son*. February 21, 2003. http://www.rogerebert.com/reviews/the-son-2003.

Foundas, Scott. "Films of the Dardenne Brothers." *The Village Voice* (blog), August 5, 2008. http://www.villagevoice.com/film/films-of-the-dardenne-brothers-6388554.

Overstreet, Jeffrey. "*The Son*." *Looking Closer* (blog). http://www.looking.closer.org/2012/09/the-son-2004/.

Scott, A. O. "A Father and the Boy Who Killed His Son." *New York Times*, September 28, 2002. http://www.nytimes.com/movie/review?res=9402EEDF1638F93BA1575AC0A9649C8B63.

Eugene Suen

27

There Will Be Blood

Sin and Its Consequences
Father/Son Relationships, Lust for Power, Original Sin

US, 2007
158 Minutes, Feature, Color
Actors: Daniel Day-Lewis, Paul Dano
Director: Paul Thomas Anderson
Screenwriter: Paul Thomas Anderson
    (inspired by Upton Sinclair's 1927 novel *Oil!*)
Rated: R (violence, language)

Synopsis and Theological Reflection

It is impossible to watch the dark opening of this film—with its discordant tones, heat steaming off the screen, chiseled sparks bursting within a dark and dangerous hole in the search for bright silver—and not be forewarned that Daniel Plainview (Daniel Day-Lewis) might be digging his own grave. It's 1898, and, like many prospectors, Plainview has traveled west where, unmolested, he can doggedly pursue a future better than the one determined by his station. Crouching by a small campfire in the wind, black storm clouds whipping around the sky, he squats and drinks a meager meal from a tin cup. Without even the comfort of sitting down, Plainview shows us from the film's first frames that he is capable of superhuman fortitude. But for what? He is able to survive a life like this for years on end, at the risk of all even *he* would

167

hold dear, so that he will not have to endure a life like this? No, there is more he is after. As the film progresses, we come to see that what drives Plainview on is power over his fellows, validation against his forebears, and vengeance against the God who has imposed on him a life beneath his ambitions. But his ravenous goals are what will turn his success to failure, his revenge to demise, his potential into the rape of his own soul. When Plainview finally achieves all he says he is after, there will be only a ghost that inhabits the life he lusts after.

It is a remarkable five minutes into the film before a word is spoken, and then it's simply Plainview's prescient "No." The loss of tools, handmade or bought, was tragic but common in that hardscrabble life; injuries in the harsh wilderness, or at the derrick or in the mine, often meant death, or worse. When the ambitious Plainview suffers a broken leg and a ruined back in a great fall, he drags himself out of the hole, stopping to check along the way for silver in the rocks dislodged by the dynamite. In spite of his life-threatening injuries, upon seeing the sparkle that his spittle uncovers, he cries, "There she is. There she is!" Plainview drags himself to town to stake a claim. Four years later, still pickaxing for silver, another mother lode oozes from the ground in the pit he is mining, and an oil fortune is set in motion.

Anderson's all-male epic of sanctimony and avarice finds its one serious antagonist in a similarly ambitious preacher, Eli Sunday (Paul Dano). The fever for fortune is a driving force for both until, as Day-Lewis put it in a 2007 interview with talk-show host Charlie Rose, "the fever itself became the thing that they lived for."

Shortly into Plainview's success, a roughneck in his employ—who has, inexplicably, an infant in tow—superstitiously baptizes his son with a forefinger covered in oil from the reserve that they have discovered. Not long after, when that worker drowns in the oil, Plainview assumes fatherhood. The child becomes his only family, introducing an important secondary meaning for the theme of blood. Plainview is fiercely attached to his "son" and yet mercenary, using the boy to promote himself as a family man to gain the trust of those whom he hopes to cheat of oil rights. We listen as Plainview completes his transformation from silent prospector to silver-tongued oilman, pitching himself to the small town as a savior who needs no speculators, contractors, or middlemen.

Plainview's journey is a tempestuous one: buying land dirt cheap; cavalierly paying the price of prospecting with the lives of his men while portraying himself as a caring foreman; squaring off with Sunday, who is just as conflicted as he is. Plainview says too often that he is a proponent of speaking "plainly," though he is hardly a man of his word. Words are tools he uses with no more duty to be true to them than he feels obligation to a hammer. People, likewise, are tools, as is mirrored by the preacher of the Church of the Third Revelation, Eli Sunday. These hypocrites fuel their passionate feuding with relentless hucksterism, and in the end, they are each other's undoing.

An hour into the film, a burst of oil brings triumph and tragedy at the same time: Plainview's son, HW, is struck deaf by the explosion that releases the oil Plainview has been drilling for. His attention divided between wounded boy and geyser, Plainview abandons his son and hurries to attend the gusher instead. But "blood ties" are not so easily abandoned. When a man claiming to be Plainview's half brother arrives on his doorstep, Plainview is surprisingly taken in, showing us this complicated man's desire for a deeper connection than oil, a *blood* connection. Eschewing his loyal right-hand man, Plainview trusts everything to the pretender, sharing an intimate confession on their first meeting: "I have a competition in me. I want no one else to succeed. I hate most people. There are times when I look at people and I see nothing worth liking. I want to earn enough money I can get away from everyone." Then, avoiding talk of his own ponderous deceits, he goes on: "I see the worst in people, Henry. . . . I've built up my hatreds over the years little by little." This is, perhaps, his most honest moment.

Shortly thereafter, Plainview tricks HW into going away to a school for the deaf, but he is visibly unmoored by the act, his hatreds, like demons, filling anew the tender emptiness of his heart. As representatives from Standard Oil offer to make him a millionaire by buying his oil-producing land, he asks without irony, "What would I do with myself?" Take care of your son, they suggest, only to receive from him an expression as blank as a statue.

When Plainview discovers that the man he accepted as his brother is, in fact, a charlatan, his degradation is nearly complete. As Plainview's bellicose misanthropy increases, Anderson's imagery on the screen becomes more apocalyptic and Jonny Greenwood's score more strident and discordant. Finally, Plainview is approached with a deal by the elderly landowner who has held out against him. The old man demands the unthinkable: that Plainview attend Sunday's Church of the Third Revelation, confess his sins, and make his heart right with God. Plainview does this, of course—what is a meaningless humiliation weighed against the ownership of the land he has been craving? But Sunday, aiming unswervingly at Plainview's single area of vulnerability, forces the rattled oilman to shout over and over, "I have abandoned my child! I have abandoned my child!" Sunday has drilled down to Plainview's soul, only to find it dry.

Playing out on the peripheral vision of the film's plot is the love story of HW and Sunday's sister, Mary, who grow up together, court, and wed. The two are a light shining from another room, something to redeem at hard cost the boozy debauchery of their families. When Plainview threatens to murder Sunday, Plainview has his comeuppance with Sunday, forcing him to decry his faith by shouting—as Plainview once did in Sunday's church—the thing hardest for him to admit: that he is a false prophet and that God is a superstition. Trying to save his life, Sunday proclaims this over and over, with increasing conviction, falling into the rhythm of his own past sermonizing. And though Sunday pleads hysterically with Plainview that "we are family, we are brothers!" Plainview murders him anyway, with the same brutality that he has lived his whole life with. When his servant comes to check on him at bedtime, Plainview—hands, clothes, and walls covered in the blood of the savagely destroyed preacher—says calmly, as if he were simply pushing away from the dinner table, "I'm finished." Viewers are left to ponder the multiple meanings of his statement.

Dialogue Texts

Make a tree good and its fruit will be good, or make a tree bad and its fruit will be bad, for a tree is recognized by its fruit. . . . A good man brings good things out of the good stored up in him, and an evil man brings evil things out of the evil stored up in him. But I tell you that everyone will have to give account on the day of judgment for every empty word they have spoken. For by your words you will be acquitted, and by your words you will be condemned.

Matthew 12:33–37 (NIV)

Beware of false prophets, who come to you in sheep's clothing but inwardly are ravenous wolves. You will know them by their fruits. Are grapes gathered from thorns, or figs from thistles? . . . A good tree cannot bear bad fruit, nor can a bad tree bear good fruit.

Matthew 7:15–18

But ask in faith, never doubting, for the one who doubts is like a wave of the sea, driven and tossed by the wind; for the doubter, being double-minded and unstable in every way, must not expect to receive anything from the Lord.

Let the believer who is lowly boast in being raised up, and the rich in being brought low, because the rich will disappear like a flower in the field. For the sun rises with its scorching heat and withers the field; its flower falls, and its beauty perishes. It is the same way with the rich; in the midst of a busy life, they will wither away.

James 1:6–11

> The sleep of a laborer is sweet,
>   whether they eat little or much,
> but as for the rich, their abundance
>   permits them no sleep.

I have seen a grievous evil under the sun:

> wealth hoarded to the harm of its owners,
>   or wealth lost through some misfortune,
> so that when they have children
>   there is nothing left for them to inherit.
> Everyone comes naked from their mother's womb,
>   and as everyone comes, so they depart.
> They take nothing from their toil
>   that they can carry in their hands.

This too is a grievous evil:

> As everyone comes, so they depart,
>   and what do they gain,
>   since they toil for the wind?
> All their days they eat in darkness,
>   with great frustration, affliction and anger.
> Ecclesiastes 5:12–17 (NIV; cf. 5:10–11)

Discussion Questions and Clip Conversations

All clips are available for viewing at ReelSpirituality.com/Books/God-In-The-Movies. We have also listed the timestamp range of the scenes for your reference.

1. What is the relationship between oil and blood? What do the two symbols mean to Plainview and Sunday? How are both men symbols of a warring that exists inside each person? How might these symbols, however exaggerated, also apply to your own life?

2. "Rehearsing" [54:31–59:44]. What is Eli Sunday's true passion? Is he an honest clergyman in difficult circumstances or a charlatan? Or both? What does the scene of Eli rehearsing on the stage of a church tell viewers about him?

3. "Bastard from a Basket" [13:16–17:26; 1:00:00–1:04:10; 1:08:04–40; cf. 1:29:21–1:34:20; 1:57:00–2:04:30; 2:08:15–2:16:18]. Over and over through the film, Plainview expresses a fierce attachment to his informally adopted son—a physical protection by literally wrapping his body around him when he is hurt at the derrick accident; a deeply rooted connection as he tricks him into staying on the train and leaves him there; and a deep affection upon his return ("This does me good, that does me good—welcome home, son!"). Yet at the end of the film he tells his son the vicious truth, "I took you in for no other reason than I needed a sweet face to buy land," and banishes him from his life. Does Plainview love the boy? Did he ever? Can he love at all? Do we sometimes betray our "blood ties" for other ambitions?

4. Were Plainview and Sunday "bad seeds" (Matt. 25), or did they make decisions that turned them each into something bad? At what point in the story did either/both take a path of no return that led them to be the men we see at the end of the film? (You might want to compare this movie with Darren Aronofsky's *Noah*; see chap. 35.)

Bonus Material

Inspirations for Anderson's film provide insight into the era of prospecting and the Wild West in which it prospered. These include Upton Sinclair's *Oil!*; the classic 1956 film by George Stevens, *Giant* (also filmed in Marfa, Texas); and John Huston's 1948 gem, *The Treasure of the Sierra Madre*, which Anderson is said to have played continuously while he was scripting *There Will Be Blood*.

Selected Additional Resources

Available DVD features: deleted scenes; fifteen-minute short on inspiration and research; teaser trailer; 1923 archival silent film, *The Story of Petroleum*.

For diving deeper into the making of the movie, consider Charlie Rose's fifty-six-minute interview with Paul Thomas Anderson and Daniel Day-Lewis (December 2007): https://charlierose.com/videos/20011.

Fuller professor Kutter Callaway's article on the movie's music (November 29, 2011): http://www.brehmcenter.com/initiatives/reelspirituality/film/articles/there_will_be_blood_music_mystery_and_milkshakes.

Guardian US chief reporter Ed Pilkington's reflection "Tell the Story! Tell the Story!" (January 4, 2008): http://www.theguardian.com/culture/2008/jan/04/awardsandprizes.

Also the *Guardian*'s review by Peter Bradshaw (February 8, 2008): http://www.theguardian.com/film/2008/feb/08/paulthomasanderson.drama.

And Jeffrey Overstreet's review for *Christianity Today* (December 26, 2007): http://www.christianitytoday.com/ct/2007/decemberweb-only/therewillbeblood.html.

Lauralee Farrer

28

Up

Friendship
Father/Son Relationships,
Hope, Loss

US, 2009
96 Minutes, Animated Feature, Color
Actors: Ed Asner, Jordan Nagai
Directors: Pete Docter, Bob Peterson
Screenwriters: Bob Peterson, Pete Docter
    (story by Pete Docter, Bob Peterson, and Tom McCarthy)
Rated: PG

Synopsis and Theological Reflection

Up is a wonderful animated film from Pixar's brilliantly creative writer-director team of Pete Docter and Bob Peterson. It is a story of love, loss, hope, redemption, and adventure—sweet, heartbreaking, hilarious, and inspiring. *Up* won the 2010 Academy Award for Best Animated Feature Film.

The protagonist, Carl Fredricksen, is, for most of the movie, a seventy-eight-year-old retired balloon salesman. As *Up* opens, Carl as a young boy reads and dreams of a world of adventure. There follows a four-minute scene, without words, in which Carl meets, falls in love with, marries, and loses Ellie, the love of his life. This remarkably tender sequence shows Carl and Ellie as they build a life together, enjoy many beautiful years, but suffer one great sadness (no children), grow old, and dream of a "trip of a lifetime" adventure to Paradise Falls in South America. They postpone their dream trip for too long, however. Ellie takes sick and dies, and Carl is left alone as a bitter and broken old man.

Carl finally decides to take the trip to Paradise Falls on his own, fulfilling his and Ellie's dream of their ultimate romantic adventure. Being a balloon salesman, Carl's transportation of choice to Paradise Falls is, of course, balloon, which allows Docter to create a colorful, whimsical airborne balloon mobile symbolizing escape, adventure, and fragility. This is not *Around the World in Eighty Days* hot air ballooning; this is Carl's old house lifted and carried by (seemingly) thousands of balloons as he sets off for Paradise Falls. Carl's trip is initially ruined—but ultimately perfected—by an eight-year-old stowaway, Russell.

In a Pixar interview Pete Docter said, "We came up with this image of a floating house held aloft by balloons, and it just seemed to capture what we were after in terms of escaping the world. We quickly realized that the world is really about relationships, and that's what Carl comes to discover." In a *Christianity Today* interview, Docter added, "[*Up*] highlights the importance of relationship, because I think that's the heart of Christianity as well. We so easily lose track of that and become self-centered. . . . The message of the film is that the real adventure of life is the relationship we have with other people, and it's so easy to lose sight of the things we have and the people that are around us until they're gone."

Much of the movie is built on the evolving bond between Carl and Russell. Carl's feelings toward Russell move from resentment to tolerance to friendship to fatherly love. Russell becomes Carl's new partner in his one great adventure trip to Paradise Falls. As this happens, Docter gently shows us the centrality of relationships to human thriving. While Russell is not a replacement for Ellie, he is, for Carl, a new partner in adventure and someone to love, protect, and mentor.

Up features talking dogs and birds, a quirky nemesis, and a moving final act of heroism. This movie is visually stunning, life-affirming, playful, and suitable for everyone but the youngest children.

Dialogue Texts

Do unto others as you would have them do unto you.

Luke 6:31

Two are better than one,
  because they have a good return for their labor:

If either of them falls down,
    one can help the other up.
But pity anyone who falls
    and has no one to help them up.

Ecclesiastes 4:9–10 (NIV)

So even to old age and gray hairs,
    O God, do not forsake me,
until I proclaim your might to another generation,
    your power to all those to come.

Psalm 71:18 (ESV)

A man of many companions may come to ruin,
    but there is a friend who sticks closer than a brother.

Proverbs 18:24 (ESV)

A friend loves at all times,
    and kinsfolk are born to share adversity.

Proverbs 17:17

Even children make themselves known by their acts,
    by whether what they do is pure and right.

Proverbs 20:11

Take care that you do not despise one of these little ones: for I tell you, in heaven their angels continually see the face of my Father in heaven.

Matthew 18:10

Discussion Questions and Clip Conversations

All clips are available for viewing at ReelSpirituality.com/Books/God-In -The-Movies. We have also listed the timestamp range of the scenes for your reference.

1. "Carl and Ellie's Life" [07:19–11:37]. What is Carl's first impression of Ellie? Do their roles reverse over time? What have they learned from each other? How do their personalities complement each other? Why do you think that Carl and Ellie's story is told without words? What is the role of the music in the "showing" of their story? In the "showing"

Carl and Russell—a journey to friendship

of their story, how do the images take on symbolic meaning? Can you give examples? Is there a part of their story that you identify with? How do their pain and joy go together? Is this true for you?

2. "Meeting Russell" [15:16–17:43]. When meeting the contractor interested in bulldozing his house, is Carl justified in being angry? Why is he crotchety? Has Carl given up? What gets him going again? Is he renewed more by his memories, his mission, or his meeting Russell? What is your impression of Russell? (Docter says his inspiration for Russell came from one of his children's best friends.)

3. "Carl and Russell" [24:11–26:22]. Why does Carl "let Russell in," literally and metaphorically? When does Carl begin to value Russell? Does the storm threaten Carl's self-reliance? Is that a blessing? When does Russell begin to feel needed? What lessons have Carl and Russell learned from their adventure? What have they learned from each other?

4. At the end of *The Wizard of Oz*, Dorothy realizes that "there's no place like home." What does the house symbolize in *Up*? The balloons? What symbols are important to you in your life and in your faith? How important is "home" for you? Why?

5. What lessons can we learn from how Carl and Russell interact with Dug (the dog) and Kevin (the bird)? What was your response to Dug saying, "I have just met you, and I love you"? What kinds of surprising or unconventional friends has God brought into your world?

6. Could this story have been told as a live-action movie? Do you identify differently with characters in an animated film than with live-action characters? How does animation invite your imagination into the story?

Bonus Material

Two of my colleagues in the Reel Spirituality Institute at Fuller Seminary have written perceptively on *Up*, one concentrating on the importance of its filmmaker, Pete Docter, and the other reflecting on his experience of the movie as a viewer who could identify with Carl and Ellie. Both creator and receiver are vital to any understanding of the theological importance of a movie. A movie's meaning does not happen in isolation from its creators or viewers. Thus, portions of my colleagues' reflections are included below to assist you in your interaction with *Up*.

Reviewing *Up* on ReelSpirituality.com, Rob Johnston wrote:

Pete Docter was born to be a storyteller, and he continues to live out that dream. The co-writer with John Lassiter on *Toy Story* (1995) and *Toy Story 2* (1999) and a co-writer with Andrew Stanton on *WALL•E* (2008), he was the co-director and lead writer for *Monsters, Inc.* (2001) and the co-writer and co-director of *Up* with Bob Peterson. He has been nominated for an Oscar six times and though only in his early forties, Docter has already received a lifetime achievement award from the Venice Film Festival. . . .

Still a kid at heart, Docter chose upon graduation not to take a job writing for the *Simpsons*, deciding instead to go to work for a start-up animation company named Pixar. There he could play laser tag in the dark with his colleagues, after spending the day collaborating in their story-telling ventures. He also joined First Presbyterian Church in Berkeley where he remains active today. From Disney, Docter says he learned in his storytelling to balance each laugh with a tear. And from his Christian faith and family, he learned the values of family, intimacy, and caring about others, all others.

From this twin base, Docter has become a central figure in shaping the stories a whole generation lives by. His stories have provided hope to young and old alike as they embody his Christian understanding of what it is to be fully human. Docter's imaginative and whimsical stories have helped all of us find joy in our lives, even as they have helped Pixar's meteoric rise to the top of the animation ladder. . . .

In *Up*, the adventure Docter creates is fun and the humor continuous, but it is the love and friendship that is displayed which proves wondrous. The hopes and disappointments of Carl and Ellie make you cry. Their love is set amidst dreams deferred and ambitions renegotiated, and is all the more real for it. But the ensuing friendship between Carl (Mr. Fredricksen) and Russell also proves to be wonder-filled. Though the trip to Paradise Falls is spectacular, the enjoyment of shared ice cream is even better.

Kutter Callaway begins his book *Scoring Transcendence: Film Music as Religious Experience* (Baylor University Press, 2013) with an extended personal reflection about the experience he and his wife, Jessica, had watching *Up*. Below is an edited version:

On the opening weekend for one of Disney/Pixar's more recent animated films, *Up* (2009), my wife and I settled into two theater seats located in the midst of a frenetically undulating sea of parents and young children. . . . [At the time], our lives were distinguished by the absence of children. After trying unsuccessfully for an extended period of time to bear children, my wife and I reveled in the joy of discovering that we had finally conceived. Yet, as the apparent randomness and absurdity of life would have it, we subsequently lost two pregnancies to miscarriage, each one further reinforcing a certain degree of helplessness and a commensurate loss of identity both as individuals and as a family. It was this very juxtaposition—our personal experience of loss along with the presence of what seemed to be a surfeit of children—that formed the immediate context for our viewing of *Up*. . . . For my wife and me, the images of Carl and Ellie wrestling with the unique but often unspoken pain of their own miscarriage [during the married life montage] . . . offered us an invitation to remember our loss and, in an important sense, functioned as an embodiment of our pain. But it was the music that expressed something that even the most explicit visual or narrative reference to our pain-filled story could not contain: the redemptive power of a hard-won hope. . . . It suggested the presence of an otherwise hidden meaning in the events it accompanied—a deeper coherence that helped to shape these events into a meaningful narrative. . . . It was a powerful, spiritual, and perhaps even revelatory experience. And it all occurred in less than four minutes.

Pete Docter's startlingly original, insightful *Inside Out*, which he cowrote and codirected, won the 2016 Academy Award for Best Animated Feature Film. In his acceptance speech, Docter echoed the sentiment of the movie when, holding his Oscar, he said: "This film was really born out of watching our kids grow up, which is not easy. Anyone out there who's in junior high, high school, working it out, suffering—there are days you're going to feel sad. You're going to feel angry. You're going to feel scared. That's nothing you can choose. But you can make stuff. Make films. Draw. Write. It will make a world of difference." And Carl would say, "Go on an adventure."

Joseph C. Gallagher

29

WALL·E

US, 2008
98 Minutes, Animated Feature, Color
Actors: Ben Burtt, Elissa Knight, Jeff
    Garlin, Fred Willard, MacInTalk, John
    Ratzenberger, Kathy Najimy, Sigourney
    Weaver, Teddy Newton
Director: Andrew Stanton
Screenwriters: Andrew Stanton, Pete Docter, Jim Reardon
Rated: G

Love
Care of Creation,
Christ Figure,
Sin and Its Consequences

Synopsis and Theological Reflection

Pixar's *WALL·E* caused a stir when it was released in 2008. Some people saw it as a blatant example of pro-environmentalism propaganda. Others saw it as a cruel condemnation of obese people. Still others saw it as a simple little love story with stellar animation and sound design in its first act and clunkily plotted second and third acts. Is *WALL·E* any of these things? Is it all of them? To answer these questions, let's go back to the beginning, to the very beginning of all things.

In the beginning when God created the heavens and the earth, the earth was a formless void and darkness covered the face of the deep, while a wind from God swept over the face of the waters. (Gen. 1:1–2)

WALL·E also begins "out there" in the heavens and descends to the surface of the earth, but the earth is hardly void. It is full of trash—cities of trash—and there is no plant, animal, or human life to be found. As the camera sweeps over the polluted expanse, it finds a little robot going about his day, humming along to his favorite song. The camera follows him as he jovially continues his work.

Just as the first man, Adam, was put on the planet to do the good work of taking care of things, so the last robot is engaged in the same work. Adam was a gardener; WALL·E is too, after he discovers one little plant growing bravely in a refrigerator and transfers it safely to a work boot.

And just as there was more to Adam than simply his calling to care for the garden, so there is more to WALL·E. As Adam worked in Eden, he discovered no one else like him. He was lonely. WALL·E is lonely too. Somehow, WALL·E knows he is made to love and to be loved. WALL·E may be built to be a worker, but deep in his circuit-board heart, deeper than his programming can reach, WALL·E is a lover. Just as Adam eventually found his Eve, so does WALL·E, and the movie that bears WALL·E's name is, at its heart, a love story.

Love stories are common in cinema, but not the kind we find here. Most center on ecstasy and instant gratification, not the kind of long-suffering and self-sacrificial love found in WALL·E. His love reminds some viewers of that love exemplified in Christ long ago, which Christ calls his followers to emulate. A Christlike love is a way of life, not simply a feeling. A Christlike love runs counter to much of what we have come to accept as ordinary life. Is *WALL·E* that kind of love story? It might seem unlikely, but according to writer/director Andrew Stanton, this is exactly the kind of love he envisioned for *WALL·E*.

In a 2008 interview with Megan Basham for *World*, Stanton said:

The greatest commandment Christ gives us is to love, but that's not always our priority. So I came up with this premise that could demonstrate what I was trying to say—that irrational love defeats the world's programming. You've got these two robots that are trying to go above their basest directives, literally their programming, to experience love. With the human characters I wanted to show that our programming is the routines and habits that distract us to the point that we're not really making connections to the people next to us. We're not engaging in relationships, which are the point of living—relationship with God and relationship with other people.

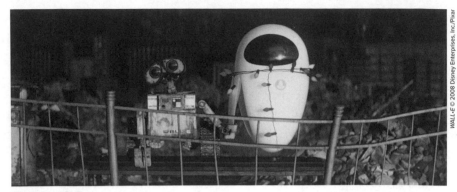

WALL·E and EVE

WALL·E is Christlike love personified (robotified?). WALL·E is patient. He is kind. WALL·E has no one to be jealous of, and the closest he comes to bragging is when he holds up a loosely-held-together block of trash to show EVE (Elissa Knight) his "directive." WALL·E isn't arrogant or rude. He spends his life for others' advantage, not his own. When EVE or anyone else slights him, WALL·E forgives immediately. There isn't an evil bolt in his body. He is truthful to a fault. In both his care for the earth and his pursuit of EVE, WALL·E puts up with anything, trusts perfectly, hopes indefatigably, and endures no matter what happens to him. WALL·E never fails in this love, even if it might cost him his life.

Everyone whom WALL·E encounters wakes up from their selfish slumber to this kind of love. Notice this throughout the film as WALL·E bumps into other people and robots and shakes them from their routines. WALL·E shows them a better way to live. He shows them that if they are going to be fully human, they're going to have to stop being lazy and self-absorbed and begin to do the good work they are called to—to take care of each other and the world once again.

In *WALL·E*, love isn't merely a feeling. In *WALL·E*, to love is to work, and to work is to love. To participate in that loving work is to participate in the re-creation and restoration of all things, as *WALL·E*'s beautiful, creative closing credit sequence shows.

Is *WALL·E* a romance? Yes. Is it about our need to take care of the planet? Yes. Is it a campaign against consumerism, sloth, and indulgence, and a campaign for redemptive work? Yes. It is all of these things, because all of these things are aspects of what it means to love the world in a Christlike way.

In *WALL·E*, Stanton does not preach, though he is sincere. The Christian undergirding of this story is implicit rather than explicit. Nevertheless, it is the core of the story. To love the world as God so loved it means we have to be tireless in our care for those we have covenanted to love. To love the world as God so loved it means we have to be good stewards of this garden God has put us in. To love the world as God so loved it means we have to serve the world and all its inhabitants instead of only pursuing our own selfish desires. To love the world as God so loved it means we have to be like WALL·E, who reaches above his base programming as his creator, Andrew Stanton, intended, to love like Christ commanded.

Dialogue Texts

In the beginning when God created the heavens and the earth, the earth was a formless void and darkness covered the face of the deep, while a wind from God swept over the face of the waters.

Genesis 1:1–2

For God so loved the world that he gave his only Son, so that everyone who believes in him may not perish but may have eternal life.

Indeed, God did not send the Son into the world to condemn the world, but in order that the world might be saved through him.

John 3:16–17

I give you a new commandment, that you love one another. Just as I have loved you, you also should love one another. By this everyone will know that you are my disciples, if you have love for one another.

John 13:34–35

Love is patient; love is kind; love is not envious or boastful or arrogant or rude. It does not insist on its own way; it is not irritable or resentful; it does not rejoice in wrongdoing, but rejoices in the truth. It bears all things, believes all things, hopes all things, endures all things.

Love never ends.

1 Corinthians 13:4–8

We know love by this, that he laid down his life for us—and we ought to lay down our lives for one another. How does God's love abide in anyone who has the world's goods and sees a brother or sister in need and yet refuses help?

Little children, let us love, not in word or speech, but in truth and action.

1 John 3:16–18

Discussion Questions and Clip Conversations

All clips are available for viewing at ReelSpirituality.com/Books/God-In
-The-Movies. We have also listed the timestamp range of the scenes for your
reference.

1. Christlike love is an act of self-sacrifice rather than a "good feeling."
   In WALL•E, we see this kind of love acted out again and again by the
   movie's protagonist and by everyone who rallies to his cause. What are
   some specific examples of this kind of love in WALL•E? What are some
   specific examples of this kind of love from the life of Christ? How do
   some characters avoid participating in this kind of love? How do we
   avoid loving others and the world in this way?

2. "Try Blue!" [39:27–42:53]. WALL•E chases EVE around the Axiom and
   encounters humans for the first time. What aspect of 2805 humanity
   do you find funniest? What aspect is the most tragic? Do you see any of
   the negative tendencies of the people in WALL•E in the lives of people
   today in the real world? Are any of those tendencies part of your life?
   How should we be acting instead?

3. "Define Dancing" [58:51–1:02:05]. What kinds of love do we see in this
   scene? Why do you think the filmmakers juxtapose love between two
   robots with blossoming love between two people and the Captain's new
   awareness of how "amazing" life on Earth was? If you have experienced
   new love, what was it like? What has it inspired you to do? WALL•E and
   EVE share a romantic moment. John and Mary notice both the stars
   and each other. The Captain becomes aware of Earth. How are the first
   sparks of romance like new awareness? Why is this?

4. "Someone to Look After You" [1:03:21–1:07:16]. EVE and the Captain
   watch the same security footage from different perspectives. What do EVE
   and the Captain each discover in this scene? When EVE sees WALL•E
   taking care of her in the security footage, what does she realize? When
   the Captain sees the globe askew on the floor, what does he realize? How
   are these things two different expressions of the same quality?

5. Which is greater—romance or care? How are both forms of love aspects
   of a greater love? What are some other ways characters in the film awaken
   to their need to care for one another and the world? Is WALL•E a Christ
   figure? Why or why not? What does the Bible say about how to love and
   care for other people as Christ did? What does the Bible say about how
   to love the world?

Bonus Material

According to Andrew Stanton in an interview with Tasha Robinson for the *AV Club*, the animation team on *WALL·E* watched Charlie Chaplin and Buster Keaton films every day at lunch during production on the film. WALL·E owes more to the Little Tramp than he does to *2001: A Space Odyssey*. One of *WALL·E*'s most indelible images—that of two hands touching—is the penultimate moment in one of Chaplin's greatest films, *City Lights*, which is another film that depicts Christlike love in an amusing and endearing way.

WALL·E is a film without a villain. The antagonist in the film—a machine named "Autopilot," or "Auto" for short—is the programming that keeps people (and robots) from loving one another. Autopilot isn't even necessarily "bad"; he's just sticking to his programming.

Selected Additional Resources

Megan Basham's entire interview with Andrew Stanton for *World* (June 28, 2008) is worth reading: http://www.worldmag.com/2008/06/walloe_world.

Tasha Robinson is one of our nation's finest critics, and she loves animation. Her interview with Andrew Stanton for *AV Club* (June 25, 2008) is stellar: http://www.avclub.com/article/andrew-stanton-14263.

Elijah Davidson

30

Water

Canada/India, 2005
117 Minutes, Feature, Color
Actors: Sarala Kariyawasam, Lisa Ray, John
Abraham, Seema Biswas
Director: Deepa Mehta
Screenwriters: Anurag Kashyap, Deepa
Mehta
Rated: PG-13 (mature thematic material involving sexual situations and brief
drug use)

Conscience and Religion
Doubt, Faith/Belief,
Human Suffering,
Loss, Prejudice/
Oppression, Theology
of Religions

Synopsis and Theological Reflection

Water opens with a wide shot of an algae-infested pond sprinkled with exquisite lotus flowers. While the expanse of water alludes to the title, the lotus flowers set the theological undertone of the film. Indian audiences immediately recognize the lotus flower as the ubiquitous symbol of an enlightened mind in Eastern religions. Others receive their clue later in the film: "The lotus is untouched by the filthy water it grows in," says the heroine. "Not everyone can live like a lotus flower," responds the hero. This opening shot prepares us to enter a world similar to that of the pond—a sisterhood of women striving to survive in a hostile world that is muddied with the oppressive customs and traditions imposed by religion.

Water is set in 1938, a mercurial time in the social history of India. The colonial power is on the verge of collapse and a new republic is beginning to emerge. The nation hears a prophetic voice through Mahatma ("Great Soul") Gandhi, who believes that the political liberation of the nation would come only through the healing of the self-inflicted wounds in the society. The protagonist of the story is a young girl, Chuyia (Sarala Kariyawasam), one of the many victims of the notorious child marriage tradition in India. As the film begins, her husband dies unexpectedly, leaving Chuyia a widow at eight years old. She is consigned to an ashram located on the bank of the Ganges, the holy river of India, where she is forced to spend the rest of her life with other widows. Madhumati (Manorama), the matriarch of the ashram, is ready to go to any extreme for survival. She is even willing to offer Kalyani (Lisa Ray), a beautiful young widow, as a prostitute to rich customers across the river. One day Kalyani runs into Narayan (John Abraham), a devout follower of Gandhi. He falls in love with Kalyani and decides to marry her despite the prohibitions against the remarriage of widows. In order to keep the business going, Madhumati now has to find a new prostitute, and her evil eyes fall on Chuyia. Shakuntala (Seema Biswas) is the only member of the ashram who has the courage to stand up to Madhumati, but the intervention comes late—perhaps too late.

As Pundit explains in the film, widows in (ancient) India only have three options: "They can burn with their dead husbands, lead a life of self-denial, or, if the family permits, marry their husband's younger brother." A widow is (or was) considered socially dead in Indian culture, and her presence inauspicious in public places. The ritualistic denigration that marks the transition of a woman into widowhood is poignantly portrayed in the film. The family takes her away from her husband's funeral in the dark of the night, after which they break her bangles, wipe off her *tilak*, and shave her head. She is forced to renounce all adornments and cosmetics and is even prohibited from eating sweets or fried food. In the end, she is dressed in a white sari and sent off to the ashram.

In telling its story, *Water* focuses on the power and mastery of sacred scriptures in the life of ordinary people. It begins with a quote from one of the oldest Hindu scriptures, establishing both the context of the story and the tone in which it is told: "A widow should be long-suffering until death, self-restrained and chaste. A virtuous wife who remains chaste when her husband has died goes to heaven. A woman who is unfaithful to her husband is reborn in the womb of a jackal" (Manusmriti 5.156–61). The film interweaves

Chuyia at the river Ganges

many scripture verses into the narrative, often in their original poetic form. For example, Narayan's father suggests to him that he could keep Kalyani as a mistress because "Brahmins can sleep with whomever they want and the women they sleep with are blessed." Narayan counters this text by referencing another verse: "Do you know what Ram told his brother? Never to honor those Brahmins who interpret the Holy Scripture for their own benefit."

In *Water*, tradition in itself is not considered evil, however. According to the film, it plays an important role in maintaining social equilibrium. Even Kalyani, one of the most tragic victims of her tradition, is prudent to recognize its cultural significance. When Narayan says, "All the old traditions are dying out," Kalyani's response is immediate: "But what is good should not die out."

The central theological theme of *Water* is the conflict between one's faith (as defined by one's religious tradition) and conscience. In 2013 I had the privilege of interviewing Deepa Mehta, the auteur of the film, during which she asserted that "it's the whole journey of trying to understand what faith is and what it means and what oppression is. . . . That for me is the crux of the whole film. . . . It is about the conflict between conscience and faith." The apparent disparity between the voice of conscience and the voice of faith, according to Mehta, is caused by the misappropriation of the sacred texts by religious leaders (something that may sound familiar to those associated with other religions of the Book). The powerful aristocrats and members of the priestly class at the pinnacle of the social hierarchy manipulate the true message of the scriptures to serve their own self-interests. When Shakuntala wonders why the news about the possibility of a widow's remarriage did not reach the ashram, Pundit responds candidly: "We ignore the laws that don't benefit us." In the words of Narayan's friend, "Avoid widows, slippery steps, and holy men. Liberation awaits."

Conflict between conscience and faith is resolved only in the enlightened mind of an individual. "Who will decide what is good and what is not?" asks Narayan. Kalyani's answer points us straight to the core message of the film: "You." What holds the key to social reformation is the transformation of an individual's heart. It is the moral compass of a believer that determines the authenticity of his or her faith. As Narayan decides to follow Gandhi, leaving his father's inheritance behind, Shakuntala also makes a radical decision to break free from the bondage of the ashram and to become an agent of change. In the final shot of the film, she turns around and looks at the audience. Mehta carefully composed this shot using a long lens to highlight her gaze, blurring everything in the background. Shakuntala has now learned that true faith comes not from sacred texts written in parchments but from the invisible words written on her conscience. In the struggle between faith and conscience, ultimate victory belongs to the conscience of an individual. This, in essence, is the message of *Water*.

Shakuntala's gaze travels through time and space and demands a theological response conditioned through our own struggle with faith and conscience. This tension between faith and conscience is a classic conundrum in every religion, including both Hinduism and Christianity. I believe that my own (Christian) tradition needs to reexamine its history through the lens of *Water*—in particular, its use of sacred texts to justify such social evils as the Crusades, the Inquisition, slavery, and even discrimination against women. Today, as we are confronted with new questions about moral and political issues, one might wonder at what point it is appropriate to listen to the voice of conscience over the voice of tradition.

In Mehta's own words, "The crisis of faith is universal." Although *Water* is set in the context of India and the plot is centered on the plight of widows, beneath its surface level the movie is targeting the general dysfunction that exists within the socioreligious system in every society. Even when the story is taking place in a particular time and in a particular location, the core issues discussed in the film resonate with viewers of all religious faiths and cultural backgrounds. In its invitation to experience the tension between the voice of faith as carried down through tradition and that of conscience, *Water*'s theological criticism transcends cultural borders and assumes universal significance.

Dialogue Texts

But woe to you, scribes and Pharisees, hypocrites! For you lock people out of the kingdom of heaven. For you do not go in yourselves, and when others are going in, you stop them. Woe to you, scribes and Pharisees, hypocrites! For you cross sea and land to make a single convert, and you make the new convert twice as much a child of hell as yourselves.

Matthew 23:13–15

> The LORD sets the prisoners free;
> the LORD opens the eyes of the blind;
> The LORD lifts up those who are bowed down;
> the LORD loves the righteous.
> The LORD watches over the strangers;
> he upholds the orphan and the widow,
> but the way of the wicked he brings to ruin.

Psalm 146:7–9

I saw all the deeds that are done under the sun; and see, all is vanity and a chasing after wind.

Ecclesiastes 1:14

Anyone, then, who knows the right thing to do and fails to do it, commits sin.

James 4:17

If you do not oppress the alien, the orphan, and the widow, or shed innocent blood in this place, and if you do not go after other gods to your own hurt, then I will dwell with you in this place, in the land that I gave of old to your ancestors forever and ever.

Jeremiah 7:6–7

They show that what the law requires is written on their hearts, to which their own conscience also bears witness; and their conflicting thoughts will accuse or perhaps excuse them on the day when, according to my gospel, God, through Jesus Christ, will judge the secret thoughts of all.

Romans 2:15–16

Our competence is from God, who has made us competent to be ministers of a new covenant, not of letter but of spirit; for the letter kills, but the Spirit gives life.

2 Corinthians 3:5–6

Discussion Questions and Clip Conversations

All clips are available for viewing at ReelSpirituality.com/Books/God-In
-The-Movies. We have also listed the timestamp range of the scenes for your
reference.

1. Though it surely helps the viewer to have a basic understanding of Indian history and culture in order to critique the social issues discussed
in *Water*, the movie also deals with a number of universal themes that
find resonance in other cultures. What significance do the social issues
presented in the movie have within your own cultural context?

2. What are some of the cultural symbols (customs, traditions, rituals,
ceremonies, etc.) you observe in *Water*? How would you interpret the
meaning of these symbols? Do they have different meaning in your
cultural context?

3. "We Ignore the Laws That Don't Benefit Us" [1:19:15–1:21:05]. Do you
think the leaders of your faith tradition would make a statement like
this? How does religion influence political and socioeconomic issues in
your culture?

4. "Kalyani's Death Is No Illusion" [1:33:35–1:35:55]. The dialogue in this
scene stems from the Hindu doctrine of maya, which assumes that all
physical entities are illusion and part of a cosmic whole. How is maya
different from the concept of vanity presented in the book of Ecclesiastes? How will this biblical book speak to Narayan and Kalyani at this
occasion?

5. "Faith and Conscience" [1:36:50–1:38:01]. How would you compare
the actions of Kalyani and Shakuntala based on the dynamics of their
understanding of faith and conscience with your decision-making process? Have you ever been in a predicament where you had to choose one
at the expense of the other? How are your life decisions influenced by
faith and/or conscience?

Bonus Material

Although India's census data from 2011 indicates that the percentage is de-
clining, 30.2 percent of all Indian women were married before they turned
eighteen years old, while only 6 percent of men married before the age of
eighteen; 2.3 percent of Indian women were married before ten years of age
(for Hindu women specifically, it was 6 percent).

Water is the third film of Deepa Mehta's controversial Elements Trilogy, which includes *Fire* (1992) and *Earth* (1999) as well. The day after *Water* commenced shooting in Varanasi, an angry mob stormed onto the set, attacked the film crew, and ransacked the place, throwing all their equipment into the Ganges River. Mehta was forced to shut down the set, fearing for the safety of her crew members. She reshot *Water* five years later by recreating the set in a remote location in Sri Lanka. The film debuted at the Toronto International Film Festival in 2005. It gained the international limelight when the Academy of Motion Picture Arts and Sciences nominated it for the 2006 Oscar for Best Foreign Language Film.

Mathew P. John

A **DECADE** FOR **SPIRITUALITY**

The 2010s began in the midst of a global financial crisis that started toward the end of the previous decade and whose ripple effects we are still feeling. The housing market collapse and the growing reliance on debt and global financial markets brought with it a level of unheralded economic anxiety, causing the beginning of a rethinking of consumer culture and materialism, as well as global political unrest. Young adults realize they will be the first generation in the modern era who will live with a lower standard of living than their parents. We also continue to live with concerns about global terror and violence, and anxiety about societal vulnerability drives much of our economic and political agendas.

Our love affair with digital technology has continued into the 2010s, and we find ourselves dependent on technologies most of us know very little about. This dependence has contributed to a general anxiety about potential disasters caused by the collapse of technology, an idea that funds some of our television and movie watching and contributes to the continuing dynamic of conspiracy theories that accompany much of life in a digital age. Traditional models of television and cinema have been challenged by the dawn of new

193

technologies—companies like Netflix and Amazon are not only redefining the way we watch films but are also creating new content and challenging old business models.

One of the great surprises to many in the latter part of the twentieth century was the continuing interest in religion. Despite the apparent triumph of "secular" society, it became increasingly clear as the twentieth century gave way to the twenty-first that religion, far from disappearing, was actually reappearing—not at the margins of society but as a central part of public life in a manner not seen for a very long time. Religious beliefs may be contested in ways that they never have been—and undoubtedly, confidence in institutional religion is at an all-time low in Western culture—but religion persists in spite of its detractors. Like many things in society, its obituary was premature. The rise of fundamentalist movements of all kinds has given credence to some who argue that religion is the source of all that is wrong with our world. But this rather naive and ill-informed assumption continues to be tempered by a growing interest in spirituality. We live, it seems, in the age of the "spiritual but not religious."

In cinema, the 2010s have seen a growing number of biblically and theologically themed films—*Calvary*, *The Adjustment Bureau*, *Exodus: Gods and Kings*, *The Tree of Life*, *Les Misérables*, *The Way*, *Get Low*, *Of Gods and Men*. This might be, as some claim, a delayed response to the success of *The Passion of the Christ*, but I would argue that it is also a sign of the ongoing and increasing interest in both religion and spirituality that characterizes our era.

In this post-secular period, many continue to struggle with aspects of life that a secularism focused solely on reason seems unable to account for. This doesn't necessarily herald a return to traditional religion, but it does point to cinema as a site for the resituating and reconceiving of the ways we live and the ways we think about the sacred.

Barry Taylor

31

The Adjustment Bureau

US, 2011
106 Minutes, Feature, Color
Actors: Matt Damon, Emily Blunt, Anthony
 Mackie
Director: George Nolfi
Screenwriter: George Nolfi (based on the short story "Adjustment Team"
 by Philip K. Dick)
Rated: PG-13 (brief strong language, some sexuality, a violent image)

Destiny and Free Will
Human Agency,
Human Identity,
Love

Synopsis and Theological Reflection

The Adjustment Bureau is one of those movies whose genre is hard to pin down. Is it an action/suspense thriller, like *The Bourne Ultimatum*, which this movie's writer and director, George Nolfi, also cowrote? Perhaps it is a political drama? But the plot revolves around a love story that is suffused with science fiction. And there are clear religious themes that invite further reflection by viewers once the movie has ended. Most cross-genre films don't work; *The Adjustment Bureau* is an exception. Nolfi has given us a movie that teenagers and adults alike will enjoy—and then ponder.

 If the movie were primarily a thriller, it would be driven by its plot. Set strikingly in New York City and given a superb sound track by Thomas

Newman, the story follows the two lead characters—David Norris (Matt Damon) and Elise Sellas (Emily Blunt), who meet unexpectedly in the men's room(!) of a major hotel on the night of Norris's concession speech, after he has blown a big lead in his race for the Senate. The rest of the movie has to do with the efforts of the "adjusters"—men in hats—to stop these two from meeting again so Norris can fulfill the "Chairman's" plan that he become president of the United States. There are strong chase scenes, taxis crashing, lots of running, and doors that open up mysteriously onto other areas of the city. Terence Stamp, as Senior Adjuster Thompson, is a worthy nemesis—as always. Can the characters escape those mysterious hatted strangers with special powers? Viewers find themselves hoping against hope that they can.

But this is because the film is also a love story, one driven by its character development. What propels the action after the opening scene is not really the suspense caused by car crashes and the bowler-hatted adjusters. Rather, it is the chemistry between Elise and David. After their kiss in the men's room, neither can stand to live apart from the other. But they also don't know how to find each other. How will they escape—or *can* they escape—the Chairman's plan, in which they both have successful careers but are not together? Viewers will root for these lovers as obstacle after obstacle is put in their path by the adjusters.

But like the short story by Philip K. Dick from which it was adapted, *The Adjustment Bureau* is not primarily a love story, nor is it a suspense thriller. In Dick's story, as in the movie adaptation, the primary power and meaning of the story lie not in the characters, however appealing they are as everyman and everywoman. Nor is the movie a mystery along the lines of *Inception* or *Memento*, where plot provides the fuel for ignition. Instead, the power and meaning come from the sense of destiny that propels the story forward. This sense, the "plan" of the Chairman, performs almost like another character in the movie and is at the movie's core. The protagonists find themselves part of mysterious plans bigger than they could have known about, plans that involve their destiny. We are beholden to this sense of a larger design that Nolfi has taken from Dick's story and then embedded within a romantic thriller.

Despite great chase scenes, and though the movie begins with real chemistry between the two leads—there is humor and candor and connection—the focus of the movie proves to be elsewhere. As we watch the story unfold, we find ourselves asking: How will Elise and David confront the plan? Can they? Or is it simply a given? And could it be that we as viewers are also somehow acting out our destiny? Do any of us really have free will, or is it somehow planned out for us—by parents? context? God? destiny? If we are married, for example, did we really choose our mate, or is there some more primary sense in which we were chosen for each other?

The Scriptures are full of such questions. "Work out your own salvation with fear and trembling; for it is God who is at work in you, enabling you both to will and to work for his good pleasure" (Phil. 2:12–13). Is it our work, or God's, or somehow both? "The human mind plans the way, but the LORD directs the steps" (Prov. 16:9). Do we choose our life, or is it chosen for us? The strength of *The Adjustment Bureau* is its ability to tell an adventure-filled love story that takes viewers deeper than they expect to be taken and causes them to ask a series of universal questions about life. Is there a "plan" for my life? Am I free to choose—free to alter that plan or to create a different plan or to live into that plan? Is there chance? Free will? Fate? Are we destined, and if so, by whom, or for what? These are perennial questions that the writer/director has embedded into his story, and the result is compelling.

At Fuller Seminary, we prescreened the movie twice at a nearby Cineplex that seats close to three hundred. Afterward, there were lively discussions about the film and about audience members' understanding of how destiny played out in their own lives. Was there, as Calvin, Luther, and Aquinas claimed, a secret will of God, something in addition to God's revealed will that governs our lives? At the second screening to a full house, a rabbi and an imam joined Christian theologian Rob Johnston and the movie's director, George Nolfi, for an interreligious dialogue about David and Elise's free will, or lack thereof. How did we understand the God of Abraham, Isaac, and Jacob, a God we all believe in, to direct the lives of men and women? The same quandaries proved common to us all.

The movie's questions have been present for millennia. But seldom have they been served up in such an engaging way. Here is a movie to see with family or friends and then afterward to stop at Starbucks to talk about not only Elise's and David's lives but also our own.

Dialogue Texts

> For my thoughts are not your thoughts,
>   nor are your ways my ways, says the LORD.
> For as the heavens are higher than the earth,
>   so are my ways higher than your ways
>   and my thoughts than your thoughts.
>   Isaiah 55:8–9

So then he has mercy on whomever he chooses, and he hardens the heart of whomever he chooses.

You will say to me then, "Why then does he still find fault? For who can resist his will?" But who indeed are you, a human being, to argue with God? Will what is molded say to the one who molds it, "Why have you made me like this?" Has the potter no right over the clay, to make out of the same lump one object for special use and another for ordinary use?

Romans 9:18–21

When God saw what they did, how they turned from their evil ways, God changed his mind about the calamity that he had said he would bring upon them; and he did not do it.

Jonah 3:10

After God pronounces to Moses his wrathful judgment on the Hebrews for building an idolatrous golden calf, and after Moses pleads with God not to do this, the text reads,

And the Lord changed his mind about the disaster that he planned to bring on his people.

Exodus 32:14

The human mind plans the way,
but the LORD directs the steps.

Proverbs 16:9

Discussion Questions and Clip Conversations

All clips are available for viewing at ReelSpirituality.com/Books/God-In-The-Movies. We have also listed the timestamp range of the scenes for your reference.

1. "David Concedes" [11:30–14:15]. How much of this speech is applicable in the lives of our political and religious leaders today? How might it relate to your own personal life, if at all? In one sense, have many of us become "company" men and women? Is this what Christ calls us to be?

2. "Meeting Thompson" [1:03:05–1:07:20]. Who writes history? Christians often portray history as a story written by God, with humans as characters playing their roles in God's story. What is the stance of *The Adjustment Bureau*? How much do you agree with the argument made

by Agent Thompson? Are humans entirely responsible for the atrocities referred to in his speech? Is the Chairman's adjustment bureau justified in taking credit for the Renaissance, the Enlightenment, and the Scientific Revolution? Must one choose between human freedom and divine providence/destiny?

3. "The Chairman's Decision" [1:36:40–1:38:53]. How does the Chairman of the adjustment bureau compare to your understanding of God? What are attributes the Chairman shares with the God of the Bible? Does the "Chairman" (God) have a plan for your life? How detailed is it? Can the plan be changed by humans? What do you make of the Chairman's decision in the end? Do you think the God of the Bible would have made the same decision? Why or why not?

4. What role does "chance" play in the film? What would have happened if Elise had never run into the men's restroom on the day of David's speech? Or if Harry hadn't dozed off in the morning? How do these events relate to your thoughts on the interplay between chance and faith in human life? Instead of being in opposition, can God's providence work in tandem with human free will to create meaning in our chaotic world? How? Would you understand this same "joint action" to be present when evil happens?

5. Do you think David and Elise have made the right choice? How would you know if their plan is better than the original plan approved by the Chairman? Does the movie suggest an answer? How would we know God's master plan for our life, assuming there is one?

Bonus Material

Philip K. Dick, the author of the short story "Adjustment Team," is often described by critics as a fictionalizing philosopher. Metaphysical questions and philosophical discussions are recurring themes in his stories, several of which have been adapted for the screen (e.g., *Minority Report*, *Blade Runner*, *Total Recall*).

Dick's short story was adapted for the screen and directed by George Nolfi, who graduated from Princeton University summa cum laude and was awarded a Marshall Scholarship at Oxford University. After studying philosophy there, he switched to a PhD program in political science at UCLA. But Nolfi had a chance encounter with Hollywood (much like the hero of *The Adjustment Bureau*) and decided that his destiny was in the film industry. Both thoughtful and unassuming, Nolfi has been a guest several times in our film and theology class at Fuller Theological Seminary, helping students in their dialogue with the movie about God's providence and humankind's free will.

Selected Additional Resources

Rodriguez, William. Review of *The Adjustment Bureau. Journal of Religion and Film* 15, no. 2 (October 2011). https://www.unomaha.edu/jrf/Vol15no2 /Reviews/AdjustmentBureau.html.

Catherine M. Barsotti and Mathew P. John

32

Calvary

Ireland/UK, 2014
102 Minutes, Feature, Color
Actors: Brendan Gleeson, Chris O'Dowd,
    Kelly Reilly, Aidan Gillen, Dylan Moran,
    Isaach De Bankolé, M. Emmet Walsh,
    Domhnall Gleeson, Marie-Josée Croze
Director: John Michael McDonagh
Screenwriter: John Michael McDonagh
Rated: R (sexual references, language, brief strong violence, some drug use)

Christ Figure
The Church, Doubt, Faith/
Belief, Father/Daughter
Relationships, the Nature
of the Human, Sin and
Its Consequences

Synopsis and Theological Reflection

In the little over one hundred years of filmmaking, Jesus Christ has been made the subject of many films. This has been done using two different genres. The first is the "Jesus" film genre, which started as early as 1902–5 with the Pathé Company's short tableau series titled *The Life and Passion of Jesus Christ*. Cecil B. DeMille's *The King of Kings* (1927) is another example. The 1960s and '70s saw a flurry of Jesus films, such as *The Gospel according to St. Matthew* (d. Pasolini, 1964), *Jesus Christ Superstar* (d. Jewison, 1973), and *Jesus of Nazareth* (d. Zeffirelli, 1977). More recent films include the infamous *The Last Temptation of Christ* (d. Scorsese, 1988), the mixed animation of *The*

201

Miracle Maker (d. Hayes and Sokolov, 2000), and the blockbuster *The Passion of the Christ* (d. Gibson, 2004).

The second genre of films is the "Christ figure" genre. Used in literature for centuries, a Christ figure or Christ image draws allusions in multiple ways between a character of the story and the story of Jesus Christ. Thus, the character might show unconditional kindness and forgiveness; perform miracles, especially the healing of others; fight for justice; be guided by the spirit of a father; be surrounded by those who want (or don't want) to learn from him or her; or walk the path to their own death—sacrificing themselves for others out of love or for causes larger than themselves. This death can sometimes take the visual shape of a crucifixion. And some novels and films even include a resurrection of some kind. Certainly this genre has a whole host of possible film examples, from the eccentric *One Flew over the Cuckoo's Nest* (d. Forman, 1975), to the classic *Superman* (d. Donner, 1978) and all its reimagined sequels (1980, 1983, 1987, 2006, 2016), to the beautifully black Christ figure of John Coffey (note his initials) in *The Green Mile* (d. Darabont, 1999), to even an animated portrayal in *The Iron Giant* (d. Bird, 1999). With the title *Calvary*, it is not surprising that in this film we meet another Christ figure.

In *Calvary* we meet Father James (Brendan Gleeson) in a most unusual way—in his church's confessional listening to a parishioner talk about the horrible and traumatic sexual abuse he suffered from a priest. Even more shocking is his promise to kill Father James in seven days' time, on Sunday, at the beach. His reasoning is that by killing Father James, a good priest, he will make more of a statement to the Catholic Church than by killing a bad priest. It will be more parallel to his own situation, in which he, an innocent boy, was assaulted. Somehow, this might set the scales of justice right. Father James has a week to carry this cross, and we as viewers journey with him.

The director, John Michael McDonagh, gives us many cues—music (e.g., the repeated instrumental tune, the lyrics of "The Dolphins" by Fred Neil, and the closing beautiful lament "Subo" by Rolando Amadeo Valladares), visuals, and colors—to help us enter into this journey of humor and despair, faith and doubt, death and life. For example, the everyday struggles of the characters are often shot in red, orange, and yellow tones, while Father James is often seen through green and blue tones. Humanity's brokenness, suffering, and despair are juxtaposed with the beautiful green-blue landscapes and seascapes of Ireland.

In that "holy" week we meet many of Father James's parishioners and colleagues, a motley crew to say the least. His colleagues include an officious supervising bishop looking for a loophole through which his priest can go to the police and a vocationless fellow priest who should have been

Father James, on the way to Calvary

an accountant. His band of parishioners include Jack, the local butcher, who has given his wife, Veronica, a black eye for having an affair with Simon, her lover; an elderly American writer who is thinking about taking his own life; Inspector Stanton, a closeted homosexual; Leo, a male prostitute; Milo, a quirky young man deciding between suicide and joining the army; Michael Fitzgerald, a pompous and empty millionaire; Dr. Frank Harte, a cynical doctor; Brendan Lynch, the pub owner; Mícheál, Father James's altar boy and a budding painter; and Freddie Joyce, a mass murderer whom Father James visits in prison. Father James serves these twelve human beings—perhaps with irony or a joke, sometimes with a hug or an admonition, with a question or a prayer, and with the Eucharist. These are his disciples, and one of them will betray him. Father James may be earthy and gritty like his community, but he is always there for them.

Besides his parishioners, two important characters enter into Father James's walk to the cross. His daughter, Fiona (Kelly Reilly), comes from London for a short visit. The bandages on her wrists betray her failed suicide attempt. Her explanation: another man has left her. Fiona is adrift since her "mum's" death and her "da's" subsequent call to the priesthood. Again, can Father James show his own daughter unconditional love so that she may be healed and their relationship restored? Their conversations, woven through the film, are a lesson in love.

Called to the hospital, Father James meets Teresa (Marie-Josée Croze). Her husband is on life support after a terrible car accident, and she has requested a priest to perform the last rites. They chat in the chapel about life, death, and faith. While Father James is there to comfort and pray with her, we sense that he is also there, in this week, to witness and be strengthened by her beautiful and strong faith.

However, his ministry is not without its bruises, both metaphorical and physical. Disappointments, losses, and accusations take their toll, and Father James goes on a bender, ending in a pub brawl. Battered in body and soul, he packs his bag to fly to Dublin. At the airport he meets Teresa, who is taking her husband's body home. Again they talk, and again her hard-won faith strengthens his, and he returns to his parish.

The next time we see Father James, he is dressing in his room. He leaves for the beach; it is Sunday. On his way, he meets several of his parishioners who are looking for him. He also calls Fiona. They forgive each other (an underrated virtue, according to Father James) and express their love for each other. He walks to the beach and sees little Mícheál painting. He waits for the one who seeks to take his life. The man arrives, dressed in a white shirt and carrying a gun. After a short conversation about the need for such a killing, the world's detachment from so many damaged children, and the pain of this abused adult, the killer shoots Father James in his side. Mícheál drops his brush and runs toward them, but Father James tells the boy to run away. When Father James tells his attacker it is not too late to stop, he is told to say his prayers. When Father James replies that he has, he is shot again. During the slow motion of this final sequence, all the parishioners flash before the viewer. Father James has come to the beach ("taken up his cross") for all of them. As the credits roll, we see Fiona visiting the perpetrator in prison, practicing the virtue of forgiveness for which her father lived.

Calvary is a spiritual drama, but obviously not of the Sunday-school variety. Rather, it weds the beauty of Ireland, the gritty ministry and ultimate faithfulness of Father James, the deep laments of his parishioners, dark Irish humor, and the "highly underrated virtue" of forgiveness. While it is not exactly typical commercial film fare, it will provide much grist for the mill long after the credits roll. Some viewers might experience the transcendent in that grist. Others might even catch a glimpse of Jesus.

Dialogue Texts

Then Jesus said, "Father, forgive them; for they do not know what they are doing."

Luke 23:34

One of the criminals who were hanged there kept deriding him and saying, "Are you not the Messiah? Save yourself and us!" But the other rebuked him, saying, "Do you not fear God, since you are under the same sentence of condemnation?

And we indeed have been condemned justly, for we are getting what we deserve for our deeds, but this man has done nothing wrong." Then he said, "Jesus, remember me when you come into your kingdom." He replied, "Truly I tell you, today you will be with me in Paradise."

Luke 23:39–43

For while we were still weak, at the right time Christ died for the ungodly. Indeed, rarely will anyone die for a righteous person—though perhaps for a good person someone might actually dare to die. But God proves his love for us in that while we still were sinners Christ died for us. Much more surely then, now that we have been justified by his blood, will we be saved through him from the wrath of God. For if while we were enemies, we were reconciled to God through the death of his Son, much more surely, having been reconciled, will we be saved by his life. But more than that, we even boast in God through our Lord Jesus Christ, through whom we have now received reconciliation.

Romans 5:6–11

What I am saying, brothers and sisters, is this: flesh and blood cannot inherit the kingdom of God, nor does the perishable inherit the imperishable. Listen, I will tell you a mystery! We will not all die, but we will all be changed, in a moment, in the twinkling of an eye, at the last trumpet. For the trumpet will sound, and the dead will be raised imperishable, and we will be changed. For this perishable body must put on imperishability, and this mortal body must put on immortality. When this perishable body puts on imperishability, and this mortal body puts on immortality, then the saying that is written will be fulfilled:

> "Death has been swallowed up in victory."
> "Where, O death, is your victory?
> Where, O death, is your sting?"

1 Corinthians 15:50–55

Discussion Questions and Clip Conversations

All clips are available for viewing at ReelSpirituality.com/Books/God-In -The-Movies. We have also listed the timestamp range of the scenes for your reference.

1. "Do not despair; one of the thieves was saved. Do not presume; one of the thieves was damned." This quote from St. Augustine starts the film. Why does the filmmaker include it? How does it speak into the film's story?

2. "Life and Death, Which Is Unfair" [37:53–41:54]. After performing the last rites, Father James and Teresa, the wife of the dead man, talk about death and faith. What strikes you about their conversation? Who is comforting whom?

3. "Do I Look Like a Monster?" [47:16–51:10]. Father James visits Freddie Joyce. Their conversation is filled with questions of forgiveness, the nature of our humanity, and the character of God. Compare your own views of these themes with the characters' views. Given the color scheme noted above, what do you notice about the colors in the prison cell, and might this be a visual representation of the human and divine? The role of Freddie Joyce is played by Brendan Gleeson's real-life son and accomplished actor Domhnall Gleeson. They are in only one scene together, but it is stunning. (Note: every conversation between Father James and one of his parishioners is worthy of further discussion!)

4. "The Walk to the Beach and the Underrated Virtue" [1:24:20–1:36:34]. Father James calls his daughter. How does their conversation strike you? Is it just a conversation or also the practice of the virtue about which they talk? When Father James is shot, we see all his parishioners. How did you feel? What did you think? Why does the filmmaker end with Fiona visiting her father's attacker in prison? Reflect on the last frame of the film and the quote from St. Augustine that started the film.

Bonus Material

John Michael McDonagh and Brendan Gleeson came up with the idea for *Calvary* during the filming of *The Guard*. The screenplay was created specifically for Gleeson, who helped to develop the character of Father James. McDonagh commented in an *IndieWire* interview about his intentions for the film: "There are probably films in development about priests which involve abuse. My remit [typical response] is to do the opposite of what other people do, and I wanted to make a film about a good priest." Again speaking to *IndieWire* he noted, "Brendan once said, 'Great art should be about making you feel less alone,' and this is entirely the way I feel about things." In a *Los Angeles Times* interview, Gleeson said, "What if you had dedicated your life to something [only] to be included in all the bile and vitriol that's associated with pedophilia? It's a smirch that never goes away. . . . If you dedicated yourself to serving the good, how would you cope with that?"

The film had its world premiere at the 2014 Sundance Film Festival. It also made its European and Irish premieres that year at the Berlin International

Film Festival (winning the Ecumenical Jury Prize) and the Jameson Dublin International Film Festival (winning Best Film, Best Lead Actor, and Best Screenplay). The film was received with critical acclaim. From the *London Guardian*: "Gleeson is majestic. . . . Here, at least, is a Christ we can relate to." Los Angeles auxiliary bishop Robert Barron wrote that the film "shows, with extraordinary vividness, what authentic spiritual shepherding looks like and how it feels for a priest to have a shepherd's heart."

Selected Additional Resources

Bishop Robert Barron of Los Angeles talks about *Calvary*: https://youtu.be /nx2CGOoRSTw.

Brendan Gleeson and John Michael McDonagh speak to NPR's Bob Edwards: https://youtu.be/yX6QeSMpuFs. Gleeson reveals that he was "touched" by a Christian Brother priest during his childhood. They also talk about the Catholic Church of Ireland and the religious impulse and search for meaning.

Catherine M. Barsotti

33

Get Low

US, 2010
103 Minutes, Feature, Color
Actors: Robert Duvall, Bill Murray, Sissy
    Spacek, Lucas Black, Bill Cobbs, Gerald
    McRaney
Director: Aaron Schneider
Screenwriters: Chris Provenzano, C. Gaby Mitchell
Rated: PG-13 (some mature thematic material, brief violent content)

Forgiveness
Confession, Peace,
Repentance

Synopsis and Theological Reflection

During his long career, Robert Duvall has given life to a host of memorable, eccentric characters—from the recluse Boo Radley in *To Kill a Mockingbird* to the insecure major Frank Burns in *MASH*; from the chilling lieutenant colonel Kilgore in *Apocalypse Now* and the lieutenant colonel "Bull" Meechum in *The Great Santini* to the self-proclaimed apostle EF who baptizes himself in *The Apostle*. And then there is his Oscar-winning performance in *Tender Mercies* as Mac Sledge, a broken-down singer who finds God through the love of another. In the 2009 independent film *Get Low*, Duvall introduces us to the backwoods hermit Felix Bush.

The movie's ostensible plot concerns a mysterious, crotchety recluse who has, after forty years, become tired of the townspeople speculating about him and his past. All they really know of him is his "No Damn Trespassing— Beware of Mule" sign, with his shotgun to back it up. So Felix, who hasn't shaved since becoming a hermit, comes to town with a plan. He first approaches a minister and asks him to preside over his funeral—to be carried out while he is still alive! When the flummoxed clergyman doesn't agree to his request, Felix is forced to instead hire the failing funeral-home owner Frank Quinn (Bill Murray) to create the funeral party. Felix wants to invite anyone and everyone from the surrounding area to tell their tall tales about him as part of the ceremony's reminiscences.

But Robert Duvall's character has other plans for the funeral as well, plans that slowly unfold throughout the movie as he interacts with the droll Quinn, his innocent assistant Buddy Robinson (Lucas Black), and two friends who knew him in days long gone—the Reverend Charlie Jackson (Bill Cobbs) and the widowed Mattie Darrow, a long-ago girlfriend wonderfully played by Sissy Spacek. Much of the fun in seeing the movie is watching consummate actors with pitch-perfect portrayals relishing their roles and enjoying the company of others similarly accomplished. In particular, the interaction between the sarcastic Frank (Murray) and the cranky Felix (Duvall) is a delight to behold. As Duvall portrays him, Felix is a mixture of orneriness, resilience, and grief, with a hint of menace thrown in for good measure. But we do know that though Felix is aware of his larger-than-life status among his neighbors, he is never fooled into confusing that myth with his reality. He is not seeking continued notoriety by the live funeral; something deeper is at play. His very humanity is at stake.

Preparations for the live funeral turn to eliciting the services of Reverend Jackson, someone out of Felix's past who is privy to the recluse's secret. By this point in the story, the viewer has come to care deeply about this old man who is suffering from some mysterious ailment—of body and soul. The story's pacing is purposely slow, giving time and space for Duvall to explore the wounded but wily soul of Felix Bush. And as with other of Duvall's roles, what the viewer experiences is the privilege of being ushered deeply into the mystery of another human being. As the credits roll, our feelings of sadness, joy, humor, and even reverence for life have been awakened. We have encountered life at a deep level.

The story was developed from the legends surrounding Depression-era eccentric Felix Breazeale, who lived alone with his mule and his shotgun in the backwoods of East Tennessee. Before dying, he did, in fact, throw himself a "living funeral," with lively music and a raffle to give his land away to help

Felix and Mattie: forgiveness and reconciliation

attract a crowd. It is said that thousands came to the event, and thus many stories about the man sprang up over time.

It is this "rural legend" that provides the movie's screenwriters with their basic plotline. But the story, as is often the case, is really about something else. Plotlines alone are not sufficient; their details must be shaped by a perspective, a lens through which the story can be viewed. A successfully told story must have a theme, a hook, an interpretive point of view through which we understand the events that happen. And so it is with *Get Low*. The plot is simply the frame on which to hang a more important exploration of the meaning of confession and forgiveness.

Felix has tried to atone for his past by punishing himself—banishing himself, to be more precise. He has tried to do good deeds as a form of penance. But the recluse comes to realize that it is only through confession that forgiveness can happen and humanity be restored. This is something he alone can do; but it is not something that can be done alone. It is difficult to portray convincingly on the screen the spiritual practice of confession. But Duvall reveals effectively to viewers both the yearning for it and its transforming power. As Felix speaks at his own funeral, secrets are revealed, truths told, and relationships given a chance at restoration. That is a lot to accomplish for one actor and one speech! But you believe Felix because you believe Duvall. You sense, as Roger Ebert suggests, that "Felix must have been rehearsing that speech for years."

To be sure, *Get Low* is not as explicitly religious as two of Duvall's other movies, *Tender Mercies* and *The Apostle*. Perhaps it is best to speak of the movie as having a "spirituality of everyday life." Forgiveness remains on the horizontal level. But though the spirituality remains in the lower case, it is nonetheless grace-filled and profound. Felix's final revelatory speech at his funeral is just that—something that provides perspective and new possibility both for those at the funeral and for the film audience watching. Some may even think of the words of Paul: "If anyone has caused pain . . . you should forgive and console him, so that he may not be overwhelmed by excessive sorrow. So I urge you to reaffirm your love to him" (2 Cor. 2:5–8).

Felix tried to forgive himself. In the end, it could only be a community event.

Dialogue Texts

> Happy are those whose transgression is forgiven,
> whose sin is covered.
>
> Psalm 32:1

Now in Jerusalem by the Sheep Gate there is a pool, called in Hebrew Beth-zatha, which has five porticoes. In these lay many invalids—blind, lame, and paralyzed. One man was there who had been ill for thirty-eight years. When Jesus saw him lying there and knew that he had been there a long time, he said to him, "Do you want to be made well?" The sick man answered him, "Sir, I have no one to put me into the pool when the water is stirred up; and while I am making my way, someone else steps down ahead of me." Jesus said to him, "Stand up, take your mat and walk." At once the man was made well, and he took up his mat and began to walk.

John 5:2–9

If anyone has caused pain . . . you should forgive and console him, so that he may not be overwhelmed by excessive sorrow. So I urge you to reaffirm your love to him.

2 Corinthians 2:5–8

Discussion Questions and Clip Conversations

All clips are available for viewing at ReelSpirituality.com/Books/God-In-The -Movies. We have also listed the timestamp range of the scenes for your reference.

1. "Get Low" [08:50–11:05]. Felix walks into church to talk to Rev. Gus Horton (note the visual images that surround them). He says, "About time for me to get low—down to business." What other meanings might "get low" have in this film? As Reverend Gus and Felix "get low," their conversation revolves around peace with God and forgiveness. With whose working definition of forgiveness does our culture most identify? Whose definition do you most identify with? Why? Why does Felix walk out angry?

2. "Confession and Forgiveness Revisited" [51:00–56:00; 57:17–58:30]. Felix visits his old friend Rev. Charlie Jackson at the church Felix built many years ago. Again the conversation centers on confession and forgiveness, but this time not just to/from God but to/from someone else. Compare the minister's and Felix's responses to your own view of confession and forgiveness. In this scene Buddy is also present. What new view of Felix does he receive from meeting Reverend Jackson and being in the church? How might forgiveness and beauty interact? Lastly, on his way home Felix goes to the grave of someone and says, "They keep talking about forgiveness. Ask Jesus for forgiveness. I never did nothing to him." Is Felix being heretical, sacrilegious, or truthful?

3. "Felix Really Gets Low" [1:23:00–1:36:00]. In this segment, after Felix's introduction by Charlie (Reverend Jackson), we hear Felix's confession and request for forgiveness (Duvall rehearsed it once and then shot it—once). What do you notice about Reverend Jackson's introduction of Felix? What can we learn from his words? What has Felix learned about confession and forgiveness by this time? What does he say about his not wanting forgiveness in the past and the consequences of such a choice? From whom does he ask forgiveness? Do the director and screenwriters want the viewer to think that forgiveness finally comes for Felix? (Think of Mattie's response, the community's response, the approach of a woman dressed in white when everyone is gone, and the final shot of Buddy with his baby.)

Bonus Material

Robert Duvall's father was a career officer in the navy, reaching the rank of rear admiral, so Duvall grew up in a military family that moved frequently (he was born in San Diego and spent his early years in Annapolis). But Duvall's extended family was rooted in Virginia, where he now lives with his wife on a farm. He graduated from Principia College as a drama/liberal arts major. The school's current byline is "At Principia, everyone is trying to understand God better. Whether you're confident Christian Science is the truth or have more questions than answers, you'll find a campus full of people ready to share ideas and support your spiritual growth."

Duvall's parents pushed him into drama, thinking that might be the only way he would graduate. Academics wasn't his forte. His first experience of acting was as a harlequin clown in a full-length mime play set to Stravinsky music! After graduation he served in the army for two years, but when approached about officer training school, he declined. He had been bitten by the acting bug and headed to New York, where he worked in live theater for many years (his first roommates were Dustin Hoffman and Gene Hackman).

Aaron Schneider was a cinematographer—*Kiss the Girls* (1997), *Simon Birch* (1998), and *Titanic* (1997)—until he wrote and directed *Two Soldiers*, an adaptation of a William Faulkner short story. It won the Oscar for Best Short Film in 2004. *Get Low* was his directorial debut of a feature-length film.

Selected Additional Resources

A. O. Scott's review of the film in the *New York Times*, "How Can You Enjoy Your Own Funeral? For Starters, Don't Die" (July 29, 2010), is worth reading to get a glimpse of a living legend in acting, Robert Duvall (who made this film at age 79): http://www.nytimes.com/2010/07/30/movies/30getlow.html.

Mary Pols's review for *Time* magazine, "*Get Low*: Robert Duvall Raises the Bar" (July 30, 2010), also sheds light on the actor and the film and its center of power and meaning: http://content.time.com/time/arts/article/0,8599,2007471,00.html.

There are various online videos of Duvall speaking about the film, his vocation and career, his approach to acting, and his love for all things Argentinian (including his wife and family), as well as for Spanish and tango. Here are some of the best:

- Duvall talking to Peter Travers about the film, about working with Bill Murray and Marlon Brando, and more: https://www.youtube.com/watch?v=POvmZ3-MUaQ
- A shorter interview with Duvall about the film ("DP/30: The Oral History of Hollywood"): https://youtu.be/aHR-sbiZYj4
- A free-form conversation at the SXSW Film Festival in 2010 with Duvall, director Aaron Schneider, producer Dean Zanuck, Bill Murray, and Sissy Spacek, including an interesting discussion of the meaning of "get low" (i.e., getting down to business, dying and being laid to rest in the ground, humbling yourself before God as in confession): https://youtu.be/GtWleEm-uR4
- Allison Krause singing "Lay My Burden Down," the closing song in *Get Low*: https://youtu.be/hayb9mZSZDQ?list=RDhayb9mZSZDQ
- Duvall singing one of his favorite hymns, "I Love to Tell the Story," with Emmylou Harris: https://youtu.be/qO7Qrhss_j8

Catherine M. Barsotti

34

Life of Pi

US, 2012
127 Minutes, Feature, Color
Actors: Suraj Sharma, Irrfan Khan, Ayush
Tandon, Adil Hussain, Tabu, Rafe Spall,
Gérard Depardieu
Director: Ang Lee
Screenwriter: David Magee (based on the novel *Life of Pi* by Yann Martel)
Rated: PG

Theology of Religions
Creation Mediating
God's Presence,
the Meaning of
Life, Wonder

Synopsis and Theological Reflection

Sometimes I tell people that I became a Christian because of a Buddhist monk. They usually laugh when I say that, but it's true. I was a sophomore in college when my creative writing professor sent us on a journey to hear the Buddhist monk Thich Nhat Hanh speak in downtown Washington, DC. Going to an event like that was outside my comfort zone because I grew up attending an African Methodist Episcopal church. The idea of visiting a Buddhist temple was not so much sacrilegious as it was transgressive, given my own cultural norms. But I went anyway, and as a result, I felt the presence of God in a way that I hadn't felt before in my young adult life. I felt God in the stillness as Hanh's voice gently cracked the hollow yet crowded room. And I saw God in the fallen cherry blossoms lying on the wet pavement as I walked home in the rain. Even though it was in a most unexpected place and in a faith tradition other than my own, I believe that Thich Nhat Hanh introduced me to a different way of experiencing God's peace, beauty, and provision. I confessed a faith in Christ not long after that experience.

For some, the film *Life of Pi* might be problematic because it seems polytheistic. That is certainly one way to read the film. But my appreciation for this film stems from my own experience that God can do the miraculous even when clouded in the mystery of other religious expressions. In *Life of Pi*, we are introduced to Piscene Patel (self-nicknamed "Pi" for short), a man recounting his 227 days of survival after being shipwrecked alone with a Bengal tiger at sixteen years of age. Pi narrates his story to a journalist who hopes that Pi's story will help him believe in God.

Through various flashbacks, we learn of Pi's affection for God and his experiences of the transcendent, both of which developed for him as a young boy growing up in India at his parents' zoo. Early on, Pi understands God's presence in unconventional ways. He is introduced to the idea of God through the Hindu god of Krishna, but he also meets Christ in the mountains. When he wanders into a Catholic church on a dare, a priest gives him water to drink, and it is here that God becomes approachable in very practical ways. God continues to reveal himself in Pi's life, later through the name of Allah, the sound of the word bringing him closer to God's peace and serenity.

In the movie, there is not a competition between these three faiths. Rather, these different faith traditions all open Pi's eyes to the importance of faith in God. Pi understands that his faith must be tested, which indeed it is after his family decides to pack up the zoo and sail from India to Canada. During a bad storm, the ship is lost, killing his entire family as well as the animals from their zoo—all, that is, except for a Bengal tiger, a zebra, a hyena, and an orangutan. Through many unbelievable events, Pi and the tiger (whom he comes to call Richard Parker) ultimately survive.

Once Pi is finally rescued, he must give an account of what happened at sea to the officials. They have difficulty believing his story, stating, "We need a story we can all believe. The truth." Pi recounts the same story a different way in which the animals in his boat serve as possible metaphors for the people in his life. While this story may be more believable for the officials, it is far more gruesome. It also brings to bear the real presence of depravity within the human soul. Pi gives the officials a choice of which story to believe, for in the end, both versions contain a similar message about survival and provision through great tragedy.

When comparing Pi's two stories, it is interesting to think about them in the context of other biblical stories on which we base our faith. For example, many believe that some of the stories in Genesis are actually derivative from preexisting Eastern literature. Thomas Mann, the German novelist, commented about the Noah story in his *The Book of the Torah: The Narrative Integrity of the Pentateuch*: "In the story of Atra-Hasis, a tremendous flood covers the earth, though one man is saved through the help of one of the gods—a story obviously very similar to the flood story in Genesis." Mann argues that the possibility of biblical stories being adaptations does not negate the validity of their words; rather, these earlier stories create a tangible narrative for the important spiritual themes and moral lessons that have become basic to our faith in God.

Life of Pi leaves out the particulars of each of the religions presented in the film, and no comparison between them is attempted. The director, Ang Lee, is directing us toward a different conclusion than the superiority of one faith over another. Just as Pi's story about his survival with a tiger may sound outrageous to some, some of the stories in the Bible may sound equally implausible to others. Yet in both cases, the stories are meant to teach lessons about truths that resonate with humankind. Biblical stories can too easily become romanticized (think of the story of Noah; see chap. 35 by Kutter Callaway on the movie *Noah*), and the real-life connection with sinful humanity can become lost in the spectacle. In a world in which skepticism and reason often seek to discredit any and all walks of faith, perhaps *Life of Pi* is asking us to consider how the religious stories of others might draw us closer to God.

Dialogue Texts

Who is like you, O Lord, among the gods?

Exodus 15:11

There is none like you among the gods, O Lord,
nor are there any works like yours.
All the nations you have made shall come
and bow down before you, O Lord,
and shall glorify your name.

Psalm 86:8–9

O give thanks to the God of gods,
for his steadfast love endures forever.

Psalm 136:2

Athenians, I see how extremely religious you are in every way. For as I went through the city and looked carefully at the objects of your worship, I found among them an altar with the inscription, "To an unknown god."

Acts 17:22–23

Because you know that the testing of your faith produces endurance.

James 1:3

Discussion Questions and Clip Conversations

All clips are available for viewing at ReelSpirituality.com/Books/God-In -The-Movies. We have also listed the timestamp range of the scenes for your reference.

1. Have you ever had an encounter with God that was outside of a church or a traditional place of worship? What was that experience like? How did it connect you to God? Have you ever experienced God in unexpected places? How did you explain your encounter to others?

2. "No One Knows God until He Is Introduced to Us" [12:23–17:55]. Young Pi says that the Hindu gods were his superheroes. He later says a prayer to Krishna, thanking him for introducing him to Jesus Christ. How does this prayer bear with the Christian belief in Jesus's divinity? Adult Pi maintains that he is a Hindu Catholic. Can such a thing exist, or is Pi misguided? Is it possible to be understanding and sympathetic toward other religions while still remaining rooted in and convinced by the Christian faith? Does finding value and beauty in other religions necessarily have to negate Christianity?

3. "Whatever Comes . . ." [59:35–1:04:05]. In this scene, Pi prays for wisdom and God gives it to him by showing him how to survive. Later (see 1:09:54–1:13:16), Pi catches a large fish and thanks Vishnu, one of the three deities in Hinduism, for coming in the form of a fish. For Pi, God has provided and saved their lives. Was this an act of God even though Pi prayed to Vishnu? Is it contradictory for him to see this provision as a gift from God? (You might recall C. S. Lewis's character Emeth in his Narnia story *The Last Battle*, in which Lewis posits a similar possibility.)

4. Do you see any parallels with how Paul relates to the Athenians in Acts 17? How is Paul able to teach them about God by mentioning gods that are already familiar to them? How is Paul able to maintain his faith while engaging with a different belief system? What can you conclude

about God's wider presence? For another interesting account where the Hebrew-Christian God speaks to a nonbeliever, and Josiah, a faithful king, is killed for not being open to this possibility, see 2 Chronicles 35:20–27.

5. "I Surrender!" [1:26:58–1:34:05]. In this powerful scene, Pi is trapped in a fierce storm. First, he praises God for the beauty of the storm; then he gets angry with God when he and Richard Parker are almost capsized. At the end of the scene, Pi acknowledges that they are dying and yet thanks God for giving him life. Are Pi's responses consistent with the Christian faith? What biblical stories have similar responses to that of Pi? Can you think of any nonbiblical stories that have similar themes? In what ways can these stories point to God's nature? Can you think of events in your own life when there was praise, then anger, then surrender?

6. "We Need a Simple Story" [1:48:45–1:56:57]. Pi tells the officials a story that is closer to the truth but is much more gruesome. After telling the story, he says to the reporter, "Neither story explains what caused the sinking of the ship. In both stories, the ship sinks, my family dies, and I suffer. Which story do you prefer?" The writer responds and says the story with the tiger is the better story, to which Pi replies, "And so it goes with God." Both of Pi's stories communicate truth—one focuses on the violence and suffering of Pi, while the animal story highlights the good that came through his experience. What is the possibility that God can be found in both the gruesome story and the fantastic story? How can we learn about God and about ourselves through such stories? How is the biblical narrative a tangle of such stories?

Bonus Material

It took Ang Lee a grueling four years to complete *Life of Pi*. It paid off, as the film won four Academy Awards in 2013, including Best Director and Best Cinematography. Lee said that after reading the book he did not see it as a film. It was only after considering filming it in 3-D that he began to see the story unfold in cinematic form. Most of the film was shot in a water tank in Taiwan, and the tiger was primarily computer generated. Tobey Maguire, who had starred in one of Lee's earlier films, *The Ice Storm*, originally played the role of the journalist. However, Lee decided that he was too big of an actor and decided to reshoot his scenes with the British actor Rafe Spall.

In a Reuters interview, Lee says that he grew up with a Christian mother, but he does not currently think of himself as practicing a particular faith.

Of the film's spiritual content, Lee says, "I am not particularly religious. But I think we do face the question of where God is, why we are created and where does life go, why we exist. That sort of thing. . . . I think life without spirit is in the dark, it is absurd. Call it illusion or call it faith, whatever you call it, we have emotional attachment to the unknown. We yearn to find out. That is human nature. It can be, in a way, unrequited love, we don't know."

Screenwriter David Magee said he wanted to write the story from the perspective of a young child looking to understand God through the lens of different religions without it becoming a lecture in comparative religions. He says much of his inspiration for the story came from the Genesis account of Noah and from the book of Job.

Selected Additional Resources

Kendrick, Ben. "*Life of Pi* Ending Explained." *Screen Rant*, November 30, 2012. http://screenrant.com/life-of-pi-movie-ending-spoilers/.

Roark, David. Review of *Life of Pi. Christianity Today*, November 21, 2012. http://www.christianitytoday.com/ct/2012/november-web-only/life-of-pi .html.

Thompson, Ann. "Writing 'Life of Pi': David Magee Talks the Mother of Adaptations." *IndieWire*, January 2, 2013. http://www.indiewire.com/2013/01 /writing-life-of-pi-david-magee-talks-the-mother-of-adaptations-240003/.

Life of Pi raises interesting questions of innate spirituality, the search for transcendence, and how the different religious traditions respond to such questions. Readers desiring a deeper inquiry into such topics might enjoy books like those listed below.

Chittister, Joan. *Welcome to the Wisdom of the World and Its Meaning for You.* Grand Rapids: Eerdmans, 2010.

Johnston, Robert K. *God's Wider Presence: Reconsidering General Revelation.* Grand Rapids: Baker Academic, 2014.

Miller, Lisa. *The Spiritual Child: The New Science on Parenting for Health and Lifelong Thriving.* New York: St. Martin's Press, 2015.

Avril Z. Speaks

35

Noah

US, 2014	***God's Righteousness***
138 Minutes, Feature, Color	*Care of Creation,*
Actors: Russell Crowe, Jennifer Connelly,	*God's Mercy vs.*
Anthony Hopkins	*Human Judgment,*
Director: Darren Aronofsky	*Pride, Scripture, Sin and*
Screenwriters: Darren Aronofsky, Ari Handel	*Its Consequences,*
Rated: PG-13 (violence, disturbing images, brief suggestive content)	*Vocation*

Synopsis and Theological Reflection

Among other things, *Noah* is a film about humanity's inexhaustible hubris, its propensity to see justice and mercy as separate realities, and the burden of living as God's chosen representatives in a world given to violence, power, and oppression. Or, to put it differently, the film is profoundly biblical. Yes, biblical. At the end of the day, Darren Aronofsky—known for films like *Requiem for a Dream*, *The Wrestler*, and *Black Swan*—very much succeeds in making a God-affirming, creation-affirming, and even faith-affirming film. It's everything we would want in a biblical epic.

In fact, just like sermons, Passion plays, and felt boards, cinematic retellings of biblical stories like *Noah* offer us an opportunity to imaginatively explore the ways in which a collection of ancient texts can inform our basic awareness of the world today. Yet we encounter these adaptations of the biblical text as meaningful, not because of their strict fidelity to some abstract notion of biblical "accuracy," but insofar as they draw us into a story that has the capacity to transform our lives.

This is not to suggest that biblical content is irrelevant. Rather, it is simply to recognize that, as it concerns both the Bible and biblical films, the core measure of a story's power and meaning does not reside in its rigid adherence to historical or linguistic data. So whether we are watching a film like *Noah* or reading a text like Genesis 6–9, our primary focus should be on clarity rather than fidelity—that is, on the interpretive insight these stories offer, the unique vision of the world each story lays bare. Whether the ark landed on Mt. Ararat is less important.

In Aronofsky's retelling, it is clearly the Creator who orchestrates everything that takes place in *Noah*. Entire forests spring forth from nothing. Barren women become fertile. Animals journey to the ark unbidden. And everyone— even the "sons of Cain"—bear witness to these miracles. At the same time, humanity exists in a painfully obvious state of disrepair. No one—not even Noah—is innocent. And the only one who can set things right is an unwieldy, mysterious, and oftentimes silent Creator.

That Noah is entrusted with the mission of rebooting the created order says as much about this Creator as it does Noah. The Creator does indeed demand justice, but it isn't a justice that is ever divorced from mercy. So the challenge that a film like *Noah* presents to viewers is not its relative "accuracy" to the biblical text but its "faithfulness" to it. The movie's challenge concerns the God that Aronofsky imagines—a God who doesn't fit within the cozy confines of nursery rhymes about floating zoos and pretty rainbows but who does fit the biblical narrative.

We normally don't want to hear anything about this kind of God because it doesn't align with our Sunday-school memories. Even when the source of this alternative vision is the Bible itself, this kind of God makes us uncomfortable. Yet, as it always does, the biblical narrative asks us to engage these uneasy realities because life is uneasy. It prods us to see with a different set of eyes and hear with a different set of ears. And if nothing else, *Noah* offers us an opportunity to do exactly that.

Dialogue Texts

When people began to multiply on the face of the ground, and daughters were born to them, the sons of God saw that they were fair; and they took wives for themselves of all that they chose. Then the LORD said, "My spirit shall not abide in mortals forever, for they are flesh; their days shall be one hundred twenty years." The Nephilim were on the earth in those days—and also afterward—when the sons of God went in to the daughters of humans, who bore children to them. These were the heroes that were of old, warriors of renown.

Genesis 6:1–4

The LORD saw that the wickedness of humankind was great in the earth, and that every inclination of the thoughts of their hearts was only evil continually. And the LORD was sorry that he had made humankind on the earth, and it grieved him to his heart. So the LORD said, "I will blot out from the earth the human beings I have created—people together with animals and creeping things and birds of the air, for I am sorry that I have made them." But Noah found favor in the sight of the LORD.

These are the descendants of Noah. Noah was a righteous man, blameless in his generation; Noah walked with God. And Noah had three sons, Shem, Ham, and Japheth.

Genesis 6:5–10

Discussion Questions and Clip Conversations

All clips are available for viewing at ReelSpirituality.com/Books/God-In-The-Movies. We have also listed the timestamp range of the scenes for your reference.

1. "The Watchers" [20:30–23:25]. Read Genesis 6:1–4. How familiar are you with this portion of the Noah story? What elements of this story are new, foreign, or strange to you? What kind of questions does this text prod us to make as readers? What did you make of Aronofsky's interpretation of the Nephilim? What happens to the Nephilim when the deluge begins? How is God gracious to them? Why?

2. "Damned If I Don't Take What I Want" [00:01–04:45]. Read Genesis 6:5–10. What do the opening scenes tell us about the context for the story? How "dark" is the Noah story that we find in the biblical text? What does it say about who God is that God was "sorry" that he had made humankind (Gen. 6:7)? What does it mean for Noah to be "righteous" or "blameless in his generation"? Is anyone entirely "righteous" or "blameless"?

3. "Let Me Tell You a Story" [1:23:15–1:28:12]. Read Genesis 6:11–8:19. What gaps exist in the Noah story (places where the biblical author

simply leaves out information)? Are there ways to explore some of these gaps without being unfaithful to the text? Why or why not? What do you make of how Aronofsky fills these gaps? For example, how does the film shed light on the creation narrative of Genesis 1 when Noah tells this story to his family while they are on the ark?

4. "Be Fruitful and Multiply" [2:00:37–2:11:31]. Read Genesis 8:20–9:29. Is this portion of the story meant to be comforting or confounding? Why do you think Noah got drunk? Why does he curse the descendants of Ham? Does Aronofsky's film raise the same questions that the biblical text raises? If not, how are they different? If you were to make a Noah film, what would it be like? What would be important to you? What would be less important? What was most important to Aronofsky?

5. How does Noah's understanding of "righteousness" change over the course of the movie?

Bonus Material

Reel Spirituality's Kutter Callaway and Elijah Davidson had the opportunity to participate in a roundtable interview with Darren Aronofsky and Ari Handel prior to *Noah*'s release. Below is a transcript of a portion of that interview.

REEL SPIRITUALITY: What about the Noah story originally inspired you?

DARREN ARONOFSKY: Well for me it was that magical teacher I had when I was thirteen years old—Mrs. Fried—at Mark Twain Junior High School in Coney Island, Brooklyn, who was a real eccentric teacher. She wore all pink and drove a pink mustang. She said one day, "Take out a paper and pen and write something about peace." And I ended up writing a poem on Noah called "Dove." I don't know why I wrote about Noah. The one memory I had recently was an early memory before this of hearing the Noah story, and I just remember being scared actually—even though it has become powerful for kids and it's like a nursery story and there is an animal-cracker box of Noah's ark and a Playmobil set. But when you really look at the story, it is a very scary story. It is the first apocalypse story. And as a kid I remember thinking, what if I'm not good enough to be on the boat? I have wickedness and sin. Would I actually get on the boat, and what would it be like if I didn't get on it? So from the beginning I think I saw that side of the story, and when I first pitched it to Russell Crowe, I said you are not going to be in a long robe with a white beard between two giraffes. It is a very, very different story, and no one has turned it into a film. Why? Why is this one of the oldest stories ever told—one of the most famous stories ever told. Everywhere on the planet people know this story, even if it is not part of your culture. In India they have their own flood story but they know the Noah story. In China, in the Amazon, the Maya—everyone has this elemental connection to the flood story, yet it has never been on the big screen. Why? So I think that was an interesting challenge for us to bring it to life.

RS: Tell us more about the rock creatures.

DA: Well the Bible talks about the Nephilim, so we knew we had to deal with that because in Genesis 6 there is very little in there, and we had to take everything and respect everything that is in there. And when you are interpreting something that is four chapters long into a two-hour movie, you have to study almost every word. So we went back to the Hebrew and thought about all the particulars of the actual original written word and what it related to and what it meant. So when it came to the Nephilim, we spent a lot of time thinking about that—about how to bring that to life, how to make that a character in the film, and an important part of the film. There is a lot of Jewish midrash—midrash is writing and discussions about that text that have been done for thousands of years—and also a lot of other sources like the book of Enoch that talk about the Nephilim, so there were a lot of places to draw from and think about to develop the characters. Of course we had to use imagination for it. But we really wanted to try and take the big themes in the film—the ideas of mercy and justice—and figure out how to create a story for these characters. So there is kind of a flip. Whereas Noah goes from a place of justice to mercy, the Nephilim go from a place of mercy toward justice and sort of bring those themes to life.

RS: As a filmmaker, why do you think the Noah story is powerful for viewers?

DA: It all comes down to the themes that are in the story. We tried to humanize it, to put ourselves as writers into that position. To say what was going on, and how would that feel? Because I think that makes it more powerful—when you can understand it as a person. That's the beauty of cinema, and the beauty of storytelling. You can relate to a six-year-old girl growing up in Iran, or you could relate to an eighty-year-old woman in France who is dying. That's the most beautiful power of cinema, to take people and help them experience human emotion. So we had to do that. We had to figure out how Noah and his family would go through this and what it would mean to them. So we talked a little about where we found that emotion, and that came out of trying to connect with and personify God's path into some type of human form for Noah and then seeing how the family relates to that. And it was sort of like Ham, being the one who is cursed. If you look at the first moment of him in the movie when he plucks the flower, he's that naughty child we all know—the one who is just a little mischievous. And he is actually a very, very balanced character where he is sort of between what Tubal-Cain is pitching him and what Noah is raising him to be. He's walking that line that we know all kids go through those temptations and those understandings. We just tried to make it modern for an audience today to ask why those are in the Bible perhaps.

Selected Additional Resources

Callaway, Kutter. "Missing the Boat: Christian Cultural Engagement and Darren Aronofsky's *Noah*." Brehm Center website, March 31, 2014. http://www.brehmcenter.com/initiatives/reelspirituality/film/articles/missing-the-boat-christian-cultural-engagement-and-darren-aronofskys-noah.

Cooke, Phil. "Should Christians Watch a Bible Movie Directed by an Atheist?" http://www.philcooke.com/christians-watch-bible-movie-directed-atheist/.

Davidson, Elijah. Review of *Noah*. Brehm Center website, March 27, 2014. http://www.brehmcenter.com/initiatives/reelspirituality/film/reviews/noah.

Johnston, Robert K. "The Biblical Noah, Darren Aronofsky's Film *Noah*, and Viewer Response to *Noah*: The Complex Task of Responding to God's Initiative." *Ex Auditu* 31 (2015): 88–112.

Kutter Callaway

36

Of Gods and Men

Original title: *Des hommes et des dieux*
France, 2010
122 Minutes, Feature, Color
Actors: Lambert Wilson, Michael Lonsdale,
   Olivier Rabourdin
Director: Xavier Beauvois
Screenwriters: Xavier Beauvois (adaptation), Etienne Comar (scenario)
Rated: PG-13 (a momentary scene of startling wartime violence, some disturbing
   images, brief language)

Vocation
Community,
Discernment, Doubt,
Faith/Belief, Theology
of Religions

Synopsis and Theological Reflection

In the history of film, movies, especially good ones, that portray genuine faith in all its humanity and glory are few and far between. But some are spectacular pieces of art and experiences of transcendence—*The Passion of Joan of Arc* (1928), *Diary of a Country Priest* (1951), *Chariots of Fire* (1981; see chap. 3), *Tender Mercies* (1983), *The Apostle* (1997), *The End of the Affair* (1999), *Into Great Silence* (2005), and *Secret Sunshine* (2007; see chap. 24). In 2010, another film, *Of Gods and Men*, ushered viewers into an equally inspiring journey of faith and vocation.

226

Of Gods and Men is based on the true story of nine Trappist monks living in the Atlas mountain region of Algeria during the civil war years in the mid-1990s. The film topped the box office in France for three weeks, won the Grand Prix at Cannes, and inspired even steely critics with its humanity and transcendence. As the film starts, the viewer hears the monks singing Psalm 81, "Sing aloud to God our strength." Little does the viewer know how much the monks will need to live into those words, as their vocation places them between Islamist terrorists and the corrupt Algerian government as they seek to serve the poor Muslim villagers that live around their monastery. While the history of French colonialism lurks in the background and is the reason for the monastery's existence, this community of Christians is portrayed as very integrated into the lives of their Muslim neighbors, and mutual love and respect are evident.

We meet these monks more as a community than as individuals, seeing them sing the Psalms together, break bread together, garden, cook, clean, pray and study in silence, and celebrate the Eucharist together. Their daily rhythms take on a transcendent beauty. While we get glimpses of all the monks and their particular personalities, joys, and struggles, only three of the monks are really developed as characters for the viewer. First, there is the leader of the monastery, Christian (Lambert Wilson), an Arabic scholar who memorizes the Koran as well as the Christian Scripture. He agonizes with his community and seeks God's will about what they should do—leave the monastery as many from the "outside" counsel them, or stay as the villagers plead with them. Christian senses that Christ is calling them to live fully into their vocation. Then there is the gentle and humorous doctor, Luc (Michael Lonsdale), who arrives at the monastery's clinic each day with a long line of villagers waiting for medical care, parenting counsel, and even advice on love. Lastly there is Christophe, who openly struggles with his faith and literally cries out to God for assurance and peace.

Certainly the viewer will walk away with memories of the other monks, especially as they journey together through doubt, fear, peace, and joy (beautifully portrayed in their last supper in the monastery, which is spent not in silence but rather listening to Tchaikovsky's *Swan Lake*, their faces bearing all as the music sets them free for a moment, and us with them). Their journey is to live into their faith knowing where it might lead—to suffering and death. The film becomes a cinematic study of faith, obedience to God, commitment to neighbor, and the concrete meaning of service and humility. Though none of the monks wear the brightly colored WWJD wristbands of recent history, they are, in fact, seeking to know how to best follow Jesus within their vocation and context.

A peacemaking community stands firm

One additional aspect of this film demands attention as it is key to the theological understanding and spiritual experience of the film. The film is structured, like a liturgy, around music—the monks' chants (Trappist monks sing for several hours each day). But in addition to the liturgical structure, the chanting monks act as a kind of Greek chorus that comments with a collective voice on the dramatic action. The monks' chants move between praise, trust, lament, supplication, and hope as the drama unfolds. Such singing also unifies the monks even when they are at odds with each other. Check out the six or seven chants listed at the end of the film; Psalm 142 is included. I will never read it in the same way after hearing it sung in this film and thinking of the monks of Tibhirine.

I saw the film during the Lenten season the year it came out, which made it even more poignant and powerful. I left the theater thinking about the words that Christian writes in his journal (spoken as a voice-over): "Should it ever befall me, and it could happen today, to be a victim of the terrorism swallowing up all foreigners here, I would like my community, my church, my family, to remember that my life was given to God and to this country. That the Unique Master of all life was no stranger to this brutal departure." Like the season, the film was austere and yet provocative, moving me closer to actual knowledge *of* God and not just *about* God.

Dialogue Texts

Sing aloud to God our strength;
    shout for joy to the God of Jacob.

Psalm 81:1

I say, "You are gods,
   children of the Most High, all of you;
nevertheless, you shall die like mortals,
   and fall like any prince."

Psalm 82:6–7

Your life shall hang in doubt before you; night and day you shall be in dread, with no assurance of your life.

Deuteronomy 28:66

He said to them, "Why are you frightened, and why do doubts arise in your hearts?"

Luke 24:38

Those who try to make their life secure will lose it, but those who lose their life will keep it. I tell you, on that night there will be two in one bed; one will be taken and the other left. There will be two women grinding meal together; one will be taken and the other left. Then they asked him, "Where, Lord?" He said to them, "Where the corpse is, there the vultures will gather."

Luke 17:33–37

Discussion Questions and Clip Conversations

All clips are available for viewing at ReelSpirituality.com/Books/God-In -The-Movies. We have also listed the timestamp range of the scenes for your reference.

1. "Birthday Prayer" [11:10–14:10]. The whole village gathers, including the monks, for a young boy's birthday. As special guests to the party, they are invited in to pray for the future of this young life. One of the Koranic prayers is "Lord, do not burden us beyond what we have strength to bear." How does this prayer for the young boy actually pertain to the monks also? How are the prayers of this faithful Islamic community similar to and different from the prayers a Jewish community might pray at a bar mitzvah or a Christian community might pray at a confirmation service?

2. The brothers meet several times to discuss whether to leave the monastery. What do their meetings reveal about living in Christian community? How does the give-and-take of community accompany each one on their journey to a final decision (think especially of Christophe)?

3. "Sidna Aissa/The Prince of Peace" [38:05–43:25]. The monks are preparing for the Christmas Eve liturgy when the feared, violent Islamicists break into the monastery. Review Brother Christian's interaction with Fayattia, their leader. What can we learn from their interaction? Think of how the readings at dinner (35:05–37:12) may have prepared Christian for this encounter and how to live into his name.

4. Brother Luc is reading Pascal's *Pensées* and reflects on Pascal's statement, "Men never do evil so completely and cheerfully as when they do it from religious conviction." How would you reflect on this statement? How are the monks trying to live into their vocation in such a way as to counter this belief?

5. "Last Supper" [1:41:08–1:47:40]. What do you know about the ballet *Swan Lake*? Why might the director have picked this ballet to play at this point in the film? Some critics saw this scene as too sentimental and manipulative. Others experienced it as transcendent. How did it affect you as a viewer?

Bonus Material

As noted above, *Of Gods and Men* is based on the true story of nine French Trappist monks from the monastery of Tibhirine, Algeria. They led quiet lives in respect and peace with all of their Muslim neighbors even in the midst of the Algerian Civil War. In late March of 1996, seven of them were kidnapped (two survived by hiding) by the Armed Islamic Group (GIA). They were held for two months by the terrorists, in hopes of a trade for one of their own leaders. In late May, when negotiations broke down, only their heads were found. The GIA claimed full responsibility for the incident. But according to other sources, including the French secret service, the monks may have been killed in a botched rescue attempt by the Algerian army.

In 2006, with the French media covering the anniversary of this tragic event, producer Etienne Comar, a Catholic who had been fascinated by the story, wanted to use film to reflect on why they had decided to stay in Algeria despite the ongoing Algerian Civil War. In 2008, after having written a draft of the story, Comar contacted director Beauvois. Together they continued to work on the screenplay—researching (including reading the writings of two of the monks, Christian de Chergé and Christophe Lebreton), meeting with theologians, and even living (Beauvois) for a week at the Tamié Abbey in Savoie. A monastic adviser was used to add historical and liturgical content as well as to review the script for authenticity. Finally, it was sent to the families of the monks, most of whom reacted positively to the portrayal and the vision of the film.

As preparation for their roles, the actors trained for a month in singing Cistercian and Gregorian chants and spent a week living as monks at the Tamié Abbey. Lambert Wilson (Brother Christian) said that through learning to chant psalms, the actors "became brothers." Olivier Rabourdin (Brother Christophe) commented, "To chant Psalms is to breathe together, to share the Breath of Life." While each actor approached his role in different ways (learning from the writings or home videos of the monks), one actor, a non-Catholic, prepared himself by praying every day for a month. The film was shot in two months at an abandoned Benedictine monastery in Morocco.

Besides its critical and commercial success and its Grand Prix honor, as well as the Ecumenical Jury Prize at the Cannes Film Festival, the film won many other prestigious awards, including the Lumières Award for Best Film, and the César Award for Best Film and Best Cinematography. It received the 2010 National Board of Review Award for Best Foreign Language Film. It was selected as France's submission for the Academy Award for Best Foreign Language Film for 2011, but unfortunately didn't make the short list of Oscar nominees.

Selected Additional Resources

Derwahl, Freddy. *The Last Monk of Tibhirine: A True Story of Martyrdom, Faith, and Survival*. Brewster, MA: Paraclete Press, 2013.

Kiser, John W. *The Monks of Tibhirine: Faith, Love, and Terror in Algeria*. New York: St. Martin's Griffin, 2002.

Salenson, Christian. *Christian de Chergé: A Theology of Hope*. Trappist, KY: Cistercian Publications, 2012.

Listen to Bishop Robert Barron talk about the actual event and the film: https://youtu.be/fWLTZqzK6XU.

Catherine M. Barsotti

37

The Tree of Life

US, 2011
138 Minutes, Feature, Color
Actors: Brad Pitt, Sean Penn, Jessica
    Chastain
Director: Terrence Malick
Screenwriter: Terrence Malick
Rated: PG-13 (mature thematic material)

Grace vs. Nature
Creation Mediating
God's Presence, Human
Suffering, Life's Mystery,
Loss, Spirituality of
Everyday Life

Synopsis and Theological Reflection

Watching Terrence Malick's *The Tree of Life* is an event—the cinematic equivalent of going to a U2 concert or the NBA Finals. Not all will want to do it, but for the devotees, it is magical, perhaps even sublime. Malick, now over seventy, is iconic—an auteur with a distinctive vision and cinematic style who in forty years made only five movies (*The Tree of Life* being his fifth). Shy in public but personable on the set; gentle, yet highly focused; mystical, but grounded in the everyday; obsessive with regard to detail, while open to wonder and the spontaneous, Malick has become a cinematic legend in his own time. Known for his breathtaking images, his whispered voice-over narration that reveals a character's inner thoughts, and his meticulously crafted sets, Malick has returned time and again to explore the place of humankind within a sacred universe. His has been a spiritual gaze.

One of the most personal of his movies, *The Tree of Life* won the Palme d'Or prize for Best Film at the Cannes Film Festival the year it came out. Finding inspiration for the movie in his own autobiography (he too had a brother tragically die when young), Malick actively worked on the script for over a decade. And even when the shooting was over, editing took another three years. Such is the care with which Malick brought his understanding of life to the screen.

The movie opens with a quotation from the book of Job:

> Where were you when I laid the foundations of the Earth? . . .
> When the morning stars sang together, and all the sons of
> God shouted for joy?
>
> Job 38:4, 7

Here is God's response to Job, who had questioned the divine as to why he, a righteous man with a caring and good family, should suffer such grievous loss. Job is never given an answer to life's pain and seeming capriciousness. But within nature, he does encounter the Answerer, the Creator of life. And that is enough. Life remains mysterious; evil continues to be present. But life is also infused with glory. It is wonder-filled, for it is graced by its Creator. Job can trust his God.

Here, in Job's story, Malick found an archetypal pattern around which to build his story; here would be the trajectory of Jack O'Brien's life story. Now a successful, middle-aged architect working in a sleek, urban skyscraper and living in a beautiful tree-lined suburb, Jack (Sean Penn) is unable to come to terms with the tragic death of his younger brother at nineteen. It is Jack's struggle that gives shape and thickness to the film. In particular, it is his perception of his parents' ongoing agony that colors all else, even Jack's present existence.

Some criticize the movie for not having a typical narrative arc, a story in three acts. But Malick's interest is elsewhere. As with Job, he is trying to understand the sometime senselessness of life. The "slaughter of an innocent" has threatened to destroy a family. It has even put the universe's meaning in doubt. "Where were you God?" "Did you know?" "I believed in you." *The Tree of Life* becomes an extended meditation on the O'Brien family's loss. And like Job, it ends with a hard-won but real epiphany of the God who holds all in his hands.

The magnitude of the O'Briens' grief begs for a cosmic response. And it is given. After helping viewers experience something of the O'Briens' loss, Malick

The Tree of Life © 2010 Cottonwood Pictures, LLC

Mrs. O'Brien and RL: the way of grace

abruptly takes viewers to the beginning of creation itself. For some viewers, the shift is puzzling. But for Malick, like Job, if we are going to contemplate the meaning of existence, it must begin where life begins. With spectacular images of nebulae and lava, starry nights and trees taking root, we are shown both the origins of the universe and the development of life on earth (there is even a sequence showing a fierce dinosaur offering a defenseless young dinosaur a surprising moment of grace). Most of this twenty-minute sequence is without words. Instead, sacred and classical music (Bach, Berlioz, Preisner, Smetana, Tavener, Górecki, Mahler) give texture and meaning to the images.

When bad things happen to good people, a host of primal questions and childlike observations often emerge. So it is with Jack. From his encounter with creation and its Creator, we are then given a flood of Jack's recollections—helping his dad plant a tree, his mom playing in the sprinklers, setting off sparklers, eating dinner, being attracted to a girl for the first time, swimming in the river, being engulfed by a cloud of DDT as it is sprayed by a truck. This is not an idealized portrayal; sin and evil are present too. Waco, Texas, in the 1950s is segregated. A neighbor child drowns while swimming at the river. The boys get in trouble when their dad leaves for an extended business trip. Malick's portrayal of Jack's life is particular and yet universal. In Jack we see ourselves and our own childhoods. Reimagining his roots carefully and lovingly, Jack (and all of us as viewers) is hoping against hope that something greater might shine through.

In this retelling of his life, Jack's remembrance begins not only with his brother's death but also with his mother reflecting that there are "two ways through life: the way of nature and the way of grace." His father represents "nature," which in this rendition means the survival of the fittest. Mr. O'Brien teaches his three boys to box, for life will be tough. He believes that everyone needs to control their own destiny, and success is how one should be judged. But eventually, after being laid off from his work, Jack's father can only tell his son, "I wanted to be loved because I was great." In the process, he confesses, "I missed life's glory." (See the discussion of *Amadeus* in chap. 1 for a similar perspective.)

Better for Jack is the way of grace, represented by his mother. Mrs. O'Brien is a nurturer. In one scene (that happened spontaneously during filming), she is dancing in the street and a butterfly lands on her. We watch her help her boys breathe fresh air and imagine life's beauty. Jack's remembrance of his mother is chiefly through images and music, though voice-overs and minimal dialogue also reveal something of her heart's longing. But though Jack's mother is graced, the family struggles as she struggles given her son's death. Can grace also include nature, warts and all? As Jack seeks to take hold of the tree of life, the grief of his parents becomes a barrier beyond which he seemingly cannot go.

As Malick shares with his viewers memories from Jack's childhood, the filmmaker is not interested in simply telling a story. Instead, as A. O. Scott writes in his *New York Times* review, his purpose is "to shine the light of the sacred in secular reality." Malick would help viewers comprehend that nothing is merely secular; even the extremities of everyday life are sacred. Malick ends his movie as Jack's elevator ride up his skyscraper morphs into a dreamlike reverie about heaven, which is to come. As his dead brother leads him to the seashore, Jack is reunited with his family and people from his hometown. Viewers are provided with what one critic has labeled "a dramatic curtain call." Pain and sorrow are vanished. We see the reconciliation of his father and mother, and young Jack is again on his father's shoulders. As Berlioz's *Agnus Dei* ("Lamb of God") plays, we see Jack's mother being freed to forgive, to release her son into God's hands—a God whose Son also died. As her boy walks out into the beyond, she is granted grace. In a final act of celebration, the movie ends with the beauty of a field of sunflowers. This is God's world.

Dialogue Texts

> Where were you when I laid the foundation of the earth . . .
> when the morning stars sang together
>   and all the heavenly beings shouted for joy?
>
> Job 38:4, 7

Out of the ground the Lord God made to grow every tree that is pleasant to the sight and good for food, the tree of life also in the midst of the garden. . . .

Then the angel showed me the river of the water of life, bright as crystal, flowing from the throne of God and of the Lamb through the middle of the street of the city. On either side of the river is the tree of life with its twelve kinds of fruit, producing its fruit each month; and the leaves of the tree are for the healing of the nations.

Genesis 2:9; Revelation 22:1–2

The heavens are telling the glory of God. . . .
There is no speech . . .
yet their voice goes out through all the earth.
Psalm 19:1–4

Consider the work of God;
    who can make straight what he has made crooked?
Ecclesiastes 7:13

Discussion Questions and Clip Conversations

All clips are available for viewing at ReelSpirituality.com/Books/God-In -The-Movies. We have also listed the timestamp range of the scenes for your reference.

1. How is the movie's story told by image and sound as well as by word? What is conveyed by the narrator's voice sometimes being that of a child? What difference does it make that the theological questions of theodicy (How can evil/sin exist if God is all-powerful and good? How can God be God if evil and pain are present?) are portrayed through a lived story rather than argued through an abstract essay?

2. "The Two Ways" [00:40–06:32]. Does Malick reject the way of nature for the way of grace? Can grace function apart from nature? Though the mother's way might be preferred, can the father's be dismissed? How are the natural and the supernatural to be held together? Does nature (as personified in the father) also love? Can grace (as personified in the mother) function without the strictures of nature and its laws?

3. "Creation" [19:39–23:45; 32:01–35:45]. How are we to understand the creation sequence? Did it work for you? What images proved powerful and what distracting, if any? How does this fit with the book of Job? How might the movie's epigraph from Job 38:4, 7 provide a key to the

movie? Is this also Malick's response to life's pain and sorrow? Does Jack receive an "answer" from God through creation? If this is not an explanation, what brings peace and reconciliation? In what way are the leaves of the tree of life healing (Rev. 22:2)?

4. "The BB Gun" [1:47:03–1:49:50]. Why does the filmmaker portray the boy drowning, Jack shooting his brother with a BB gun, the kids fighting, Jack's fascination with his neighbor's lingerie, and so on? What is the purpose of juxtaposing these scenes with a butterfly landing on the mother's shoulder, the father teaching his sons to fight, or the reverie of a family at play? In what sense is this family like all our families? Is it archetypal? Do you find yourself in Malick's story? If so, in what way? And which character are you?

5. "Eternity" [2:04:05–2:11:38]. Heaven has been difficult to portray in film, for we must use symbols and metaphor. But some movies have done so memorably. Do you recall *Places in the Heart* (see chap. 9)? How has Malick used the images of Revelation 22 to complete this meditation on life and death? Did they work for you? What role does the music play in the final scene? How can it help with your interpretation?

Bonus Material

In giving voice to the relationship between nature and grace as the movie opens, Jack's mother's words are almost an exact quotation from Thomas à Kempis in his *Imitation of Christ* (bk. 3, chap. 54; see John McAteer, "The Nuns Taught Us . . ." *Video Ut Intellectum* [blog], July 21, 2011, https://film philosopher.wordpress.com).

The music that is playing in the opening scene as the mother receives the telegram of her son's death is the "Funeral Canticle" by John Tavener. Its words set the tone for the whole movie: "What earthly sweetness remaineth unmixed with grief? / What glory standeth immutable on earth? / All things are but shadows most feeble, / But most deluding dreams. / Yet one moment only, / And death shall supplant them all."

The film's music also includes Giya Kancheli's "Morning Prayers" as the mother walks through the woods after learning of her son's death; "Lacrimosa 2" by Zbigniew Priesner as the mother continues to grieve and again later when Jack grieves after shooting his brother in the finger with a BB gun; Smetana's *Vltava*, a symphonic poem that evokes the flow of the river Vltava through the Czech countryside, and perhaps by extension the river of life in Revelation 22; and the "Domine, Jesu Christe" movement from Berlioz's

Requiem, Opus 5, as the family achieves a final reconciliation in heaven, their mother giving her son to God. Although the music's words are often in Latin, the music itself provides a strong interpretation, giving voice to what viewers see on the screen.

Selected Additional Resources

Detweiler, Craig. "*Tree of Life*—From Genesis to Revelation." http://www
    .brehmcenter.com/initiatives/reelspirituality/film/articles/tree-of-life-from
    -genesis-to-revelation/.
McCracken, Brett. "The Divine Guide in Terrence Malick's 'Tree of Life.'"
    http://brettmccracken.com/2012/05/21/the-divine-guide-in-terrence-malicks
    -tree-of-life/.

Robert K. Johnston

38

True Grit

Justice/Vengeance
Human Identity, Loss,
the Meaning of Life,
Morality/Amorality

US, 2010
110 Minutes, Feature, Color
Actors: Jeff Bridges, Matt Damon, Hailee
   Steinfeld
Directors: Ethan Coen, Joel Coen
Screenwriters: Joel Coen, Ethan Coen (adapted from the novel *True Grit*
   by Charles Portis)
Rated: PG-13 (intense sequences of Western violence including disturbing images)

Synopsis and Theological Reflection

Joel and Ethan Coen's 2010 film *True Grit* is a remake of the 1969 version
starring John Wayne (his only Oscar win for Best Actor). Although both are
screen adaptations of the Charles Portis novel by the same name, the Coens'
version stays closer to the source material. Still, by repurposing this preexisting
material, *True Grit* is able to draw upon the cultural power and meaning of
not only the Western genre but also one of the most iconic actors in cinematic
history (i.e., John Wayne).

   Historically speaking, the Western has served as the American genre par
excellence. Often featuring independent, morally upright protagonists who
conquer the untamed land (and its inhabitants) and commit themselves with

religious-like devotion to Manifest Destiny, Westerns represent a number of core elements that have come to define the American imagination. But in the hands of the Coen brothers, *True Grit* is more than a romantic vision of the American West or a nostalgic longing for a bygone era of filmmaking. Instead, Joel and Ethan Coen are auteurs who are interested in the moral ordering of the world—a framework rooted in their Jewish religious tradition. And like so many of their other films (e.g., *Raising Arizona, Fargo, No Country for Old Men, A Serious Man*), *True Grit* exemplifies their willingness to explore these religious questions in and through the medium of film.

The plot of *True Grit* is pretty straightforward. Mattie Ross (played masterfully by Hailee Steinfeld) seeks to avenge her father's murder by capturing Tom Chaney (Josh Brolin). She enlists the help of US Marshal Rooster Cogburn (Jeff Bridges) and Texas Ranger LaBoeuf (Matt Damon). Together, this unlikely trio carries out Mattie's single-minded goal of retributive justice. Nothing here is altogether surprising. In fact, in terms of the plot, the Coens follow the generic conventions of the Western rather faithfully. However, if we pay closer attention to the opening and closing segments of the film, we get a glimpse into how the Coens are making use of the genre to speak in new ways to contemporary audiences.

The opening sequence begins in complete silence. Opening credits typically serve as a buffer for the audience—a kind of airlock between the "real" world outside the theater and the world of the film. In the case of classic Westerns like the original *True Grit*, a title song will often play over the opening credits, offering commentary on the soon-to-unfold narrative. But in the Coens' version, we have only silence. It spans the entire title sequence, from the appearance of the corporate logos to the *True Grit* title card. This text then disappears, and for a moment we are left with a black screen and no sound. Here, everything is completely still—absolute cinematic silence.

Out of this silence, written text, music, and dialogue appear. The text is taken from the book of Proverbs: "The wicked flee when none pursueth." The music is an instrumental version of the hymn "Leaning on the Everlasting Arms," and the voice-over narration reminds us that "you must pay for everything in this world one way or another. There is nothing free, except the grace of God." In other words, what emerges from the initial silence is a near liturgy, complete with a sacred text, religious music, and a homily.

The quoted text from Proverbs 28:1 seems clearly to affirm some form of retributive justice. The voice-over "homily" by Mattie echoes this same line of thought: there is a moral order that governs the universe. The good prosper while the guilty are brought to justice. And according to the music, it is clear

Mattie as an adult looking for Marshall Cogburn

who is honorable and who is evil because the morally upright are those who are "leaning on the everlasting arms."

But this moral certainty is immediately called into question when we consider the second part of Proverbs 28:1, which is conspicuous by its absence. It challenges the rightness or perhaps even the "righteousness" of the characters and the story we are about to see and hear. The full passage reads: "The wicked flee though none pursueth, but the righteous are as bold as a lion." The Coens frame the entire film with only the first half of this proverb. The righteous, it would seem, have no place here. Like the second half of the proverb, they have been literally cut off.

Here, then, is the fundamental question the film explores: In this world of cowboys and lawmen and young women who are seeking to avenge an unjust murder, who can we reasonably say is righteous? Who is leaning on the everlasting arms? By the end of the film, we realize the answer: no one. No one has entirely pure intentions. In spite of the morally straightforward world that the Western genre assumes, things are far more ambiguous than they seem. There is nothing free in this world—not even for the righteous.

All of this moral ambiguity culminates in the final scene. In fact, the ending features a parallel to the opening, only with a slight twist. The voice of an aging Mattie confirms the passage of time. Another instrumental variation of the "Everlasting Arms" motif plays until the credits roll, at which point we hear lyrical accompaniment by Iris DeMent (see the full lyrics below).

If it was unclear at the beginning of the film, there is no doubt now about the song we have been hearing all along. As Mattie walks toward the horizon and snow falls in silence, she offers a final reflection on the story of her life: "Time just gets away from us."

This statement is a far cry from the Proverbs epigraph and her opening statements about paying for everything in this world one way or another. Thus, even though the film is quoting Proverbs, it seems to be more at home in Ecclesiastes, a book within Israel's Wisdom literature that commends humility in the face of life's fundamental mystery. What began as a liturgy filled with moral certitude has transformed into something of a moral quandary—a quandary that was written into the film from the very first frame, if only we had the ears to hear it.

Before it is anything else, *True Grit* is of course a Western. But it is also a vehicle for exploring expressly theological questions—questions that have to do with life and its meaning in the midst of a seemingly amoral world. It is not simply a critique of the American imagination but a re-visioning of its possibilities. Rather than denying the value of what it means to be an American, *True Grit* rejects a rigid and triumphant interpretation of that identity—one that uncritically embraces our own position as inherently "righteous" or exceptional. The film is thus a critique of both the interpretive tradition that Mattie's character embodies (i.e., a certain strain of Protestant Christian Americanism) and its contemporary representatives. Recognizing that life is basically ambiguous, *True Grit* seems to take a cue from Israel's Wisdom tradition and commends not righteousness but humility.

Dialogue Texts

> The wicked flee when no one pursues,
>   but the righteous are as bold as a lion.
>   Proverbs 28:1

> In my vain life I have seen everything; there are righteous people who perish in their righteousness, and there are wicked people who prolong their life in their evildoing. Do not be too righteous, and do not act too wise; why should you destroy yourself? Do not be too wicked, and do not be a fool; why should you die before your time? It is good that you should take hold of the one, without letting go of the other; for the one who fears God shall succeed with both. . . .
>   Surely there is no one on earth so righteous as to do good without ever sinning.
>
>   Ecclesiastes 7:15–20

> A good name is better than precious ointment,
>   and the day of death, than the day of birth.

> It is better to go to the house of mourning
>   than to go to the house of feasting;
> for this is the end of everyone,
>   and the living will lay it to heart.
> Sorrow is better than laughter,
>   for by sadness of countenance the heart is made glad.
> The heart of the wise is in the house of mourning;
>   but the heart of fools is in the house of mirth.
> It is better to hear the rebuke of the wise
>   than to hear the song of fools.
> For like the crackling of thorns under a pot,
>   so is the laughter of fools;
>   this also is vanity.
>
> Ecclesiastes 7:1–6

Discussion Questions and Clip Conversations

All clips are available for viewing at ReelSpirituality.com/Books/God-In-The-Movies. We have also listed the timestamp range of the scenes for your reference.

1. "Prologue" [00:01–02:45]. Considering the film and the text from Proverbs, who do you most naturally identify with—the righteous or the wicked? Are you Mattie Ross on the hunt for her father's murderer? Or are you Tom Chaney? In what ways might our Christian discipleship become distorted if we always identify with the righteous? How might we benefit from placing ourselves in the position of the wicked in our reading of Proverbs?

2. "Rooster Cogburn" [14:10–20:51]. Is Rooster Cogburn a righteous person? Is he just? Is he moral? Is there any way to mete out retributive justice like Cogburn does while remaining morally upright? What happens when the two become blurred? What makes someone righteous or not according to the biblical witness? What do you make of Ecclesiastes 7:20 in light of reading Proverbs 28?

3. "True Grit" [20:51–22:40]. Mattie wants nothing more than to make Tom Chaney pay for his wrongdoing. And her desire is morally justified. So how might Mattie's single-minded focus shed light on what it means for the righteous to "perish in their righteousness" (Eccles. 7:15)? Mattie is also concerned that, because her father is unknown to those

in power, no one will come to his defense. No one will pursue justice. How do we enact justice without becoming self-righteous?

4. "The Crackling of Thorns" [37:30–40:20]. Both Cogburn and LaBoeuf are cowboys, but they are far from being the "strong, silent types" represented by icons like John Wayne. In fact, they are almost always talking—even when LaBoeuf has bitten through his tongue! How do the two characters change and grow over the course of the film in this regard? In particular, how do their words and actions shift from being like the crackling of a campfire to something more along the lines of what Ecclesiastes 7 describes?

5. "Time Gets Away from Us" [1:43:19–1:45:59]. In light of who Mattie becomes, do you think the lyrics in this song are ironic? Or do they represent where Mattie finally lands as a character? In what sense does she lean on (i.e., trust) God to bring about justice in her life? To what extent does she reject the possibility that God might enact justice without her own efforts? In your own experience, how do you know the difference between truly seeking wisdom and righteousness, and failing to trust God by attempting to seize control of your circumstances?

Bonus Material

"Leaning on the Everlasting Arms"

What a fellowship, what a joy divine,
Leaning on the everlasting arms;
What a blessedness, what a peace is mine,
Leaning on the everlasting arms.

(chorus) Leaning, leaning,
Safe and secure from all alarms;
Leaning, leaning,
Leaning on the everlasting arms.

Oh, how sweet to walk in this pilgrim way,
Leaning on the everlasting arms;
Oh, how bright the path grows from day to day,
Leaning on the everlasting arms.

(chorus)

What have I to dread, what have I to fear,
Leaning on the everlasting arms?

I have blessed peace with my Lord so near,
Leaning on the everlasting arms.

(chorus)

(Written by Anthony Showalter
and Elisha Hoffman, 1887; performed
in the movie by Iris DeMent)

Selected Additional Resources

Broxton, Jon. "Hymns of the Old West." *Movie Music UK* (blog), December 21, 2010. http://moviemusicuk.us/2010/12/21/true-grit-carter-burwell/.

Kirk, J. R. Daniel. "*True Grit*: A Proverbial Pelicula." http://www.brehmcenter.com/initiatives/reelspirituality/film/articles/true_grit.

Kutter Callaway

39

12 Years a Slave

US/UK, 2013
134 Minutes, Feature, Color
Actors: Chiwetel Ejiofor, Lupita Nyong'o,
   Michael Fassbender, Sarah Paulson, Paul
   Giamatti, Benedict Cumberbatch, Brad Pitt
Director: Steve McQueen
Screenwriter: John Ridley (based on *Twelve Years a Slave* by Solomon Northup)
Rated: R (violence/cruelty, some nudity, brief sexuality)

Prejudice/Oppression
Faith/Belief, Freedom,
Human Agency,
Human Suffering, Scripture

Synopsis and Theological Reflection

12 Years a Slave centers on Solomon Northup, a free black man in the 1840s living in New York state, who is kidnapped and sold into slavery in Louisiana. The movie is based on his memoirs, which he published following his rescue in the 1850s.

The film is difficult to watch because director Steve McQueen, director of photography Sean Bobbitt, and editor Joe Walker do not shy away from showing us the brutality of the system of slavery. The violence in *12 Years a Slave* is terrible, but the film is no more explicit than *The Passion of the Christ*. The comparison is especially apt, because *12 Years a Slave* models the beatings and whippings Solomon and the other slaves receive after Christ's scourging. Just as the Jewish authorities believed they were acting in God's name when they beat Christ, so the slave owners believed they were acting righteously when they beat their slaves. The perspective of history makes the injustice of their actions evident to all.

12 Years a Slave is a film that should be seen at least twice. The first time, you are so waylaid by the movie, so emotionally rent, you are unable to do much of anything besides weep—a perfectly appropriate response.

The second time you see it, you are able to reflect on what you are seeing and how the film is affecting you. You know what you are going to see, so you aren't shocked by it. You are able to anticipate it, the effect it will have on you, and to surrender more completely to the emotional and aesthetic experience of the film. More importantly, you are able to talk about it afterward. See it with the same group of people both times if you can.

12 Years a Slave contrasts different expressions of Christianity as practiced by the characters. The faith of the white slave owners is moralistic, used to gain power, and easily discarded when it would otherwise preclude selfish action. The faith of the slaves is vital, sustaining, and neither easily won nor easily discarded. *12 Years a Slave* is a harrowing testament to the various expressions of the Christian faith among the powerful and the weak both then and now.

Which of its characters you identify with will determine how you respond to *12 Years a Slave*. Do you count yourself among the weak and marginalized people in the world? Is your faith all you have to hold onto as the powers that be take advantage of you or worse? Or do you identify with the powerful and privileged people in the world? Do you enjoy economic, political, and cultural freedom? Is your faith socially advantageous? Does it make you "part of the club" rather than causing you to be ostracized from it? Is it an accessory to your life rather than the source of it?

You must answer those questions for yourself. Certainly, the powerful aren't always depraved, and the powerless aren't exceptionally spiritual necessarily, but this is the dichotomy the film presents us with, so we would do well to hold it loosely for a moment.

Seeing the vibrancy of the slaves' faith in Christ in *12 Years a Slave* makes me, a white man born into privilege and power in society, question whether I have any rightful claim to faith in Christ at all. I know nothing of low places, low esteem, and the vibrant life that is only found in close proximity to death. I know nothing of truly needing Christ. The only injustice I know is as one who has, at best, benefitted from it and, at worst, participated in enacting and enfranchising it.

My ancestry is that of the slave owners. They are my people. I am heir to the wickedness of buying and selling people, of profiting from the breaking

Solomon Northup

apart of families. Watching *12 Years a Slave*, I feared for my immortal soul, for what rightful claim do I have to eternal goodness, having experienced so much goodness in this life? My demise, both instantaneous and final, would be entirely justified by even the most generous reckoning of guilt.

If there is room for me, a white man of Southern blood, in God's mercy, God's mercy stretches wider than I am able to comprehend.

This film convicts me. I wonder who the afflicted are in my day. I wonder what systems I have bought into and what groups of people are falling by the shrapnel of those systems. Liberation eventually comes for Solomon because a privileged person stoops down to identify with him. Is that what God is calling me to do as well?

The filmic testimony of Solomon's life experiences gave me new eyes to see. If I am to be included in God's mercy, I am thankful. I pray that mercy makes me humble and responsive to the needs around me. I pray it will set me down among those closest to God's grace. I pray that I will identify with them, lift them up, even hazard my life if that's what God needs me to do.

Dialogue Texts

The Lord replied, "Who are the faithful and wise managers whom the master will put in charge of his household servants, to give them their food at the proper time? Happy are the servants whom the master finds fulfilling their responsibilities when he comes. I assure you that the master will put them in charge of all his possessions.

"But suppose that these servants should say to themselves, My master is taking his time about coming. And suppose they began to beat the servants, both men and women, and to eat, drink, and get drunk. The master of those servants would come on a day when they weren't expecting him, at a time they couldn't predict. The master will cut them into pieces and assign them a place with the unfaithful. That servant who knew his master's will but didn't prepare for it or act on it will be beaten severely. The one who didn't know the master's will but who did things deserving punishment will be beaten only a little. Much will be demanded from everyone who has been given much, and from the one who has been entrusted with much, even more will be asked."

Luke 12:42–48 (CEB)

Look at your situation when you were called, brothers and sisters! By ordinary human standards not many were wise, not many were powerful, not many were from the upper class. But God chose what the world considers foolish to shame the wise. God chose what the world considers weak to shame the strong. And God chose what the world considers low-class and low-life—what is considered to be nothing—to reduce what is considered to be something to nothing. So no human being can brag in God's presence.

1 Corinthians 1:26–29 (CEB)

Don't do anything for selfish purposes, but with humility think of others as better than yourselves. Instead of each person watching out for their own good, watch out for what is better for others. Adopt the attitude that was in Christ Jesus:

> Though he was in the form of God,
> he did not consider being equal with God something to exploit.
> But he emptied himself
>   by taking the form of a slave
>   and by becoming like human beings.
> When he found himself in the form of a human,
>   he humbled himself to the point of death,
>   even death on a cross.

Philippians 2:3–8 (CEB)

Maybe this is the reason that Onesimus was separated from you for a while so that you might have him back forever—no longer as a slave but more than a slave—that is, as a dearly loved brother. He is especially a dearly loved brother to me. How much more can he become a brother to you, personally and spiritually in the Lord!

So, if you really consider me a partner, welcome Onesimus as if you were welcoming me.

Philemon 1:15–17 (CEB)

Discussion Questions and Clip Conversations

All clips are available for viewing at ReelSpirituality.com/Books/God-In -The-Movies. We have also listed the timestamp range of the scenes for your reference.

1. *12 Years a Slave* is a difficult film to watch because it does not let you look away from the suffering of Solomon, Patsey, and the other slaves. The film depicts the physical terror of slavery in frightening detail. Do you think this explicitness is justified? Why or why not? Would the film be as compelling if it implied the suffering instead of showing it? How do the actors' performances help you process the pain these real-life people experienced? The women and men depicted endured much worse brutality than this. Should we avoid seeing this kind of brutality ourselves?

2. "That's Scripture" [52:28–55:40]. In this pair of scenes, we see Ford (Benedict Cumberbatch), a man whom we thought well of up to this point, refuse to help Solomon out of fear for his own safety. This scene is followed immediately by Epps's sermon in which he twists Scripture to justify his brutal treatment of his slaves. Together, these two scenes present a depressing picture of the ways the Christian faith can be used to legitimize injustice. Have you ever used your faith to legitimize not doing something to help a fellow human being, as Ford does in his scene? Have you ever seen someone do something similar? Have you ever twisted Scripture to your benefit, as Epps does in his scene? Have you ever seen someone do this? How should we respond both to our own misuses of the Christian faith and to others' misuse of Scripture?

3. "Roll, Jordan, Roll" [1:39:03–1:41:49]. In this scene, Solomon encounters the vibrant Christian faith of his fellow slaves. At first he is hesitant to participate in their faith. Then he is won over and joins in. In contrast to the scenes we watched before, this scene shows how invaluable the Christian faith is to people who have nowhere to turn except to Christ. Have you ever felt like you had nowhere to turn except Christ? What part did your faith play in that circumstance? Are instances of faith like the ones we see in these scenes more or less valuable than the faith we practice in less trying times?

4. Who are you in this story? We live a long time after slavery, and none of us would buy or sell slaves now, but the power dynamics that rule that time still rule ours. People are still privileged or powerless today. Who are you in this story? What does this story suggest about how you should order your life if you are either the powerful or the powerless? What does the example of Christ—God become man—suggest to you about how we should order our lives if we are either powerful or powerless? What systems rule our day? How are we complicit in them? What chains should we break, and for whom should we break them?

Selected Additional Resources

This is a rich, complex film, and many writers have considered it from a variety of perspectives. For thoughts on the religious imagery used in the film, both the brutal and the beautiful, read "*12 Years a Slave*: A Journey through Brutality to Grace" from *Variety*'s Justin Chang (now a reviewer for the *Los Angeles Times*): http://variety.com/2013/film/news/12-years-a-slave-a-journey-through-brutality-toward-grace-1200749270/.

For the perspective and experience of an African American filmmaker, film scholar, and theologian, read "The Horror and Humanity of *12 Years a Slave*" by Avril Speaks: http://www.brehmcenter.com/initiatives/reelspirituality/film/articles/the-horror-and-humanity-of-12-years-a-slave.

For a more pragmatic investigation of the film's technique and effect, listen to this episode of *Filmspotting*: http://www.filmspotting.net/reviews/1081-466-12-years-a-slave-top-5-movies-set-in-the-south.html.

For help coming to grips with the violence featured in the film, read Kenneth Morefield's review at *Christianity Today* (October 18, 2013): http://www.christianitytoday.com/ct/2013/september-web-only/12-years-slave.html.

Elijah Davidson

40

Zero Dark Thirty

Justice/Vengeance
Morality/Amorality,
Vocation

US, 2012
157 Minutes, Feature, Color
Actors: Jessica Chastain, Joel Edgerton,
  Chris Pratt, Jason Clarke, Kyle Chandler,
  Harold Perrineau, Jeremy Strong, Reda Kateb
Director: Kathryn Bigelow
Screenwriter: Mark Boal
Rated: R (language, strong violence including brutal, disturbing images)

Synopsis and Theological Reflection

There are films made for women, and there are films made by women. And then there is Kathryn Bigelow. Of course, the definitions for each of those categories are flawed, but Bigelow has carved a niche for herself that defies industry expectations of what it means to be a female filmmaker. Throughout her career, Bigelow has managed to avoid the typical "chick flick." Her work has challenged the notion that women can only tell stories that revolve around relationships, the home, or children. Her film *The Hurt Locker*, which won Academy Awards for Best Picture and Best Director in 2010, has one lone woman in it. Without relying on female characters, she tells a gripping story about what happens when our noble ambitions get the best of us.

Zero Dark Thirty has a similar theme. In this film, a woman does take center stage as we are introduced to Maya (Jessica Chastain), a CIA intelligence analyst who is at the helm of an extensive manhunt for Osama bin Laden. In the course of the movie, Maya's pursuit of al-Qaeda's leader morphs from a job assignment with a measure of moral worth into an obsession in which self-sacrifice is a necessary by-product.

The film is unapologetic in its depictions of torture-induced intelligence, which has been one of the major critiques of the film. Although Maya is very much a part of this machine because of her position, her inner conflict over the use of brutal force on the detainees is evident, at least in the beginning. She is slow to participate in the violence, often standing in the shadows of the room while the most brutal of tactics are used. Yet she proves to be a woman who can hold her own, and by the end of her task, she is ordering hits herself. She becomes just as convinced of her own knowledge, expertise, and authority as she is determined to find bin Laden. It is her persistence that leads her to walk a thin line between seeking justice and seeking retaliation in the name of national defense.

Things get complicated in the last thirty minutes of the film when the Navy SEALs finally find and ransack bin Laden's compound. In true Bigelow fashion, this is where the issues at stake become more than just news headlines and political platitudes. As the soldiers storm the home, women and children are disrupted from their home routine. Some are killed. Bigelow's decision to present these moments quietly resists our temptation to turn the scene into something triumphant. Instead, in these moments we are reminded of the fact that even a criminal has family, and we are made to wrestle with the question of whether a terrorist, even one as infamous as bin Laden, deserves to be treated with any sort of dignity. Once bin Laden is killed, it would seem that we are supposed to do a victory lap for catching the bad guy. Instead, we feel the awkwardness of not knowing what to do next. Should we cheer? Should life just go on?

Although Bigelow has called the intense search and the eventual raid on bin Laden's home "one of the greatest stories of our time," this film has courted more than its share of controversy. Many feared that the film would perpetuate a sense of American bravado, something unwelcome by those who already found American involvement in the Middle East to be problematic. The biggest issue, however, was the film's implied politics surrounding torture and waterboarding. Many accused the film of being a work of propaganda, since the CIA gave the filmmakers access to classified information that even journalists were never allowed to see. Critics warned that it would validate a false view that the use of torture was beneficial in finding the real bin Laden.

Maya

Yet Bigelow is meticulous about pushing more than just a government agenda. She tries to refrain from patting anyone on the back and instead brings the audience a nuanced performance from Chastain that leaves us in the gray area of what is right and wrong in the politics of war.

Whether Bigelow has a political agenda or not, Maya's internal struggle is a reminder of the still-present climate of fear that has dominated our culture since September 11, 2001. Violence may be morally wrong, but what if it is a means to a "good" end? Does that make it morally right? Who really suffers as casualties of war—the victims themselves, those they leave behind, or the perpetrators? As much as our current political sphere is divided over torture, Bigelow doesn't let us feel any sense of blind justice in watching Maya and the CIA's actions. There are consequences, and Maya endures the hazards of what it's like to pursue one's intuition, even when deep down inside you know it could lead you down a very dark path. In the end, Bigelow leaves us to wrestle with the possibility that perhaps in our nation's pursuit of an end to the war on terror, we may have lost an essential part of ourselves.

Dialogue Texts

What does it profit them if they gain the whole world, but lose or forfeit themselves?

Luke 9:25

Then your light shall break forth like the dawn,
    and your healing shall spring up quickly;
your vindicator shall go before you.

Isaiah 58:8

The spirit of the Lord GOD is upon me,
    because the LORD has anointed me;
he has sent me to bring good news to the oppressed,
    to bind up the brokenhearted,
to proclaim liberty to the captives,
    and release to the prisoners;
to proclaim the year of the LORD's favor,
    and the day of vengeance of our God.

Isaiah 61:1–2

Beloved, never avenge yourselves, but leave room for the wrath of God; for it is written, "Vengeance is mine, I will repay, says the Lord."

Romans 12:19

Discussion Questions and Clip Conversations

All clips are available for viewing at ReelSpirituality.com/Books/God-In-The-Movies. We have also listed the timestamp range of the scenes for your reference.

1. Maya's main focus was on locating a terrorist known to be a major threat. In order to accomplish this task, she allowed the abuse of detainees, a practice that many feel is morally wrong. Is there ever a time where it is acceptable for moral beliefs and convictions to succumb to what is necessary for the greater good? How do you decide what is "good" in those situations? Have you ever found yourself in a situation where you had to make a decision between doing two things that could be seen as equally wrong or problematic? How do you make these types of decisions?

2. "Protecting the Homeland" [1:18:24–1:20:22]. In this scene, Maya confronts her commander, demanding that she receive the resources necessary to find bin Laden. She accuses Joseph of not actually wanting to protect the homeland but in fact just wanting to look good through increasing his body count. This scene shows Maya's confidence and her convictions about what she knows to be true about finding bin Laden.

This scene is also significant because it shows both Maya's willingness to stand up and fight against all the odds and her unraveling in the process as her obsession with finding bin Laden continues to take over her life. What does Maya really care about in this scene? Is she more concerned about the homeland or about being taken seriously? How can one remain committed to a cause without losing one's sense of self?

3. "For God and Country" [2:15:40–2:23:30]. In this scene, a soldier eerily whispers Osama's name while women and children cower and cry in their pajamas. Shots are fired and we learn that bin Laden is dead and his home pillaged. In some theaters, audiences cheered after this scene. Was this an appropriate response to bin Laden's death? Do you think Bigelow made the film in order for the United States to brag about its victory? How might you put this scene in dialogue with Isaiah 61's call to liberate captives and to release prisoners? How would you define America's present moral stature when it comes to war and peace? In the movie, does patriotism demand compromise of biblical values?

4. "Where Do You Want to Go?" [2:26:20–2:30:00]. When the pilot in the final scene asks Maya this question, she is at a loss for words. What do you think is going through Maya's mind? Has Maya gained anything by spending so much time and energy on this mission? What did Maya lose throughout the course of this mission? Do you see Maya's determination throughout the film as an act of heroism or of self-interest? Or both?

Bonus Material

Zero Dark Thirty is a military term for half past midnight when no one can see you. To that end, Bigelow said she sees the film as a tribute to those military personnel who "work in the shadows." SEAL Team Six was the real-life special forces unit that was credited with killing bin Laden in his notorious compound in Abbottabad, Pakistan. Wanting to put the audience on the ground with these operatives, Bigelow had former Navy SEALs serve as advisers on the set, and the actors went through extensive military training in order to accurately simulate the raid.

In 2015, PBS's *Frontline* aired a documentary called *Secrets, Politics and Torture*, which highlighted the discrepancies between CIA accounts and a Senate committee report on whether the use of torture was effective in finding Osama bin Laden. According to the documentary, *Zero Dark Thirty* was a part of this debate because, it claimed, the film was endorsed by the CIA as a Hollywood spin on an otherwise divisive topic. The film was so contested within Congress that during an advanced screening of the film, Senator Dianne Feinstein walked out of the theater, stating that the film was entirely false.

The documentary also asserts that despite international law that prohibits torture (also referred to as "enhanced interrogation techniques"), the CIA maintains that they felt a moral obligation to get the information they needed to protect the American people by any means necessary. Several cover-ups were made to justify the methods used, even though their actions qualified as war crimes. In an op-ed piece in the *Los Angeles Times*, Bigelow wrote about her own stance regarding the film and the accusations:

> I think Osama bin Laden was found due to ingenious detective work. Torture was, however, as we all know, employed in the early years of the hunt. That doesn't mean it was the key to finding bin Laden. It means it is a part of the story we couldn't ignore. War, obviously, isn't pretty, and we were not interested in portraying this military action as free of moral consequences.

Bigelow's film maintained that dilemma from beginning to end, and it earned the film five Academy Award nominations, including Best Picture.

Esquire magazine published an interview with "The Shooter," the unnamed Navy SEAL who actually shot Osama bin Laden. In the article, he talks about his own inner conflict over the shooting, stating, "I remember as I watched him breathe out the last part of air, I thought: Is this the best thing I've ever done, or the worst thing I've ever done? This is real and that's him." He says that when bin Laden went down, it was chaotic and people were screaming. Perhaps Bigelow's choice to shoot that scene quietly speaks to her intention not to glorify the situation but instead to create a work of art that challenges us to think about what it means to seek justice in times of war.

Selected Additional Resources

Bigelow, Kathryn. "Kathryn Bigelow Addresses 'Zero Dark Thirty' Torture Criticism." *Los Angeles Times*, January 15, 2013. http://articles.latimes .com/2013/jan/15/entertainment/la-et-mn-0116-bigelow-zero-dark-thirty -20130116.

Maass, Peter. "Don't Trust *Zero Dark Thirty*." *Atlantic*, December 13, 2012. http://www.theatlantic.com/entertainment/archive/2012/12/dont-trust-zero -dark-thirty/266253/.

Roark, David. "Zero Dark Thirty." *Christianity Today*, December 21, 2012. http://www.christianitytoday.com/ct/2012/december-web-only/zero-dark -thirty.html.

The National Religious Campaign against Torture (www.nrcat.org) was founded in 2006 by George Hunsinger of Princeton Seminary and has a membership of 260 American religious organizations.

Avril Z. Speaks

ACKNOWLEDGMENTS

This book would not have been possible without the collaboration of our nine colleagues and friends (Avril, Barry, Craig, Elijah, Eugene, Joe, Kutter, Laura-lee, and Mathew) who worked *en conjunto*, as Latino theologians have taught us. Together we created this book—from the initial brainstorming sessions to heated and hilarious discussions about which films should be included; from deciding who should write on which film (some of us had to park our passions and our pride when someone else seemed more appropriate to write on a particular film) to meeting deadlines and graciously receiving our editorial comments. Bound together by the love we all share for God and neighbor, we also shared the desire to create something that would evoke enthusiasm for the films as well as provide practical tools to put faith and film in dialogue.

We also want to thank Ralph Winter, not only for writing the foreword to our book, but also for his continuing support of Reel Spirituality since its inception. Ralph was the codirector with Rob of our first Reel Spirituality Conference in the late nineties and is an ongoing, active member of the advisory board of our institute. He has cotaught with Rob a theology and film class at Fuller Seminary several times and has helped all of us deepen our understanding of film as an artistic medium. Why would this accomplished film producer (four movies in the Star Trek series, four in the X-Men series, two Fantastic Four movies, *Planet of the Apes*, *The Giver*, and many more) care about helping ministers dialogue with popular culture? Because he is both committed to Jesus Christ and a churchman. Thanks, Ralph, for all you do for Fuller and the Reel Spirituality Institute.

A special shout-out goes to Elijah Davidson, Brehm Center web manager and codirector of the Reel Spirituality Institute, who formatted the chapters, and Steve Vredenburgh, who provided the still photographs used in the book.

We also want to thank Joe Gallagher, operations director for the Brehm Center, for supporting the project with his chapters and with his enthusiasm and encouragement. And last but not least, we want to express our gratitude to Baker Publishing Group for the continued support of our publications in theology and film and especially for the advocate that we have in our editor, Robert Hosack.

Likewise, a word of thanks goes to the movie group (a rotating group of friends from our neighborhood, church, and life's adventures) that we have hosted for the last twenty-plus years in our home. We gather to watch and discuss films once a month. The discussion takes place while we eat a meal together in the style of the selected film (yes, even cooking a "Babette's Feast"). These friends (Bob, Dale, Liz, Lyn, Mathew, Joanne, Maureen, Nancy, Peter, Rusty, Tim) have been our dialogue partners and coaches, helping us to understand better what we have seen. We also want to thank our students—those who attend Centro Hispano de Estudios Teológicos and Fuller Theological Seminary, as well as the many Young Life staff who have studied with us.

Just as the production of a movie is a corporate act, this movie book has been a community event. We trust that the Spirit of God will evoke communion with God and neighbor as you use it in your life and ministry.

Appendix 1

Movies Listed by Biblical Text

Old Testament

Genesis

1:1–2—*WALL•E*
1:27—*The Elephant Man*
2:9—*The Tree of Life*
2:18—*Three Colors: Blue*
4:8–9—*Munyurangabo*
6:1–10—*Noah*

Exodus

15:11—*Life of Pi*
20:8–10—*Chariots of Fire*
20:12—*Field of Dreams*
32:14—*The Adjustment Bureau*

Leviticus

25:47–55—*The Shawshank Redemption*

Numbers

14:17–19—*Munyurangabo*

Deuteronomy

5:12–15—*Chariots of Fire*
14:22–26—*Babette's Feast*
15:7—*Lars and the Real Girl*
28:66—*Of Gods and Men*

Job

4:15–17—*Wings of Desire*
7:13–18—*Secret Sunshine*
38:4, 7—*The Tree of Life*
38:19–20—*Secret Sunshine*
40:1–14—*A Serious Man*
42:1–6—*A Serious Man*

Psalms

8:4–6—*Wings of Desire*
19:1–4—*The Tree of Life*
23—*The Elephant Man*
32:1—*Get Low*
68:4–5—*Places in the Heart*

71:18—*Up*
81:1—*Of Gods and Men*
82:6–7—*Of Gods and Men*
86:8–9—*Life of Pi*
91:11–12—*Wings of Desire*
96:1–2—*Three Colors: Blue*
127:3–5—*The Son*
136:2—*Life of Pi*
146:7–9—*Dead Man Walking,
     Water*

Proverbs

10:1—*Field of Dreams*
10:28—*The Shawshank
     Redemption*
13:12—*Field of Dreams, The
     Shawshank Redemption*
14:32—*Field of Dreams*
16:9—*The Adjustment Bureau*
17:17—*Up*
18:24—*The Shawshank Re-
     demption, Up*
20:11—*Up*
23:18—*The Shawshank
     Redemption*
27:6—*The Shawshank
     Redemption*
28:1—*True Grit*

Ecclesiastes

1:1–9—*A Serious Man*
1:9—*Groundhog Day*
1:14—*American Beauty, Water*
2:1–2—*Groundhog Day*
2:11—*American Beauty*
2:16–17—*Groundhog Day*

2:24—*Groundhog Day*
3:1–2—*To Live*
4:4–6—*Amadeus*
4:9–10—*Three Colors: Blue, Up*
4:9–12—*Lars and the Real Girl*
4:13–14—*Magnolia*
5:7—*Magnolia*
5:12–17—*There Will Be Blood*
5:15—*Magnolia*
6:12—*To Live*
7:1–6—*True Grit*
7:13—*The Tree of Life*
7:14—*To Live*
7:15—*Crimes and Misdemeanors*
7:15–20—*True Grit*
8:1—*Magnolia*
8:14–15—*Crimes and
     Misdemeanors*
9:1–7—*Babette's Feast*
9:7–9—*American Beauty,
     Wings of Desire*
9:7–10—*Groundhog Day, To
     Live*
9:11—*Magnolia*

Isaiah

9:6—*Children of Men*
11:6—*Munyurangabo*
29:13—*The Piano*
55:8–9—*The Adjustment
     Bureau*
58:8—*Zero Dark Thirty*
61:1–2—*Zero Dark Thirty*

Jeremiah

7:6–7—*Water*

13:13—*The Shawshank Redemption*
14:32–35—*The Piano*
15:50–55—*Calvary*

2 Corinthians

2:5–8—*Get Low*
3:4–6—*Water*
5:18—*Field of Dreams*

Galatians

3:27–29—*The Piano*
4:4–5—*Children of Men*
6:9—*Chariots of Fire*

Ephesians

2:1–10—*Groundhog Day*
4:31–32—*The Son*

Philippians

2:1–8—*Amadeus*
2:3–8—*12 Years a Slave*
3:14—*Chariots of Fire*

Colossians

3:12–13—*The Son*

1 Thessalonians

4:9–18—*Places in the Heart*
4:10–11—*American Beauty*

1 Timothy

1:12–17—*The Mission*

Philemon

1:15–17—*12 Years a Slave*

Hebrews

1:14—*Wings of Desire*
10:24–25—*Lars and the Real Girl*

James

1:3—*Life of Pi*
1:6–11—*There Will Be Blood*
3:13–4:3—*Amadeus*
4:17—*Crimes and Misdemeanors, Water*

1 John

2:9—*Do the Right Thing*
3:11—*Lars and the Real Girl*
3:16–17—*Lars and the Real Girl*
3:16–18—*WALL•E*

Revelation

3:20—*Babette's Feast*
22:1–2—*The Tree of Life*

Appendix 2

Movies Listed by Theological Topic

A boldfaced movie title indicates that the topic is a major theme in the movie.

Art/Play

Art/Play Mediating God's Mercy

Babette's Feast, *Three Colors: Blue*

Art/Play Mediating God's Presence

Amadeus, American Beauty, Chariots of Fire, Field of Dreams

Beauty

Amadeus, American Beauty, Babette's Feast, The Piano, The Shawshank Redemption

The Church

Calvary, Lars and the Real Girl, The Mission, Places in the Heart

Community

Babette's Feast, Of Gods and Men, Lars and the Real Girl, Places in the Heart

Confession

Get Low

Conscience and Religion

Water

Creation

Care of Creation

Noah, WALL•E

Creation Mediating God's Presence

Life of Pi, The Tree of Life

Destiny

Destiny and Chance

   Children of Men

Destiny and Free Will

   The Adjustment Bureau

Discernment

   Of Gods and Men

Doubt

   Calvary, Of Gods and Men, Water

Faith/Belief

   Breaking the Waves, *Calvary, Chariots of Fire, Children of Men, Of Gods and Men, 12 Years a Slave, Water*

Father/Son and Father/Daughter Relationships

   Calvary, Field of Dreams, Munyurangabo, **The Son**, *There Will Be Blood, Up*

Forgiveness

   Babette's Feast, Calvary, **Get Low**, **Munyurangabo**, *Places in the Heart, The Son,* **Unforgiven**

Freedom

   The Piano, Three Colors: Blue, 12 Years a Slave

Friendship

   Munyurangabo, The Shawshank Redemption, **Up**

God

God's Mercy vs. Human Judgment

   Babette's Feast, Breaking the Waves, The Elephant Man, Noah

God's Presence

   Life of Pi, The Tree of Life

God's Righteousness

   Noah

Grace vs. Nature

   The Tree of Life

Gratitude

   Babette's Feast

Hope

   Children of Men, The Shawshank Redemption, *Up, Wings of Desire*

The Human

Human Agency

   The Adjustment Bureau, **The Piano, Three Colors: Blue**, *12 Years a Slave*

Human Dignity

Dead Man Walking, The Elephant Man, To Live, The Piano

Human Identity

The Adjustment Bureau, The Shawshank Redemption, Three Colors: Blue, True Grit, Unforgiven

Human Suffering

The Elephant Man, Magnolia, Munyurangabo, The Piano, Secret Sunshine, Three Colors: Blue, The Tree of Life, 12 Years a Slave, Water

The Nature of the Human

*Calvary, Dead Man Walking, **The Elephant Man**, To Live, The Shawshank Redemption, Wings of Desire*

Jesus

Christ Figure

***Calvary**, Dead Man Walking, WALL•E*

The Incarnation

Children of Men

Justice/Vengeance

*Crimes and Misdemeanors, Dead Man Walking, Do the Right Thing, Munyurangabo, Secret Sunshine, **True Grit**, **Zero Dark Thirty***

Life

Life's Mystery

Crimes and Misdemeanors, Magnolia, A Serious Man, The Tree of Life

Life's Vanity

American Beauty, Crimes and Misdemeanors, Groundhog Day, Magnolia, A Serious Man

The Meaning of Life

***American Beauty**, Children of Men, **Crimes and Misdemeanors**, **Groundhog Day**, Life of Pi, To Live, **Magnolia**, **Secret Sunshine**, **A Serious Man**, True Grit*

Loss

Field of Dreams, Munyurangabo, Places in the Heart, Secret Sunshine, A Serious Man, The Son, Three Colors: Blue, The Tree of Life, True Grit, Up, Water

Love

*The Adjustment Bureau, Breaking the Waves, Groundhog Day, Three Colors: Blue, **WALL•E**, **Wings of Desire***

Redemptive Love

*Breaking the Waves, Dead Man Walking, **Lars and the Real Girl**, Magnolia, The Son*

Morality/Amorality

*Crimes and Misdemeanors,
The Son, True Grit, Zero Dark
Thirty*

Neighbor?, Who Is My

Dead Man Walking, **Do
the Right Thing**, *The
Elephant Man*, **The Mission**,
Munyurangabo, **Places in the
Heart**

Otherness

Do the Right Thing

Peace

Get Low

Play

Chariots of Fire, Field of Dreams

Prejudice/Oppression

*Do the Right Thing, The
Elephant Man, The Piano,
Places in the Heart,* **12 Years a
Slave**, *Water*

Reconciliation

Do the Right Thing, **Field of
Dreams**, *Munyurangabo, Places
in the Heart*

Religions, Theology of

Of Gods and Men, **Life of Pi**,
The Mission, Water

Repentance

Get Low, The Mission

Resistance, Peaceful/Violent

The Mission

Sabbath

Chariots of Fire

Scripture

Noah, 12 Years a Slave

Sin

Idolatry

Amadeus, American Beauty

Jealousy

Amadeus

Lust for Power

There Will Be Blood

Original Sin

There Will Be Blood

Pride

Noah

Sin and Its Consequences

*Calvary, Crimes and
Misdemeanors, Magnolia, The
Mission, Noah, The Piano,*
There Will Be Blood, *WALL•E*

Spirituality of Everyday Life

To Live, *Places in the Heart*, *Secret Sunshine*, *The Son*, *The Tree of Life*

Vocation

Amadeus, *Babette's Feast*, *Chariots of Fire*, *Field of*

Dreams, *Of Gods and Men*, *Noah*, *Zero Dark Thirty*

Wonder

Field of Dreams, *Life of Pi*, *Wings of Desire*